D1201680

Born Yesterday

BORN YESTERDAY

Inexperience and the Early Realist Novel

STEPHANIE INSLEY HERSHINOW

Johns Hopkins University Press | BALTIMORE

© 2019 Johns Hopkins University Press
All rights reserved. Published 2019
Printed in the United States of America on acid-free paper
9 8 7 6 5 4 3 2 1

Johns Hopkins University Press
2715 North Charles Street
Baltimore, Maryland 21218-4363
www.press.jhu.edu

Library of Congress Cataloging-in-Publication Data

Names: Hershinow, Stephanie Insley, 1982– author.
Title: Born yesterday : inexperience and the early realist novel / Stephanie
    Insley Hershinow.
Description: Baltimore : Johns Hopkins University Press, 2019. | Includes
    bibliographical references and index.
Identifiers: LCCN 2018046669 | ISBN 9781421429670 (hardcover : alk.
    paper) | ISBN 9781421429687 (electronic) | ISBN 1421429675 (hardcover :
    alk. paper) | ISBN 1421429683 (electronic)
Subjects: LCSH: English fiction—18th century—History and criticism. |
    Characters and characteristics.
Classification: LCC PR858.C47 H47 2019 | DDC 823/./0927—dc23
LC record available at https://lccn.loc.gov/2018046669

A catalog record for this book is available from the British Library.

*Special discounts are available for bulk purchases of this book. For
more information, please contact Special Sales at 410-516-6936 or
specialsales@press.jhu.edu.*

Johns Hopkins University Press uses environmentally friendly book
materials, including recycled text paper that is composed of at least
30 percent post-consumer waste, whenever possible.

Suppose her to have received from Nature the seeds of common sense; do these require no attention to raise them? or is this most useful plant to be reared without the aid of experience? But where, or how, is that to be obtained by a girl?

—JOHN FORDYCE, *Sermons to Young Women* (1766)

By what process of logical accretion was this slight "personality," the mere slim shade of an intelligent but presumptuous girl, to find itself endowed with the high attributes of Subject?

—HENRY JAMES, *The Art of the Novel* (1934)

Contents

Acknowledgments

It has become something of a running joke that the writing of this book on unformed characters has been formative for me. The project had its earliest beginnings as a dissertation written at Johns Hopkins University, and I find it difficult to articulate just how influential my training there has been on my thinking. I could not have written this book without the example and encouragement of Frances Ferguson, whose writing remains my model of serious engagement with difficult ideas and rewarding texts. She has given me the gifts of friendship, patience, and pickled okra, and I hope this book can go some small way toward repayment. It is only since leaving that I've realized just how special the years I spent at Hopkins were, and I still cannot believe my luck at having stumbled upon that Brigadoon. The first glimmer of the topic of this book emerged in an essay written for Amanda Anderson's class; she has since continued to help me ask the right kinds of questions, and the prospect of making her laugh has gotten me through many a tough stretch. Coursework and conversations with Sharon Cameron, Simon During, and Richard Halpern make their marks here, and I am especially grateful to Richard and to Patricia Kain for teaching me how to teach. While they arrived too late for me to study with them, I found in Doug Mao, Jared Hickman, Jesse Rosenthal, and Drew Daniel models of style both on and off the page. I thank my classmates for making a tiny department feel cozy rather than claustrophobic (well, most of the time); among them, I wish especially to thank Beth Steedley, Christiane Gannon, Nick Bujak, Doug Tye, Roger Maioli, Robert Day, Rob Higney, Elisha Cohn, Dan Stout, Cristie Ellis, and Tara Bynum. Rebecca Brown and Sam Chambers were condescending in the very best eighteenth-century sense. Jessica Valdez, Maggie Vinter, and David Schley have continued (across a stretch of continents and time zones) to hold me accountable (and listen to my excuses). Claire Jarvis has fielded the most bizarre questions and has read many versions of most of these pages. My thanks to these fellow travelers are even warmer.

At the Rutgers Center for Cultural Analysis, Billy Galperin, Jonah Siegal, and Jonathan Kramnick helped ease me out of my bubble, as did my fellow participants in the "Formalisms" seminar. The feedback I received from that group improved this project greatly. Rachel Feder and Katherine Schaap Williams were especially tireless interlocutors and readers, as they have continued to be. A text thread with Rachel Feder and Nan Da saw the first draft of this book through to completion.

This project became a book at Baruch College, and I could not have made this transition without the friendship and guidance of (among many others) Nancy Yousef, Mary McGlynn, John Brenkman, Tim Aubrey, Jessica Lang, Shelly Eversley, Cheryl Smith, Tatiana Emmanouil, Matt Eatough, Rick Rodriguez, Amina El-Annan, Laura Kolb, Allison Deutermann, and Sean O'Toole. As department chair, Eva Chou guided me through the trials that accompany even the smoothest journey down (up?) the tenure track; Jessica Lang, in lately assuming these duties, has already offered her mentorship, time, and wisdom. Three deans—Jeff Peck, Al Romero, and, in an interim capacity, Allison Griffiths—supported this project both morally and materially. Grants from the PSC-CUNY research award program gave me the time and resources to conduct the bulk of my research. Staff at the Peabody Library, the Folger Library, the British Library, and (my home not too far away from home) the New York Public Library proved invaluable for this stranger to the archive. At a key moment, the project benefitted from the interdisciplinary writing group underwritten by the Faculty Fellowship Publication Program; I thank my co-participants and our group leader, Nancy Yousef, for helping me consider audience and for sharing their own truly fascinating work. Final revisions and a last-minute research trip were supported by the Provost's Award for Faculty Book Publication. That trip would have been far less comfortable were it not for the hospitality of Donna and Richard Vinter. I am ever grateful for my union, the Professional Staff Congress, for supporting the research of junior faculty and for fighting for better working conditions for all of my colleagues, including the adjuncts who do the majority of teaching at CUNY. And I thank my students, across institutions, for their verve and their willingness to join me on a number of improbable journeys.

In New York, the Columbia University Seminar on Eighteenth-Century European Culture quickly became my intellectual home. I thank chairs Al Coppola and Kathy Lubey for their leadership and their camaraderie. I have also been grateful for the collegiality of my fellow seminar members, especially Jenny Davidson, John Richetti, Wendy Lee, Abigail Zitin, Slaney Chadwick Ross, Lynn Festa, Dan Gustafson, Kathleen Urda, and Dustin Stewart. I am grateful to the Leonard Hastings Schoff Publication Fund for their help with publication. Portions of this project have been presented over the past years at the Columbia University Seminar and also at the International Society for the Study of Narrative, the Modern Language Association, the British Women Writers conference, and several meetings of the North American Society for the Study of Romanticism and the American Society for Eighteenth-Century Studies. I thank audiences at these venues and at Yale University for tough questions, keen insights, and even every "comment more than a question" that helped me refine my argument. A number of interlocutors at conferences over the years have influenced this project, including Deirdre Lynch, Jess Keiser, Gena Zuroski, Kasia Bartozynska, Anne Stevens, Heather Keenleyside, Stephanie DeGooyer, and Mark Vareschi (my only friend). Jonathan Kramnick, Scott Black, Andy Franta, Ruth Mack, and Sandra Macpherson have made the silly notion of an academic family tree seem like good sense; I thank them for being the best big siblings this oldest child could hope for. A well-timed NEH summer seminar, "Postsecular Studies and the Rise of the English Novel, 1719–1897," granted me the stimulation and fellowship of a brilliant group of scholars. I am grateful for the leadership, encouragement, and unflappability of Lori Branch and Mark Knight. An unforgettable conversation with Misty Anderson helped clarify thorny questions (and raise new ones that I'll keep trying to answer). In a particularly supportive group, Jeff Galbraith and Kevin Seidel were exceptionally generous with feedback, and John Wiehl made for a fast and forever friend. In a big city where, as Joseph Andrews laments, "next-door Neighbours don't know one another," I have been lucky to find the neighborly goodwill of Tricia Matthew, Karl Steel, Matthew Harrison, Vim Pasupathi, Andrew Wasserman, and Debapriya Sarkar. Anna Kornbluh and Adam Grener were gracious enough to share unpublished work when I needed a last push of inspiration. My Brain Trust (Kathy Lubey, Gena Zuroski, and Kasia Bartozynska) deserves repeated thanks for their timely validation and generous reading. While Twitter delayed publication considerably, friends, colleagues, and total strangers on my timeline also reminded me that the book had an audience out there somewhere.

Catherine Goldstead at Johns Hopkins University Press believed in this project and had the patience to see it through to completion. Her generosity and good humor are a salve, and her editorial expertise always invigorates (whether dispensed poolside or otherwise). Anonymous readers for the press made this book immeasurably better; I thank them for seeing in that manuscript the book I was trying to write and for offering encouraging and perceptive suggestions. (I beg their forgiveness for remaining absences and infelicities.) I am likewise grateful for the care and perspicacity of Carrie Watterson, whose thoughtful copyediting made my writing better. I thank Thomas Broughton-Willett for bringing his expertise to the index. An early version of chapter 1 appeared as "Clarissa's Conjectural History: The Novel and the Novice," in *The Eighteenth Century: Theory and Interpretation* 56.3 (2015): 297–319. An early version of chapter 2 was published as "When Experience Matters: Tom Jones and 'Virtue Rewarded,'" in *Novel* 47.3 (2014): 363–82. I thank the anonymous readers for these journals for helping me to articulate my arguments at that early stage in my thinking. I am likewise grateful to the editors of those publications and to the University of Pennsylvania Press and Duke University Press, respectively, for permission to reprint here.

My family and friends have likewise been patient as I assured them that, yes, I was still finishing that book. I thank Kathy and Rickey Wood along with my brother Rickey, and I hope that I honor the memory of Otis and Linda Insley by finishing what they only could see me begin. For their support and good company, I also thank Shel and Lorna Hershinow; Kim Evans; and David, Ruby, and Star LaRocca. Lisa Grimes guided me when I was but a novice myself, and she remains my model of a good (which is to say voracious) reader. Brian Wilkins and Mary McDonough have offered enduring friendship across variable distance. Megan McLaughlin, Laura Gallo, Lauren Klemmer Foley, Megan Selheim, Shannon Lewis, Beth Marchessault, Katherine Frattini, Jennifer Lucado, and (especially, especially) my dearest friend and neighbor Meredith Fortin have provided much-needed running commentary on my adult life. Lolo and Ira have provided companionship and literal warmth for the duration of this undertaking. But for the existence of Harvey Hershinow—born yesterday, give or take—this book would have been finished sooner but would likely have been far worse. His goofiness and tenderness sustain me. Without the loving care of the women of Smile and the Garden of Mustard Seeds nurseries, this book would still be a draft; I thank them for attending to one of my big projects so that I could finish up the other one.

I encountered David Hershinow just as I was entering the world; ours is a bond that has survived—thrived—through expatriation, a lengthy transnational separation, shared graduate coursework (I *know*), several jobs and moves, one baby, and nearly simultaneous book completion deadlines, which only further proves this book's claims about the pleasures inherent in duration, stability, and constancy. He has read every word of this book several times over and has performed the herculean (persean?) work of coaxing me to translate my wild and tangled thoughts into intelligible and concrete form. I thank Rotary International for its efforts in eradicating polio and for introducing me to Dave. In a superfluous gesture if there ever was one, this book is dedicated to him.

Born Yesterday

Entering the World

My dear child, I often think you were born but yesterday,
only, by some accident, you came into the world, like Minerva,
grown up and ready dressed.
—LIONEL TO CAMILLA IN FRANCES BURNEY, *Camilla*[1]

About halfway through Frances Burney's third novel, *Camilla: A Picture of Youth* (1796), Camilla Tyrold's brother Lionel—the profligate fool who hastens her downfall—captures something fundamental to her character even as he uses that same insight to dismiss her.[1] In this admonition, Lionel accuses Camilla of inexperience for expecting him to repay a large sum of money he has borrowed on the credit of his relation to her. That he has borrowed the sum from Camilla's wealthy (but unwelcome) suitor further complicates the matter, as she now finds herself with an obligation that can be repaid only with an engagement she is loath to accept, and this trap, in turn, catalyzes a series of misunderstandings that, in true sentimental fashion, leave our heroine alone and on the brink of death by the novel's tenth and final book. Lionel's condescension stems from his disbelief that Camilla might hold him to a set of expectations (namely, a commitment to duty and honor) he has no intention of recognizing: "What makes you think I mean to pay him?" Assuming Lionel's adherence to a code of behavior he regards both irrelevant and irritating, Camilla reveals herself to be out of touch. Her belief in the persistence of aristocratic values in a modern, commercial age makes her into something of a time traveler, or a stranger in a strange land. Even, as Lionel cannily figures her, an entirely new being, one with the appearance of a young woman but all the savvy of a mewling babe.

Given what we know of the sentimental novel, Lionel's accusation of wide-eyed simplicity—of a morality that is also a liability—is likely unsurprising. More intriguing is his suggestion that not only is Camilla being naïve in this moment, but that she is, on the contrary, repeatedly born again ("I *often* think"), encountering the iniquity of the world anew in each successive moment. After all, Lionel's dependence on this fact—on the expectation that Camilla lacks the shrewdness either to anticipate or to prevent his wrongdoing even when presumably familiar with the history of his exploits—explains why he accepts the dubious loan in the first place. Lionel's appraisal of Camilla captures both his worldliness and her artlessness, his experience of the world and her recent entrance into it. "I am too knowing," he tells her, and she too ignorant of the ways of the fashionable set. And, crucially, his characterization captures the impression that experience, for Camilla, recurs without accumulating—the uncanny way Camilla has of *encountering* experience without thereby *becoming* experienced.

This book is about characters like Camilla, those whose inexperience lingers even as their novels' plots take shape. In focusing on these characters, it is also a book about how character functions in the early novel as a site of suspended possibility rather than as a catalyst for development. If the eighteenth-century novel emerges alongside the modern subject, as scholars have long argued, then this book centers on a question that commonplace raises in turn: whether it is even possible to imagine the subject without *Bildung*.[2] "Born yesterday," the idiom this book takes as its title, is an expression that we most often encounter—both in the eighteenth century and today—in the form of a disavowal. "What do you think, I was born yesterday?" is a rhetorical question that assumes both an affirmative answer (apparently you think this, or you wouldn't try to con me) and also the force of correction (now you know just how wrong you are). "I wasn't born yesterday" uses that workaday rhetorical figure litotes, understating the speaker's presumably considerable experience of the world by conjuring the fantasy of spontaneous maturity. But in the case of Burney's Camilla, it is also a charge the heroine cannot really deny. And indeed she does not; instead, she implores Lionel to consider "justice and honour" (523). He laughs at her. Camilla's virtue—and, more to the point, the capacious goodwill that repeatedly leaves her the gull of those less scrupulous—really does make her appear, in each episode, as if she had no experience of the world behind her that might inform her future decisions. Again and again, she finds herself victimized by those who would take advantage of the distance between her naïve idealism and the practical venalities of modernity.

While this Teflon goodness marks Camilla as exceptional within her narrative, the model of inexperience she embodies pervades eighteenth-century novels, which consistently feature protagonists who encounter the dangers of the world without ever learning to avoid them. I argue in the pages that follow that the persistence of inexperience—across diegetic time, across the nascent canon of eighteenth-century novels—marks not an aesthetic failure but rather the height of the novel's formal innovation in this period. In a time when adolescence as a conceptual category receives new cultural energy, fiction sees youth as an economical strategy for representation: inexperienced characters require explicit and expansive depictions of social life (its conventions and assumptions laid bare).[3] At the same time, youthful protagonists can act as hostile agents, revealing the hard work and dubious rewards of perceptual agility and social accommodation. Novel theorists have come to recognize these dual commitments—social expansiveness and psychological acuity—as the hallmarks of the realist novel. But, again and again, implicitly and explicitly, novel theory has likewise understood these commitments as brought into relation by the organizing principle of *Bildung*, wherein protagonists break out in psychology as if it were a side effect of their development. In illuminating figures who do not trace paths of development, this book both identifies and offers a counternarrative, one that encourages us to revisit our ways of thinking about plot and character, self and society, experience and its fragile but enduring alternatives.

Before encountering Lionel's description of Camilla a few years ago, I had long associated the expression "born yesterday" (as you might, as well) with the 1946 Garson Kanin play, later made into a film (and, yet later, a remake). In a star-making turn by Judy Holliday, the play's heroine Billie Dawn finds herself agog at the pretensions of Washington, DC, when dragged there by her corrupt tycoon fiancé, Harry Brock. The story is part fish out of water, part Pygmalion, as Brock hires a tutor to smooth Billie's rough edges. (He will, almost inevitably, come to soothe her in other ways as well.) The play's twist is that the dumb blonde requires only the slightest access to cultural capital to reveal herself as an incisive critic of Washington corruption, patriarchal violence, and the everyday banalities we all employ to make up for a variety of ignorances. Billie wasn't born yesterday because she exemplifies a common sense that can cut though the most intimidating obfuscations of Washington bureaucracy, and yet she *is* born yesterday in that her inexperience with the world of government—and her refusal to acclimate fully to that world—is precisely what enables her critique, her vision for a better politics, and ultimately the play's marriage plot.

Although the play captures the idiom so forcefully as to produce something of a folk etymology, I would venture that the expression is a particularly eighteenth-century one, capturing the period's vexed fascination with both novelty and origins. The earliest reference I have found is in Eliza Haywood's 1723 comedy *A Wife to Be Lett*. There, a wronged woman, refusing to be duped, uses the phrase as we might expect. Learning that she has been conned into marrying someone below her station, she recovers her reputation by asserting her worldliness: "A Footman! A Footman! but I'll have him hang'd, he's a Cheat, he has marry'd me in a false Name; but you shan't think to carry it so—I was not born yesterday: I'll go to a Lawyer immediately."[4] While Haywood's heroine has been fooled, her discovery of the scheme puts an immediate end to it; to uncover the plot is to undo its work so effectively that the marriage seems to dissolve even before the annulment can be arranged. For Burney, writing later in the century, the expression performs a different kind of work, collapsing social acuity and infancy rather than prying them apart. Camilla may be unsuccessful in unraveling the plot into which she has been thrust, but it is her *un*worldliness, we are led to believe, that enables her to identify the plot and, in turn, to reject the market-driven sociality on which it is founded. Even as she remains stuck in a tangle of debt and dependency, Camilla serves as the novel's moral center, and her immaturity only solidifies that position. What Burney reminds us in using the phrase not once but twice in *Camilla* is that the eighteenth-century novel becomes preoccupied not only with newness as an aesthetic imperative—what we might think of as the novel form's preoccupation with novelty—but also with *persons* who are new, with characters who embody the very conditions of possibility that the genre embraces.[5] In the interest of keeping that conflation of aesthetics and character in view, I will call these figures "novices" in the pages that follow. Likewise, I will use the anachronistic term "novel" heuristically throughout this study to acknowledge and to underscore the extent to which midcentury writers held the ambition of newness at the forefront of their efforts, whether or not we judge them to have succeeded. As Anna Laetitia Barbauld puts it, even if prose fiction has a long and venerable history, "there are some periods which make, as it were, a new era in this kind of writing," and the mid-eighteenth century is one of them.[6]

Burney is a master of depicting the ways that the crucible of female adolescence (the moment, as she puts it in *Evelina*, of a "young lady's entrance into the world") heightens and complicates the typical plot of the courtship novel.[7] That phrase, "entrance into the world"—now closely associated with Burney but used widely in this period—evokes precisely the same infancy/maturity dyad as "born yesterday": the expression marks both literal birth and the threshold into adulthood. Both capture Camilla's essential contradiction, a toggle between biological states: per Lionel, she is a "child" *and* she is "grown up." The suggestion is that infancy and adolescence are life stages during which one is particularly vulnerable to experience's effects. One's formative years—as we often call them—are those when character is malleable and identity as yet unset. Later, I will have more to say about how this *second* entrance into the world recapitulates the Enlightenment investment in the first: infancy as a laboratory for uncovering the workings of sensory experience and, especially in later responses to this tradition, the accretion of that sensory experience into individual identity. The ballroom, on this model, is another nursery. If our infantile encounters with the world make us individuals, then our adolescent encounters with the world make us adults. The novel's focus on the novice's entrance into the world fastens the conceptual link between phenomenal experience and worldly experience—our perceptual encounters with things and our social encounters with persons. At the same time, in the hands of the authors central to this study, this second entrance into the world also complicates and even revises those same philosophical accounts of experience and identity by suggesting that they are less formative than the analogy would initially propose. In other words, the novice both takes advantage of the affordances of this familiar eighteenth-century comparison while, at the same time, evincing skepticism toward the very terms of the analogy. Both maturity and subjectivity are held up for inspection rather than taken as given.

At the risk of belaboring the point, allow me to observe that we *know* Camilla has not *actually* sprung fully formed from the head of Jove—or of anyone else for that matter; the novel's action follows her from age nine to seventeen. Lionel may invoke the radical contingency of romance—"some accident" that might render Camilla a goddess instead of a girl—but he is only joking. After all, Burney's novels are also what we tend to call "realist": characters do not just materialize, they age and grow in predictable ways, and even characters of mysterious parentage (like the purportedly illegitimate Evelina) are of woman born. Yet Burney's interest in her heroines' "coming out" into society does not correspond to an interest in their "coming of age" in the sense that we usually understand that generic category: as the representation of incremental development and growing maturity, an investigation of character that focuses on how characters change over time.[8] And Burney's suggestion that Camilla is herself a "picture" (or *Bild*) of youth in the novel's subtitle (and elsewhere) does not mean, in turn, that we should take this novel to be a bildungsroman.[9] On the contrary, it is Camilla's stasis, her resistance to change, that the novel most clearly illuminates.[10] I will demonstrate this at further length in chapter 4, where I take on *Camilla*'s suggestion that minority, for all its limitations, offers a compelling model for ethical engagement. For now, it will suffice us to note that Lionel's patronizing joke cannily captures this conflation of Camilla's moral dignity (even, as the reference to Minerva suggests, her wisdom) with her tenacious and puzzling inexperience.

Where literary scholars have recognized character consistency of this sort in eighteenth-century novels, we have tended to attribute it to one of three possibilities. First, we can see characters as continuing to operate within the generic constraints of romance (or, in what amounts to the same move, as parodying those constraints via their exposure). According to this line of argument, the novel, as it emerges, holds on to the flatter, more typological figures of romance —its damsels, its saviors, its villains—as it struggles to differentiate itself from its antecedent fictional mode and to develop and codify a new set of generic conventions.[11] Second, to follow another line of argument, we can see these stubbornly consistent figures not as nostalgic but as precisely symptomatic of their historical moment, especially as novels represent young women who, by this account, are prevented not just narratively but culturally from fully maturing into adulthood, isolated as they are from key experiences of social and political life reserved for men.[12] (Here the constraints that novels reveal are ideological rather than formal; they inhere in *what* early realism represents rather than *how* it represents.[13]) Finally, we can see these consistent characters as examples of inept characterization, usually understood as missing or primitive *Bildung*: the novel is slow to develop a model of character fully imbricated with and responsive to the complexities of historical time; only when it does so can the novel achieve the full potential of its form.[14] All these possibilities find their way into this project, but I should be clear at the outset that I aim throughout this book to carve out a way of thinking about consistently inexperienced novelistic characters on their own terms: as neither backward nor forward looking, neither hobbled by formal demands nor yielding to historical pressures, but as a central, affirmative component of the novel project in the second half of the eighteenth century.[15] This focused span of attention, this temporal constraint, necessarily means that this book addresses a literary historical topic (the British novel's early strategies), but the questions I ask here are typically formal in nature: about what a character is, how narrative works, and what realism can do.[16]

Realism's Awkward Age

The present study takes as its provocation the fact that the early realist novel so consistently chooses as its subject the figure of the adolescent without predictably following adolescence into adulthood. Over the course of the following chapters, I explain why eighteenth-century novels find attractions in stubbornly youthful figures by illuminating the formal problems attendant to early realism that the figure of the adolescent promised to address—foremost among these, the technical difficulty of representing both everyday, lived experience and, at the same time, exemplary conduct. Enter the novice: youthful protagonists, in crossing a threshold from private to public life, approach the wider world differently than those understood as already belonging to it. As we shall see, this difference of approach finds narrative presentation in the suspension of counterfactual logics: the novice believes that an encounter is working in a way that his interlocutor, or witness, understands not to be the case (and this distance between their understandings is often exploited at the novice's expense). Take, for example, Clarissa Harlowe's belief that she finds herself imprisoned not in a brothel but in a respectable boarding house, a mistake so fundamental as to raise questions about her powers of perception. The unthinkable, for one of Clarissa's virtue, shades into the unseeable, and the tension between moral and empirical demands structures the long novel's minimal plot. Such a misunderstanding further divorces the novice from the society that understands how things "really" work but, in doing so, grants the novice a position of moral authority from which to understand that society—or even, by comparing it to a more idealistic vision, to improve upon it. And so, while I may appear to echo Lovelace's charge that Clarissa is "a mere novice" in matters practical, my use of the term leverages an entirely different rhetorical and evaluative energy.[17] There is no "mere" about it—the novice is, I propose, the central figure of the early realist novel, encapsulating its formal, epistemological, and moral aims.

By illuminating this figure, this study lingers in realism's awkward age, its growing pains. While the early novel centers on young characters, I argue that it is less interested in charting a naturalistic process of maturation than in using adolescence to stage and work through the formal problems that attended the emergence of realism (not least of which was the question of just how *real* the novel must be). That is, this book aims to sever the too-easy alignment of novelistic form with individual formation, arguing that to understand the emergence of the British novel we must learn how to read its skepticism toward character development. While both phenomenal and social experience are at times understood as inevitable and unavoidable—that is, one cannot help but experience the world—these novels work to disentangle experience from development, and that disentanglement raises important questions about what the novel form could—and can—accomplish.[18]

In referring to the period boundaries of this study—roughly the second half of the eighteenth century—as "early realism," I wish to stress the provisionality of the realist project in this moment, the sense that realist representation was being figured out in real time and with considerable urgency. Most centrally, I want to light up the coincidence of the eighteenth-century novel's loose mimeticism with its tendency toward idealization. Indeed, early realism is always an idealizing mode—*selecting* what is fit for representation rather than striving for thoroughgoing verisimilitude.[19] Samuel Johnson puts it this way in an oft-quoted (and oft-taught) passage from *Rambler* 4:

> It is justly considered as the greatest excellency of art, to imitate nature; but it is necessary to distinguish those parts of nature, which are most proper for imitation: greater care is still required in representing life, which is so often discoloured by passion, or deformed by wickedness. If the world be promiscuously described, I cannot see of what use it can be to read the account; or why it may not be as safe to turn the eye immediately upon mankind, as upon a mirror which shows all that presents itself without discrimination.[20]

Literary scholars have long recognized the conservatism of Johnson's injunction here, his insistence that it just is not "safe" for fiction to represent "life" that is "discoloured" or "deformed." This warning marks the pinnacle of the mid-century debate over so-called mixed character, to which I turn in the first two chapters of this book as I engage with Richardson's and Fielding's surprisingly parallel approaches to this problem. But perhaps because of a distaste for Johnson's conservatism, scholars of the novel have neglected the implications of his theory that imitation should be discerning, that fiction, in deciding what aspects of life to capture, can effectively create new life. If early realism is conservative in Johnson's vision, it is likewise fundamentally generative. With special attention to this latter quality, this study shows early realism to be both descriptive and conjectural, tethered to the lived world of its readers but always aspiring to drift away from it in order to limn the contours of another world. As Jed Esty notes in a forceful essay, "Realisms are neither replicative of the real, nor unexperimental. . . . The most apparently mimetic modes of narration still register an artistic impulse to transform the world as well as imitate it."[21] This perceptive observation is central to early theories of the British novel. In what we might justly consider the first theorization of the novel as such, the preface to *The British Novelists* (1810/1820), Anna Laetitia Barbauld stakes out a remarkably generous terrain for the genre that similarly highlights its transformative capacity: "It is pleasant to the mind to sport in the boundless regions of possibility; to find relief from the sameness of every-day occurrences by expatiating amidst brighter skies and fairer fields; to exhibit love that is always happy, valour that is always successful; to feed the appetite for wonder by a quick succession of marvelous events; and to distribute, like a ruling providence, rewards and punishments which fall just where they ought to fall."[22] Barbauld takes up Johnson's theory of realist idealization, then, but grounds it not in a paternalistic caution against moral hazard but instead in readerly enjoyment. Selectivity is a tool for heightening pleasure, delimiting the suitable by eliminating the soporific as well as the suspect. By "insist[ing] on the fictiveness of even the most probable of novels, [Barbauld] posits no firm binary between romance and novel, ancient and modern fiction, or probability and improbability," and she establishes realism as a capacious mode of representation that centers idealization as an imaginative technique that yields significant rewards.[23]

Realism so understood includes, indeed elevates, the depiction of the unrealized. Barbauld's reference to the "boundless regions of possibility" opens up the field on which the novel might "sport," but the game of plot is nevertheless delimited, if only because the length of the novel is delimited (Richardson's experiments in prolixity notwithstanding). We may be reminded of Paul Ricoeur's observation: "It is the function of a plot to bend the logic of *possible* acts toward a logic of *probable* narratives."[24] But pace Ricoeur, the logic of possibility lingers in realist narratives, structuring the probability of plot by revealing diegetic narrative always to be one possibility among many. In a moving essay in a special issue of *Representations* devoted to counterfactual narratives, Andrew H. Miller refers to counterfactual logics as the "optative mode," after the grammatical mood of *what if?*, and he argues that they are central to realist fiction: "To the extent that realism proposes to tell us how things really were, a space naturally opens up within that mode to tell us how things might have been, but were not."[25] To see the counterfactual as inherent to realism, as Miller does, is to see realism distill and reflect upon a principle essential to narrative tout court. Focusing on the nineteenth-century novel, Miller sees the optative as casting a light—better still, a shadow—on lives unled and paths not taken, most powerfully harnessing feelings of remorse and regret. This principle is certainly at play in the novels I center here; narrative works by delimiting the possibilities that the novice protagonist encounters: a field of suitors narrows to *the* one on whom both the heroine and the courtship plot will focus their attentions. Tom Jones does not ultimately go to sea, as he is determined to early in Fielding's novel, nor does he join the king's forces to quash the Jacobite rebellion. Moments of entering the world are, of course, particularly prone to the generation of counterfactuals of this sort, as the demands of momentous life decisions force the optative to seep out. Early novels, like those of nineteenth-century high realism, highlight narrative's capacity to create value through the depiction of counterfactual, *un*realized alternatives to a primary narrative seen as correct, worthwhile, and, as Miller suggests, *real.*

Yet, in the readings that follow, I see at once a more extraordinary and more mundane counterfactual structure in eighteenth-century novels. Plots follow protagonists who *live out lives parallel to their own*, their inexperience forking each encounter into the real and the illusory, the empirical and the merely possible. To recognize this counterfactual structure is to notice what Ian Watt calls, tugging at a thread that runs from *Clarissa* though to *Middlemarch* and *The Portrait of a Lady*, "the all but unendurable disparity between expectation and reality that faces sensitive women in modern society," but it is also to place considerably more pressure on the trajectory of expectation than we have previously. This is because the moral weight of eighteenth-century fiction encourages experience as such to be foreclosed, meaning that hypothetical experience—to wit, *in*experience—is only further heightened. Novices bring to their stories a variety of dubious assumptions about the world that shape their paths, from the mundane (shopkeepers ask fair prices) to the profound (people are ultimately good). I am advocating for a method of reading that finds as much narrative heft in the assumptions of the novice as in the eventual correction of those assumptions. And I aim to emphasize the way that those unreal narratives threaten to take precedence, even when revealed to be empirically bogus, ontologically undone. Even faced with the relentless assertion of the ontology of the empirical world, counterfactual inexperiences assert themselves.

Not all the characters I analyze here (or that may have been included) are young women, and yet I will suggest that the novice is prototypically female. This is in part because the kind of sustained inexperience I track in the following pages is the cultural inverse of an expansive worldly experience reserved for men, just as the provincial upbringing of many of these characters opposes itself to the experiential scale and density of the metropolis and the grand tour. But, moreover, I associate the kind of counterfactual logic set in motion by the novice with women's encounters with a world that is often hostile to them. To point this out is by no means to endorse the conservative "protection" of women from presumably fuller and richer lives. Rather, it is to suggest that the novice's benevolent vision of the world is nevertheless a kind of embedded utopianism, assuming (with varying degrees of hesitancy) the possibility of free movement and ready hospitality. At its boldest, the vision the novice projects is of a world where women are not raped. This visionary projection *remains* one way that feminists make claims about the world, and, thus, inexperience can be understood as operating according to an abiding feminist logic: women should be able to wear what they please, walk alone at night, have a drink in a crowded bar, without those actions inviting violation. That is, we must live as if the world has no rape in order to hold rapists accountable for rape's existence in the world. We must project the world we wish to inhabit. The danger of elevating inexperience is that it goes hand in hand with the misogynistic privation of women, the diminution of their experiences by patriarchy. I have no desire to dispute this, and I take as given that a pervasive culture of misogyny is inherent in the stories I tell. At the same time, I have been struck over the years, as I have worked on this study, by the force of even those narratives that trace women's lives at their most minimal, unmarked by developmental eventfulness. My aim is not to recuperate inexperience so much as to notice what else is happening in these narratives of extreme constraint. To appreciate these narratives, we must be willing to hold two propositions in tension: one, that these figures speak to conditions of sociopolitical limitation and privation; two, that they at the same time offer complex and even powerful encapsulations of aesthetic and ethical ideas. As such, this argument requires what I sometimes think of as a kind of suspension of feminist disbelief: a willingness to think through the terms of a constrained life without (or before) emphasizing what is left out.

I suggest that the optative mode in eighteenth-century realism offers a modest sort of utopia, a gesture toward another sort of world.[26] We might think of this gesture in generic terms as the irruption of romance into the space of the otherwise verisimilar. "Romance," Miller writes, "can be said to serve as the expression of the optative mode for realism—its dream of an alternative life," and this doubling occurs as much within fictional narrative as it does among narratives.[27] (That is, I am encouraging a model of reading that recognizes that the windmills are also—on a parallel plane, in a neighboring possible world—dragons.) Once we abandon our expectations of development and instead focus on inexperience itself, we see such counterfactual narratives with considerably more clarity and capture their diegetic recapitulation of the visionary work that fiction performs more broadly. Like Dorothy Van Ghent, I understand this project to stand in tension with our typical understanding of the novel's indebtedness to empiricism: "Being a hypothetical structure, the novel is able to give leverage to the empirically known and push it into the dimension of the unknown, the possible. Its value lies less in confirming and interpreting the known than in forcing us to the supposition that *something else might be the case.* It is for this reason that the novel is a source of insight."[28] And so, when I call the early novel conjectural or speculative, I refer not to what we now think of as early speculative fiction (of the sort we might identify with Margaret Cavendish or, later, Mary Shelley), but something more routine: the world conjured by a young person whose expectations and hopes bear little resemblance to the "real" (likewise diegetic) world that threatens to quash them. Early novels regularly offer up competing visions of the world within their pages—signaled by the proliferating and contested meanings of the word "world"—and they just as regularly endorse those worlds that are most remote from lived experience.[29] When "the world" is both comprehensive and restrictive, heavenly and secular, when it names the cosmopolitan and the parochial, public flourishing and private retreat, we would be wise to ask just what world the novice enters into and just what the novice lacks when she is deemed unworldly.[30]

The novice's counterfactual potential begins to explain why such figures proved so popular to early novels even as the lives of young people could by another vantage be seen as offering little by way of instruction or entertainment. When Oliver Goldsmith's narrator, the Rev. Dr. Charles Primrose, turns to provide the novel's cast of characters in *The Vicar of Wakefield* (1766), he stops short once he comes to his adolescent children. He gives the reader their names, a brief sketch of their more prominent features, and then he seems to reach the limits of his descriptive capacity: "But it is needless to attempt describing the particular characters of young people that have seen but very little of the world."[31] Of course, Primrose's dismissal ultimately proves apophatic: these young people *are* described throughout the novel, and, indeed, their encounters and obstacles drive the sentimental novel's plot. But, by Primrose's account, to be young is to be, in some sense, without a character—or, what amounts to the same thing under the protocols of realism: to share a character in common, to be a type.[32] This is true even when the qualities he ascribes to this type (they are "all equally generous, credulous, simple and inoffensive") are qualities that he himself shares. Goldsmith suggests, as do the other novelists examined in this book, that young people constitute a *special* type, one that fundamentally reveals the operations of novelistic character even as they confound description. Far from being ill suited to representation because of their limited experience, their representation drives fiction's testing of empirical claims.

Developing the protocols of early realism, midcentury novelists turned to young protagonists both to exploit and to manage narrative's potential. As J. Paul Hunter observes, "Almost all eighteenth-century novels . . . concentrated on character[s] and situation[s] with which the young could readily identify, and novelists ever since have continued to be preoccupied with the crises of the decisive moments in adolescence and early adulthood."[33] Hunter explains the prevalence of young characters by reference to the novel's eighteenth-century readership, seeing the depiction of youthful characters as both a matter of mimetic representation and of didactic utility. In other words, novelistic characters imitated their readers so that their readers could, in turn, imitate them. Even if we set aside the actualities of the burgeoning reading public, the novel reader is repeatedly *figured* as youthful, both in defenses of the emergent form's instructive value and in warnings about its seductive dangers. In that latter category, perhaps most famously, Samuel Johnson figures the novel's readership as "the young, the ignorant, and the idle," suggesting that these categories might contain significant overlap that the wrong kind of novel would only exacerbate.[34] While she cautions that early novels in fact had a particularly diverse readership, Teresa Michals recognizes this gravitation toward adolescence as well: when the reader's age was considered by early novelists and novel theorists, "the most important member of that audience was 'the young person' rather than the adult."[35] Mirroring these young readers both real and imagined, early novels begin, again and again, with characters on the brink of adulthood, wide-eyed naïfs teetering on the edge of a wider world. More strikingly, as we will see, these inexperienced characters tend to remain on that threshold—*entering* the world without ever having fully entered—a suspension of the figure's possibility that turns out to complicate its claims to didactic utility.

While I am indebted to work on eighteenth-century readerships, this book resists relying on readership as a ready answer to the questions raised by adolescent characters—not least because I simply do not see these characters following the patterns of initiation sketched by the conduct books and apprentice manuals to which scholars have long seen them adhering.[36] (To take just a couple of late examples, think of books like Susan Nicklin's *Address to a Young Lady on her Entrance into the World* [1796] or manuals for visitors to London like Richard King's *The New Cheats of London Exposed; or, the Frauds and Tricks of the Town Laid open to Both Sexes. Being a Guard against the Iniquitous Practices of that Metropolis* [1795].) Fiction certainly boasted of offering credible models of initiation. But I depart from studies focused on readership by emphasizing two key complications of that professed aim. First, I want to point out the limits and challenges of (even realist) representation. As we have seen, early realism's emphasis on selectivity opened a gulf between fiction and the life of its readers. Just what did it mean for these highly idealized characters to represent their ordinary readers? Second, while I agree with generations of scholars of the early novel that the form must be understood as—in Michals's apt phrase— "proudly didactic," I contend that its lessons were never as clear as a cautionary model would have us believe.[37] Avoiding in real life the perils faced by these novices would, in case after case, require abandoning a moral fortitude that these characters, however gullible, consistently embody. Credulity, in these novels, goes hand in hand with moral vision, and so the elimination of the first endangers the second—constituting a serious ethical hazard no matter how assured the practical rewards may be. To put it plainly, if novel protagonists were young because they served as avatars of their imagined readers, it is nevertheless true that the work of readerly identification with literary characters was (and remains) tricky and ever shifting.[38]

The difficulties of imitation are unmistakable in conduct books' self-conscious discussions of young people's experience. As the Rev. John Fordyce makes clear, the problem of female inexperience (in particular) raised a number of intractable questions, foremost, "where, or how, is [experience] to be obtained by a girl?" Fordyce's sermons would come to inspire derision and parody (just think of the sniggering and snoring they elicit when read aloud by Austen's Mr. Collins), but they were also enormously popular. The problem

Fordyce lays out—how are women to be expected to gain the experience necessary to cultivate their native good sense while also avoiding the dangers experience was expected to bring—was central to eighteenth-century moral thought,
and the answer he arrives at was likewise a common one: women must pursue
experience vicariously, through judicious reading (of conduct and devotional
literature, specifically). In fact, conduct books recognized a paradox at the center of their task: they aimed to proliferate experiences that might model conduct,
while they also encouraged young readers to avoid experience at all costs. "It is
a melancholy consideration," writes Hester Chapone, "that the judgment can
only be formed by experience, which generally comes too late for our own use,
and is seldom accepted for that of others."[39] Conduct book writers arrive at a
number of acrobatic solutions to this central problem. Addressing her advice to
a beloved niece, Chapone arrives at an amusingly specific recommendation; she
advises that young women befriend *slightly* older women (she recommends aim-
ing for around twenty-three or twenty-four), taking advantage of the narrow
window in which vicarious experience promised to be fresh and not yet bitter.
We might think of the most useful conduct books, then, as the twenty-three-
year-old friends of the print media social circle. But the novel—especially as it
continued to return to the lives of young people—could not manage to thread
this needle. The problem faced by the novelist is the same faced by the moral-
ist: what does a life without experience look like? (To paraphrase Henry James,
how does a girl become a subject?) Here, the challenge is technical as much as
moral. Indeed, my proposition is that the form's moral and aesthetic aims were
altogether different from those articulated by conduct books. Rather than im-
part a worldly discernment in its young (and not so young) readers, the novel
instead invited and capitalized on the generative potential of unworldliness.

More New Than Any Other Characters

By focusing on the novice as a character type, this book has both a narrow and
a broad task. On the one hand, I elevate the novice to the pantheon of well-
known eighteenth-century character types (the coquette, the picaro, the libertine, and so on) and, in doing so, illuminate a figure that has been largely
neglected inasmuch as it has never quite rewarded the kind of inquiry until
recently dominant in eighteenth-century studies: namely, a model shaped by
the methodologies of historicism and cultural studies.[40] Yet, on the other hand,
considering this type means that we must conceive of novelistic character dif-

ferently. Rather than conceiving of novelistic character tout court as operating according to the protocols and expectations of *Bildung*, I refuse to consider the depiction of character over narrative time as conterminous with psychological maturity.[41] I will be tilting time-honored debates about character "depth" on their axes: finding varieties of shallowness or depth that do not map onto a timeline of growth or development.[42]

To resist the pull of the *Bildung* model on these characters (let alone on character more broadly conceived) is no straightforward task. Some readers will find axiomatic the suggestion that eighteenth-century characters escape *Bildung*, while others will greet the proposition with skepticism. That both reactions can coexist is, in part, due to the slipperiness of the bildungsroman as both a literary historical genre and as a theoretical topos. As Marc Redfield reminds us, perhaps no literary critical concept has been more successful than the bildungsroman, a subgeneric model that has long threatened to become synonymous with the novel itself, reaching past its initial locus in the nineteenth-century European novel and finding its way into nearly every aspect of our understanding of the genre.[43] Its insinuations find a mixed reception in studies of the eighteenth-century British novel. Take, for example, *The Cambridge History of the English Novel*, a reputable, student-directed resource that we can take to express a more general sentiment within the field: "It is tempting to include in a history of the English bildungsroman earlier literary landmarks such as *Robinson Crusoe* (1719), *Clarissa* (1748), *Tom Jones* (1749), *Tristram Shandy* (1759–1767), the novels of Fanny Burney and a number of those of Scott and Austen. Indeed, the fact that most eighteenth- and nineteenth-century English novels are concerned with self-development suggests that the term bildungsroman should be considered as describing a central tendency of the English novel *sui generis*."[44] One of the aims of this study is to challenge this "temptation" to consider the British novel and the bildungsroman as coextensive. To reject *Bildung* as the governing model of the early novel is not simply to resist, in the name of a better literary historicism, the creeping anachronism of a model invented at a later date and codified at yet a later one, though I certainly endorse Patricia Meyer Spacks's caution against "read[ing] the nineteenth-century novel back into the eighteenth."[45] I also want to assert the presence of a competing model that will enable us to bring the same critical attention to the novice that we have continued to bring to the bildungsroman.[46]

With this goal in mind, I refer throughout this book to "inexperience" in an attempt to capture a persistent (if not permanent) state, rather than a condition only to be subsumed into experience. I welcome the slight infelicity of that word—inexperience—the noun form lending a bit of solidity to a concept that has tended to be understood as fleeting, evanescent, subordinated to its hegemonic opposite. No doubt, as we have already seen, a constellation of terms collects around the figure of the novice: naïve, innocent, ignorant, immature, uneducated, simple. These will all find their way into this study. Why, then, focus on "inexperience"? I do so because the term captures the curiously antagonistic relationship to philosophical empiricism I see foregrounded by these narratives.[47] In these novels, experience of the world is not absent (nor indeed could it be), but it is consistently subordinated, questioned, and even expunged. This claim will no doubt strike some readers as controversial. Indeed, readers familiar with scholarly accounts of identity in eighteenth-century fiction and culture may find curious my assertion that experience can be decoupled from identity. Scholarship on the early novel in eighteenth-century Britain, especially since Ian Watt, has focused on the centrality of empirical philosophy to Enlightenment culture and has, by extension, considered the representation of individual experience as central to the early novel's particular brand of realism and, with it, realistic character development.[48]

Despite decades of revision by later scholars, Watt's theory of the eighteenth-century novel has continued to shape the field, not least, I suggest, because of its capacious mobilization of two related, but quite distinct, models of what experience means to novelists who are attempting to differentiate an emergent realist mode from its precursors. First, and most famously, Watt begins with John Locke's *Essay concerning Human Understanding* (1690) and, specifically, Locke's insistence that knowledge results from sensory experience: "Let us then suppose the Mind to be, as we say, white Paper, void of all Characters, without any *Ideas*; How comes it to be furnished? . . . To this I answer, in one word, from *Experience*. In that all our knowledge is founded; and from that it ultimately derives itself."[49] Rejecting the notion that we come equipped with innate ideas, Locke posits instead that ideas are generated by the experience of direct sensory impressions. Watt sees Locke's claim as influencing the way the novel presents its characteristic specificity, "particular individuals having particular experiences at particular times and at particular places."[50] This account of the registration of sensory impression in narrative form, a technique Watt calls "formal realism," slides easily into an account of the characterological effects that those experiences provoke. As he puts it in his discussion of the form's temporal precision, "The novel in general has interested itself much more than any other literary form in the development of its characters in the course of time."[51] This second variety of lived experience, which operates according to an extrapolation and extension of sensory experience, is most evident in Watt's move from formal realism, which he also calls "realism of presentation" (290), to a quite different novelistic innovation: "realism of assessment" (291). More related to plotting than to description, realism of assessment is discernable in the novel's orchestration of various scenes of social life—scenes that the protagonist encounters and that are then either reflected upon by the narration or that serve via juxtaposition as counterpoints to each other.[52] In moving between these two varieties of experience, Watt's account extrapolates from encounters with objects to encounters with society, raising questions of how experience shapes our understanding of the world, how experience changes us, and what experiences come to matter and why.[53] It is realism of assessment that alerts the reader to the author's evaluative stance toward the novel's characters and events, producing an almost paternal, "wise assessment of life" (Watt 288). The term registers the felt sense that the reader is in the hands of a master of social experience. If formal realism is about the novelist's depiction of a world, realism of assessment is about the novelist's depiction of worldliness.[54]

While Watt's theory of formal realism has been widely influential in subsequent scholarship, critics have often accused him of underdeveloping his second term, realism of assessment.[55] This charge stems in large part from the sense that the term seems to be present in Watt's argument primarily to account for the novels of Fielding, which show comparably little investment in the formal realism favored by Daniel Defoe and Richardson. In noticing this disequilibrium, critics have neglected to note that the collision of these two kinds of experience recalls the central analogy in eighteenth-century thought between our first sensory experiences and our first social encounters. Semantically connected through variations on the phrase "entrance into the world" (which will serve as something of a leitmotif of this book), the analogy captures the precariousness of these moments of initial encounter. But whereas this connection would suggest that the novice, a newly blank slate, will be overwritten, formed, by the social experiences to which she is exposed, this assumption of development is repeatedly challenged once we turn to the novels themselves. Indeed, it is worth noting that Locke himself turns away from the infamous blank slate metaphor (and, indeed, most writing metaphors) over the course of his investigations. If the palimpsest is a problematic figure for empiricist subjectivity, then it proves only more troublesome for character.[56]

Eighteenth-century novels emphasize character beginnings over character development, with the novice epitomizing this widespread tendency. Central to the formation of this figure is Milton's *Paradise Lost*, especially in its reception by eighteenth-century critics. Take the theory of character Joseph Addison articulates in the *Paradise Lost* essays first published in *The Spectator*. Addison understands Milton's radicality to hinge on the poet's depiction of his characters as belonging to poetry rather than history. That is, Adam and Eve are not historical figures; we have no human testimony that narrates their lives. Yet Milton's account is authoritative in its attempt to divine the logical and psychological bases for their actions, for how they *should have been* given their circumstances. This logic invests particular meaning in their newness with respect both to the created world and to literary history. In favorably comparing *Paradise Lost* to classical epic, Addison argues, "We have . . . four distinct characters in [Adam and Eve]. We see Man and Woman in the highest innocence and perfection, and in the most abject state of guilt and infirmity. The two last characters are, indeed, very common and obvious, but the two first are not only more magnificent, but more new than any characters either in *Virgil* or *Homer*, or indeed in the whole circle of nature."[57] From the perspective of Christian cosmology, Adam and Eve are the newest characters of all; they are without precedent. In this light, Addison's comparison to the classical masters seems unjust, as the *Aeneid* or the *Iliad* simply cannot represent such extreme novelty. But Addison is not just firing yet another volley in the Quarrel of the Ancients and the Moderns. The fact that Adam and Eve are newer than any character "in the whole circle of nature" does not undermine their plausibility but instead changes the terms by which a character might be considered plausible.[58] Milton not only provides the reader with a "newer" cast of characters than those of Homer and Virgil, his ability to reconstruct the origins of humanity undermines the very assumption that one must take discrete historical facts into account to produce a reliable narrative. This shift renders classical history constitutionally derivative, a collection of disconnected and often contradictory reports. Milton is, we might say, at his most modern when completely rejecting the timeline of ancient-before-modern in favor of a timeless *pre*history that fundamentally revises how history might be understood. In this sense, Milton does not rewrite Genesis but instead re*creates* who Adam and Eve must have been if we accept as true the situation described in Genesis.

In underscoring (and delighting in) the novelty of Milton's protagonists, Addison employs a kind of critical shorthand in which newness signals not only the moral perfection of the prelapsarian condition but also a fresh perspective on the world (newly created or otherwise). Thus Aeneas and Odysseus, while necessarily imperfect for their paganism, are yet more so for having already passed, wearily, through the trials of war before their narratives begin. Though twenty-first-century readers might associate the uniform innocence of the unfallen Adam and Eve with a lack of narrative interest, such a reaction is utterly alien to Addison's thought. On the contrary, it is the fallen state, the state in which we find ourselves, that is mundane. The novice is new. Accordingly, the narrative of the fall, the series of steps that move Adam and Eve past their flawless condition, is indispensable for their fallen state to hold any narrative interest whatsoever. Beginning with the new (the *un*worldly) is what allows the mundane to become intelligible, to bear meaning. Richardson will echo Addison's sentiment explicitly in his lament to his friend Lady Bradshaigh over the success of *Tom Jones* (1749): "Has not the world shown me that it is much better pleased to receive and applaud the character that shows us what we are (little of novelty as one would think there is in that) than what we ought to be? Are there not [those] who think Clarissa's an unnatural character?"[59]

Unnatural, yes, and yet vital for early realism's attempt to fashion a world both plausible and carefully curated. Addison's striking reading of *Paradise Lost* is central to his aesthetics of novelty more generally. Critics tend to read Addison's conception of the novel as a way of explaining the rapidly changing social world of eighteenth-century England.[60] Yet, in the above passage, Addison is associating not just novelty alone, but novelty at its *utmost*, with a definitively presocial, premodern world—one that seems to invoke the novice's wariness of sociality more than the rake's urbane mastery of it. Furthermore, Addison attaches this conception of novelty not to the first-person observations of the essay form but, crucially, to the creation and depiction of fictional characters. Novelty need not register only the contemporary or current (what is newly emerging right now) but can also index the *radically* original (what was new at the very beginning).

We can trace this insight across eighteenth-century narrative and in a range of figures both beloved and infamous for the misfit between their perspectives and their worlds. The defamiliarizing affordances of the novice are legible in the speculative imaginings of the viewpoint of so-called noble savages like Addison's own King Sa Ga Yean Qua Rash Tow or Voltaire's "Child of Nature," where inexperience is racialized and experience coded as proximity to the colonizing center.[61] This is true even when (as is often the case in descriptions of

these encounters) it is the West that comes in for criticism. Consider this ex-
cerpt from Burney's extensive description of meeting Omai, the Pacific Islander
who returned with Captain Cook and became the toast of London society:
"Indeed, he seems to shame Education. . . . [H]e appears to be a perfectly rational & intelligent man, with an understanding far superior to the common race
of *us cultivated gentry*. . . . [He] appears in a *new world* like a man [who] had
all his life studied *the Graces*."[62] Often less about the contact between two independent cultures, these interactions show what Northrop Frye calls "philosophical man abstracted from his social context," encountering the so-called civi-
lized world as if first encountering the social as such. Here, the novice is "an
abstract model of a human being, a laboratory specimen, as it were, used as
a basis for a study of human behavior in general, without regard to a specific
historical period or social setting."[63] Mary Shelley would take this abstraction
to the extreme—well, to the laboratory—creating out of a number of men a creature who is both a composite man and a new kind of being entirely. Less spec-
tacularly, consider the period's popular depictions of youthful inexperience as
attached to an aging man—Fielding's Parson Adams, Goldsmith's Dr. Primrose, Sterne's Uncle Toby, or Burney's Sir Hugh Tyrold. Each is likened to a
newborn babe, each undergoes a series of humiliating encounters that charts
the distance between the knowing world and the naïf. The advanced age of these
characters testifies to the period's interest in the sustainability of inexperience
over time, the possibility that we might find youthfulness decoupled from the
biological stage of youth. It is not, then, to be clear, that the adolescent is the only
figure to capture the affordances of inexperience or to evince the eighteenth
century's attraction to such a state. Nevertheless, as we shall see, adolescence
holds a privileged place in this story for the ways that it distills character's formal operations.

Characters Drawn on Dust

Distinguishing the early novel from established forms like the epic or the romance, novel theorists have tended to train our attention on the ways that
characters undergo experiences that change them and that promise to change
the reader in turn. As I show in this final section, theorists of character have
more recently complicated this picture—yet character development (and, in
particular, character development *over diegetic time*) remains stubbornly central. For an explicit statement of assumptions undergirding most classic ac-

counts of novelistic character, we can turn to Mikhail Bakhtin, whose capacious theory of the novel (as voraciously consuming all other genres with which it comes into contact) would seem to allow for a similarly flexible conception of character. And yet, in contrasting the novel with the epic, Bakhtin emphasizes the novel's point of contact with an ever-shifting present moment and the epic's corresponding containment of a past that is over and done with, an "absolute past" that is both set apart from and valorized by the present-day world of the reader.[64] This distinction, for Bakhtin, maps onto the ways each genre presents fictional characters. Because the novel is the only genre to emerge within modernity, in what Bakhtin calls "the full light of the historical day," it has a special relationship to its own time.[65] And this connection to the present ensures that the novel will always be a form that is curiously formless, never reaching the moment of highly polished completion that we might see with ancient genres, and instead seeming always to be a work in progress.[66] A work *in* progress, but also a work *about* progress, as Bakhtin makes clear when he establishes an analogy between each genre and its heroes: the epic contains characters who are fully formed, and the novel's plasticity requires characters who are equally unfinished and malleable. The special relationship between the novel and its time ensures that the genre be attuned to the procedures through which we might understand a protagonist's encounter with and accommodation to his present. Indeed, one of the principles of the early novel that Bakhtin sees arising from contemporaneous critical accounts, such as those Fielding incorporates into his novels *Joseph Andrews* and *Tom Jones*, is that "the hero should not be portrayed as an already completed and unchanging person but as one who is evolving and developing, a person who learns from life."[67] While he is right to emphasize the flux of novel time—its capacity for heightening character potential—Bakhtin goes a step further in taking the novel's formlessness to necessitate characters who undergo formation. Indeed, novel theory, when it has considered character at all, has tended to assume that character as such indicates the sum of such changes, the accretion of experience over the time of the novel's plot.[68] Here, individual development *is* character development; characterization is successful to the degree that maturation is achieved. This tendency is only exacerbated in many studies of the eighteenth-century novel in particular, where the vast intellectual movement of the Enlightenment is seen as imposing a model for the microcosmic tracing of characters' individual lives—as if taking literally Kant's answer to the question, "What is Enlightenment?": "Enlightenment is man's emergence from his self-imposed immaturity."[69] But this account of how novel characters work is, at best, incomplete and, at worst, wholly inadequate to the task of theorizing the novel's taking up of questions of fictional personhood and impersonality.

I suggest such a resistance to progress can be contained in a model of character, urging a distinction between fictional character and the expectations we have of real persons. Over the past twenty years or so, scholars of eighteenth-century novels have been particularly open to considering the ways in which characters might be less than human, while still prompting human responses from their readers. Catherine Gallagher, in *Nobody's Story* (1994), argues that fictional characters—"proper name[s] explicitly without . . . physical referent[s] in the real world"—provoked powerful cultural effects precisely because they were not fully human.[70] Because novelistic characters did not refer to actual persons, as did the scandalous romans à clef that preceded them, readers were free to sympathize without the risk of forming inappropriate attachments. But perhaps no other scholar has done more to enrich our understanding of eighteenth-century character than Deidre Shauna Lynch, who, in *The Economy of Character* (1998), argues that readers did not look for roundness in characters until late in the eighteenth century, when they started to use character depth to mitigate their own anxieties about the emerging market economy that threatened to make them feel rather instrumental themselves. Lynch in particular draws out the multiple contemporary significations of "character"—as fictional personage, ethos, and currency. In examining the cultural practices converging around the new market culture, Lynch is most interested in how characters were read as marks on a page (yet another meaning of the word "character") and not as deep, psychologically complex quasi-persons until well into the Romantic period. If Locke asks us to think of the mind as a sheet of white paper, then Lynch asks us to think about how many *kinds* of character converge in the process of cognition: "The imprinting of a surface and the acquisition of characters produce 'character,' or personality, where before there was a blank."[71] The present study builds on this understanding of character while, at the same time, questioning whether these marks of character are truly indelible, or whether they are, as Locke says of the unretained thoughts of the soul, "characters drawn on Dust, that the first breath of wind effaces."[72] Novelistic character, I suggest, capitalizes on associations with marking or imprinting (as figures for formation or development) but never fully incorporates the model of formation those parallels would appear to necessitate. Youthful characters, it turns out, as less *impressionable* than we might think.

What does it mean, then, to understand novelistic character outside of the model of development so powerfully articulated in work on the bildungsroman? I take one cue from Frances Ferguson's groundbreaking 1987 essay "Rape and the Rise of the Novel."[73] Through a formal analysis of rape law, Ferguson argues that the psychological novel (inaugurated in Richardson's *Clarissa*) emerges as a registration of the incommensurability of two ways of thinking about mental states (a term Ferguson prefers to the more commonly used "interiority"): on the one hand, what we might think of as *actual* mental states (what a rape victim is thinking), and, on the other, formally (that is, legally) stipulated mental states (what she *must* be thinking). Perhaps one of the more neglected contributions of Ferguson's essay is its claim that young people in particular reveal the unremittingly formal operations of character. In a crime like statutory rape, for example, the victim's consent or non-consent is confronted and even *replaced* by the law's insistence that she, being underage, *cannot* consent, no matter her intention. (Indeed, this is perhaps even more striking for young men: the law designates an age under which a boy cannot be said to *commit* rape.) Rather than seeing this opposition as intractable, and then concluding that character is irrelevant, I take from Ferguson that we must instead say this opposition is intractable and so it must inform our understanding of how character operates. Indeed, character is more important than ever once we recognize this formal operation. As she puts it, "The importance of the notion of a mental state, the importance of the notion of subjectivity itself, may be guaranteed precisely by eradicating its relevance in an actual situation, precisely by denying the capacity of a particular individual to have a meaningful mental state."[74]

The consequences of this observation for the novice are twofold. First, it is crucial to note that adolescence in particular illuminates this formal problem, even if the confrontation of stipulated and actual mental states structures subjectivity more broadly conceived. Instead of pushing for a more robust historicism in order to get a granular account of all the different ways that we have tried to arbitrate the boundaries of adolescence/adulthood (what rights accord to individuals when), Ferguson enables us to see adolescence as a formal mechanism that confounds our desire for such specific terms. This is not to ignore the historical fact that, for example, the Hardwicke Marriage Act of 1753 established twenty-one as the age under which those who wished to marry were required to seek parental permission. Nor is it to deem irrelevant the fact that, by one contemporary measure, human life was understood to progress through regular intervals of seven years (with twenty-one again marking the momentous arrival of adulthood). It is, however, to recognize that the establishment of such an age marker is an attempt to remedy the essential ambiguity of young adulthood.[75] Discomfort with adolescence's slipperiness is as potent today as it was in eighteenth-century Britain. As I write this, the United States is mired in a heated debate about the limits of minority: at what age should an individual be permitted to buy a firearm? to vote? to participate in civic discourse? to be tried as an adult in a court of law? to be sentenced to capital punishment? That this conversation is so urgent in 2018 speaks less to the timeliness of this study than to the endurance of these questions and, what follows, the lasting amorphousness of adolescence as a conceptual category into which persons might be slotted—an instability further compounded by the uneven attribution of adolescence as a category across gender and race. Some young people, we know, are expected to mature very quickly; others, for good or ill, are permitted to remain young indefinitely.[76] At stake in these debates is our understanding of what inexperience means and what its affordances can be. So, while the characters most closely analyzed in this book are teenagers and I attend occasionally to the rights granted upon the achievement of certain arbitrary milestones (especially in chapter 4's discussion of legal minority), this is not a work of social history but of literary criticism. I remain most invested in uncovering inexperience as a largely symbolic liminal state, a heightening of possibility that makes multiple futures more visible. A threshold time.

The second point I take from Ferguson: to encounter the novice is always to tell her that, given her limited experience, she may say that she thinks *X*, but it is only because she does not know any better. Rather than understand these novels as depicting either the correction of young persons by outside forces or the process of reconciliation between young persons and their worlds, I wish to hold onto the incommensurability between those worlds as a way of understanding character as such.[77] Indeed, it *matters* that this incommensurability is not subject to a process of reconciliation but rather that it allows us to linger in the possible worlds created by the irreconcilability of naïve vision and empirical reality. The figure of the novice offers theorists of the novel the clearest example for understanding novelistic character as offering the promise of individuation without the fulfillment of that promise, such that individuation does in fact resemble a *theory* of the novel without accurately describing its praxis. Indeed, the novice figures promise itself: the potential of futurity as such without any of the messy negotiating of the future's terms and conditions.[78] When I say "promise," I do not mean simply the illusion of humanness that we sometimes say is inherent in character because of its fundamental referentiality (its quasi-humanness). In that model, a character's referential promise is akin to a chicken-wire skeleton onto which we slather the papier-mâché of imagined personality, rounding the limbs and producing the expression—taking the minimal frame and creating out of it something resembling ourselves. Rather, and more specifically, I see the novice as figuring the promise of lived experience itself, the future possibilities of a life lived, while holding the elimination of possibilities ever in abeyance.

The novice underscores the operations of novelistic character in the ways that he appears *individualizable*. That is, the novice gives us the illusion of character as process, of individuation in the making. These characters give the impression of persons-to-be but not persons, not quite. Here is Henry James on Tom Jones: "He has so much 'life' that it amounts, for the effect of comedy and application of satire, almost to his having a mind, that is to his having reactions and a full consciousness."[79] Tom "almost . . . [has] a mind," but he does not. The delicacy with which his bewilderment—his high-flying, youthful inexperience—is drawn brings his character just to the precipice of personhood. Tom's inexperience pulls character in two directions: on the one hand, he can strike us as a bit of a dolt, his lack of "imagination" signifying an utter inability to place himself in another moment, to be anything other than he is. On the other, it is precisely his lack of psychological flexibility that makes him impetuous, that leads him to love when the odds are against him, to care when a wiser man would not. Tom is inert in a way that draws our attention to his flatness while torquing that flatness into something approaching its human analog: dependability, reliability, the sense that we could say of someone, "Oh, that's *so Tom*." In other words, all characters are almost-persons, but novices in particular both expose and obscure this underlying configuration by attaching character's formal operations to the real social operations of incipient adulthood, with all of the cultural difficulties that attend those who, because of their age and thus their oblique relation to the social, are difficult to pin down, difficult to know fully, and yet, at the same time, knowable precisely as figures of youth.

This is why, despite the portability of inexperience across age and gender, race and nation, the paradigmatic novice is, to my mind, Richardson's Pamela, whose tender age is emphasized from the novel's earliest pages. "For, tho' God has bless'd you with Sense and Prudence above your Years," her parents write, "yet, I tremble to think what a sad Hazard a poor Maiden of no more than Fifteen Years of Age stands against the Temptations of this World."[80] That Richardson focuses on a figure of little apparent importance (a servant girl, no less) is, so the story goes, one of the things that makes the novel a novel. Despite her flowery name, Pamela is no romance heroine, and her very mundanity bespeaks the genre's investment in the project of depicting real life.[81] Yet, I propose that from our vantage, after nearly three hundred years of the novel's ordinariness, the audacity of Richardson's experiment lies less in its choice of focus than in its suggestion that someone so young could provoke powerful changes in those around her, while remaining little changed herself. The novel famously stages its heroine's steadfastness and its transformative effects (most notably, and rather notoriously, in reforming her would-be rapist and eventual companionate husband, Mr B). One of the novel's earliest readers finds Pamela's moral tenacity, the fact that she "carries on a determin'd Purpose to persevere in her Innocence," to be "an astonishing Matter" (7).[82] Astonishing indeed. In young Pamela's story, we find no compromise, no accommodation to the world, no gradual recognition and acceptance of its demands. *Pamela* is not, that is to say, a coming-of-age novel.[83]

How is Pamela both mundane and unworldly—both of the world and ignorant of that world? How could the novel, a form that emerges to show the world as it is, take as its subject characters who remain so insistently isolated from the world's operations? Separated from her parents, mourning the loss of her beloved mistress, Pamela Andrews has little experience of the world and even less of society (high or otherwise). She has few life lessons to draw upon when her new master's advances thrust her into a plot we have alternately called imperilment and courtship. And though both this master, Mr B, and her parents repeatedly insist that Pamela has "sense above [her] Years" (16), we have the impression that this preternatural good sense may not be enough. Pamela, we are also told, is prudent, and yet prudence is exposed as a rather flimsy virtue, for we understand that this young servant girl's forethought can be grounded only on her severely sheltered past. In other words, it is clear to us, even from the novel's earliest pages, that, no matter her precocity, Pamela is still a young girl who does not understand how the world works—and who is thus particularly vulnerable to its dangers. Like Pamela's parents, we "tremble," and we do so from the first page of the novel, even when—*especially* when—Pamela assures us that there's nothing to fear: "As yet I see no Cause to fear any thing. . . . Sure they can't *all* have Designs against me!" (15). We recognize Pamela's sense of security as an overconfidence born of inexperience. She does not "see . . . cause to fear anything" because of a juvenile myopia that constrains her judgment. What to her parents (and the reader) seems like reasonable precaution strikes the inexperienced Pamela as something closer to paranoia—or worse, cynicism. (She calls that menace "suspicio[n]" [15].)

Richardson's genre-defining risk, I contend, is in centering a narrative on the limits of his protagonist's perspective while ultimately endorsing and confirming that perspective. This is not to say that Pamela is correct to extend good faith to her master and fellow servants, but instead to point out something that should strike us as rather more extraordinary: that Pamela's naïve goodwill exerts a world-building effect of its own, shaping her circumstances, redeeming her fellows, until the reader's initial sense of precaution comes to look ungenerous and, what is more, uninspired. That this is true even when our protection of Pamela was warranted (that is, Mr B does indeed prey on her as we suspected) is precisely the risk, even the danger, of endorsing her limited view. (Indeed, Richardson would struggle with the consequences of this gamble for the remainder of his career.) Far from cautionary, Pamela's story ultimately rewards her virtue but also, just as influentially, her inexperience. This plot-level resolution asks us to hold in tension our (presumably) superior knowledge about the world's operations and Pamela's more speculative vision of a better (which is to say *more good*) world in this life. To maintain this tension is no simple task, but this is precisely the work that the novel form requires of its readers as it brings together a verisimilar representation of ordinary life and the more challenging figure of a character who defies the expectations and demands of life as we know it. Richardson's ratification of Pamela's essential goodness is moralism, yes, but it is a generative and formally complex moralism that probes the nascent novel's limits.

As Pamela's example suggests, novices urge their novels to test the limits of literature's engagement of abstract ideas, of how to use literary representation to recast real life. I point to the ways that novice characters in particular cleave to a standard of character that was considerably more abstract (and thus less particularized) than many commenters on the early novel would have us believe.[84] If the novice connected the early novel to the real world of its readers, she likewise marked an almost unbearable immateriality. This is because, not yet having entered into the world, the novice is consistently figured as only hypothetically a person (as a minor, not a person at all in the legal sense and, if a woman, perhaps never a legal person if married before adulthood). Not yet particularized through experience of the world, the novice invoked a theoretical constellation remote from the workings of instantiated, empirical life: perfection, goodness, youth as a conceptual ideal rather than a biological stage. In other words, the early realist novel attempts at once to capture lived experience of the world while *also* depicting characters who begin (and remain) unchanged by that world, a collision of imitation and idealism at the heart of the early novel's project.

While Pamela's example looms over this study, I begin my readings with Richardson's second novel because it attempts to correct for what I have called the danger of endorsing Pamela's inexperience (quite literally the danger of rape) by, in effect, doubling down on inexperience as both a moral coordinate and as a model of character. In abandoning the claim to facticity in the writing of *Clarissa* (and softening it to a principle of "Historical Faith" in later editions of *Pamela*), Richardson suggests that faithful verisimilitude would be less important to his "new species of writing" than the use of the world as a point of departure from which fiction could make a case for a morally superior, if practically more vulnerable, way of life. My first chapter focuses on Clarissa Harlowe's stasis, especially as her story is set against the plot of development (followed by her friend Anna Howe) and the plot of conversion (followed by her executor John Belford). Clarissa not only lacks experience at the beginning of Richardson's novel but also continues to do so until her early death, refusing to derive meaning from events or milestones that are the conventional building blocks of a life story. Rather than understand herself through her approach to marriage or motherhood, for example, Clarissa remains focused on her death, not only after her traumatic rape but even from her very first letter of the epistolary novel. This is because Clarissa evaluates herself against what Anna calls the "should-be," a way of thinking I connect to the eighteenth-century philosophical project of conjectural history. Rather than explicate historical progress, conjectural histories (including, I argue, Clarissa's) show how a careful consideration of the origins of a particular practice or idea helps us to understand its logical path rather than its historical course. Clarissa believes that her personal "should-be" requires her early demise, a conclusion that is disturbing for the reader but that is also consistent with her repudiation of socially imposed ways of determining her value.

In a reading of Henry Fielding's *Tom Jones* in the second chapter, I show how the novel is positively influenced by the example of naïve virtue and class conversion found in Richardson's *Pamela*. In doing so, I challenge the long critical history surrounding the representation of experience in the novel, particularly attending to Sophia Western's choice at the novel's end to act in ignorance of her knowledge of Tom's experience when she agrees to marry him. In other words, I demonstrate that Sophia does not act prudently (where prudence would require her to remember and understand past actions so that she might be able to accurately project future consequences) but instead demonstrates an almost symptomatic understanding of the operations of class in her society. Tom's society, in recognizing him as Allworthy's heir, erases his past experiences, seeing the actions of gentlemen not as constitutive of identity but instead as purgative and temporary. My reading shows that the idea of catharsis, then, operates in the moment of society's embrace of Tom and not in his horror at the threat of incest, because this horror is quickly rendered parodic and the incest purely fictional. Founded on a false impression, Tom's seeming repentance ("all the dreadful mischiefs which have befallen me, are the consequences only of my own folly and vice") is an absurd parody of Aristotelian anagnorisis, the movement of the tragic hero from ignorance to knowledge.

The second half of the book takes up the two subgenres of the early novel—the Gothic and the sentimental—that Ian Watt argued undermined the fragile credibility of the novel as an esteemed literary endeavor. Watt subordinated these subgenres, I propose, because of the ways that they departed from his understanding of novelistic character as both particularized and developmental. By challenging that model of character, I see more continuity across these texts. My third chapter begins with the observation that the ignorant domestics in *The Castle of Otranto*—for whom Horace Walpole famously apologizes in his preface—are proven correct over the course of the novel. These characters have traditionally been read as a rather amateurish appropriation of Shakespeare's use of low life for comic relief, but I contend that they represent a valid knowledge system, one that need not be continually updated. As Walpole himself points out, "Many passages essential to the story . . . could not be well brought to light but by their naïveté and simplicity." These characters' belief in the supernatural is validated by the novel's fantastical plot (which insists that there really is a giant in the castle), even though the characters are not themselves credited or reevaluated within the diegesis. Walpole's tacit validation of naïveté inaugurates, I argue, a close relationship between the Gothic and naïveté that is further complicated by Ann Radcliffe's novels. Radcliffe's signature use of the "explained supernatural" in novels like *The Romance of the Forest* and *The Mysteries of Udolpho*—in which seemingly otherworldly effects are found to have altogether mundane causes—serves to render the heroine's already limited experience (that is, her experience of paranormal phenomena) as permanently incomplete and her knowledge ungrounded. This creates the impression of a heroine who herself does not change. While the early novel tends to set the worldly against the parochial or regional, Radcliffe's novels render the provincial otherworldly. Her heroines' naïve insistence upon seeing the supernatural marks them as otherworldly themselves, even when events in the novel turn out to be resolutely ordinary.

My fourth chapter considers Burney's famous immolation of her juvenilia at the age of fifteen (a scene recounted in the preface to her final novel, *The Wanderer*) as emblematic of her fascination with adolescence as a time of rebirth. This is perhaps most obvious in the pressure she places on the idiomatic expression "entrance into the world" (the subtitle to *Evelina*), which, as we have seen, refers in this period both to birth and to the process of "coming out" into society. Burney, I argue, is particularly interested in the idea of newness, of unfamiliarity with the world, as a model of theoretical personhood: a way of being that is untried but that may, nevertheless, offer valuable moral and epistemological insights. I read this perspective alongside, first, the cultural apparatuses that maintained it—in particular, changes in eighteenth-century legal liability that rendered minors incapable of entering contracts and incapable of causing harm—and, second, the literary form that enabled its perpetuation—specifically, the sentimental novel.

As has no doubt already become clear, this book is only historicist at its edges, even though it tells a literary historical story—of the brief but exciting period between the emergence of realism as a fictional mode and the dominance of *Bildung* as a novelistic project, from roughly Pamela to Fanny Price (likewise "a girl of fifteen! the very age of all others to need most attention and care").[85] Even that story is an incomplete one. The novice did not disappear; she was only submerged for a while, popping up from time to time in more or less threadbare guises. In an epilogue, I demonstrate the flexibility and formal ubiquity of the novice as a figure, following the logic of the project to some unexpected places: Jane Austen's *Emma* (1815), a novel supposedly invested in its heroine's self-cultivation, and Suzanne Collins's *The Hunger Games* (2008), a novel that places adolescent idealism in extremis. What does it mean to enter the world? To enter the world is always to conjure a new one, to project onto the world another version of itself, to place alongside a series of worlds yet another version, another option, another vision of what a world might be. As the writers I study make clear, entering the world requires, necessarily, the sorting of a variety of conceptions of world and of the self's place in them.

CHAPTER 1

Clarissa's Conjectural History

The Novel and the Novice

> In my opinion, the world is but one great family; originally it was so; what then is this narrow selfishness that reigns in us, but relationship remembered against relationship forgot?   —CLARISSA HARLOWE IN SAMUEL RICHARDSON, *Clarissa*[1]

Samuel Johnson's quip "if you were to read Richardson['s *Clarissa*] for the story, your impatience would be so much fretted that you would hang yourself" never really gets old. It delights and relieves students, and it provides a bitter sort of solace when one is looking, yet again, for which letter a particular something was said in, somewhere nestled in all those endless pages. No matter how assiduously we conjoin the crack with its more reflective (and more clearly admiring) follow-up ("but one must read him for the sentiment, and consider the story as only giving occasion to the sentiment"), the force of the charge (what Johnson's interlocutor has called "tediousness") remains, even for the most avowed Richardson partisans.[2] While Johnson suggests that "sentiment" is not just a consolation prize but even a superior reward for the persevering reader of Richardson, he does not attempt to account for the deficiencies of Richardson's plotting, to diagnose the problem that could lead to a frustration so overwhelming as to prompt suicide. This chapter does just that: I argue that *Clarissa* (1747–48) does not have much of a plot because Richardson experiments, with his protagonist, in crafting a character whose relationship to plot is nearly frictionless. That is, Clarissa's character is not constituted through her encounters with the world but rather through her ability to detach from the world even so far as to remain impervious to its realities and demands.

Take Clarissa's argument for universal kinship: her claim that "the world is but one great family" is curiously abstract given its context. In divulging to Anna Howe her confusion about her legal position with respect to her family and her proposed marriage to the vile Mr. Solmes, Clarissa moves quickly past the technical terms of inheritance and alliance to an argument that seems only tenuously connected to the situation at hand. The Harlowes are interested in maximizing their property holdings, and Clarissa's marriage to Solmes will secure an adjacent estate. Acknowledging this but then changing the register, Clarissa's account bypasses the local demands imposed by her family in favor of a conception of human interaction that would seem to dilute the claims of those blood relatives considerably and, moreover, to propose the dissolution of the very idea of personal property. Clarissa later suggests—in similarly conjectural terms and with a kind of commandment force—that filial duty carries a compulsion so strong that it exists prior to life itself: the duty of a child to a parent "must be a prior duty to all other duties: a duty anterior, as I may say, to your very birth" (479; 3:197). Filial duty for Clarissa requires no experiential precedent or confirmation. On the contrary, even though the beginning of Richardson's novel relentlessly reminds us that Clarissa's experience of family life (cruel, arbitrary, violent) should undermine her commitment to it, she remains unshaken—refusing to modify her assumptions about what the family should be. Clarissa's meditations on anteriority can appear contradictory—one makes her parents' claims upon her more tenuous, the other makes them more binding—but what remains clear is the shared project through which they excavate the terms on which Clarissa sees her life operating. This deployment of conjectural logic is, I argue, central to Richardson's *Clarissa* and to the novel's understanding of experience. With this reading, I aim to continue a conversation—begun by scholars like Michael McKeon, Catherine Gallagher, and John Bender—about the mid-eighteenth-century novel's turn to manifest fictionality. These critics agree that the novel at this moment shifts from a "claim to simple factuality as a basis for its truth" to an investment in "higher" truths independent of factual authentication.[3] I understand *Clarissa* to epitomize this significant shift in the novel's epistemology; in subordinating empiricism to the level of subplot, Richardson's novel threatens to untether the form from its earlier epistemological underpinnings. Where I depart from this work is in finding in Clarissa herself a localized expression of fictionality's aims—her version of her life, falsified as it is by the reality of her predicament, rises to the level of intradiegetic fictionality. Less delusion than vision, Clarissa's inexperience is heralded as enacting a higher truth than do the lives of her peers. Observing this, we can appreciate the novel's endorsement of the foundational claim of realist fiction at this moment: its limning of a world instructive by virtue of its superiority, and not its fidelity, to the real world.

To think about how Clarissa's narrative operates in the absence of lived experience is to notice how consistently she is set apart. Clarissa's invocation of a conjectural story of human origins helps make intelligible her troubled relationship to the social world, even as the gesture's reductive simplicity threatens to make her appear to be simple-minded herself. Flagged initially as "opinion," Clarissa's assertion soon takes on the status of what we might call prehistorical truth ("originally it was so"). But rather than remaining prehistorical, this knowledge provides Clarissa with the conditions for an alternative, conjectural present in which her own thoughts and actions are entirely reasonable, even if— perhaps *especially* if—they are rejected by those around her.[4] She is able to deduce from her understanding of this original state a set of axioms that will guide her actions. This generally "forgot[ten]" knowledge carries for Clarissa a kind of moral authority—and an explanation for her own convictions—that widely accepted social conventions simply cannot provide. As we shall see, this narrative strategy finds its analogue in a tradition of long eighteenth-century writing that finds significance, and relevance, not in what *has* been but in what *should have* been.

As Anna observes at the novel's conclusion, after Clarissa's trajectory has found its objective in her early death, "upon the whole, [Clarissa] knew what every subject required, according to the nature of it: In other words, was an absolute mistress of the *should-be*" (8:209).[5] Anna's nominalization of the modal auxiliary—making the verb phrase "should be" into the unfamiliar noun "the *should-be*"—is not simply an instance of Richardson's famous predilection for neologisms. It also reveals, in its strangeness, the conflation of the two potential meanings of the word: on the one hand, "should" as suggesting a moral opinion and, on the other, "should" as suggesting the logical work of deduction. One way to characterize my reading of *Clarissa* is as an extended consideration of the coexistence of these two possible interpretations of "should be," this grammatical toggle that exposes an implicit connection between the didactic and the formal.

Conjectural Origins

I want to step back to situate Clarissa's own formal project within the Enlightenment genre of conjectural history, for Clarissa's investment in origins speaks
to a broader Enlightenment interest in speculating on the advent of charged
concepts and categories. Of course, this was not itself a new project. While
Clarissa offers no source for her genealogy, it can be assumed that she is basing
her account at some level on the one found in Genesis: "The world is but one
great family," that is, because we are all descended from Adam and Eve. Critics
have long read Richardson's novel alongside the biblical account of Eve, but
superimposing the story of the fall over the narrative of Clarissa's rape and death
often produces unsatisfying results, in part because the sheer density of textual
material resists reduction to the level of plot points (in this case: innocence,
temptation, fall). Here I am more interested in the implications of the Genesis
story for thinking about the premises of Richardson's novel, specifically regarding the possibility and implications of creating an original character—a project
central to the novel's radical epistemology.

By using the word "original," I mean to stress not only that Clarissa is herself
unique, sometimes to the point of peculiarity, but also that she is interested
in origins and indeed finds herself at a point of origin. Similarly, when Joseph
Addison underscores the novelty of *Paradise Lost* in a series of *Spectator* essays,
he is not merely agreeing with John Dennis's earlier assessment that Milton
"was the first . . . to present the world with an original poem; that is to say, a
poem that should have his own thoughts, his own images, and his own spirit."[6]
As you recall from my introduction, for Addison, Milton is not simply a genius
because he was innovative but more fundamentally because he suggested that
we could adequately understand the origins of humanity through a purely conjectural account. Adam and Eve are, for Addison, exemplary characters because they are entirely new to the created world—more so, indeed, than any
ancient hero could possibly be. They likewise have the advantage of universal
investment, both by virtue of kinship and of representation: while Greek readers may delight in Homer, Roman readers in Virgil, "it is impossible for any of
[*Paradise Lost*'s] Readers, whatever Nation, Country or People he may belong
to, not to be related to the Persons who are the principal Actors in it" and,
moreover, "the principal Actors in this Poem are not only our Progenitors, but
our Representatives. We have an actual Interest in every thing they do, and no
less than our utmost Happiness or Misery is concerned, and lies at Stake in all

their Behaviour." Milton's exceptionality in choosing Adam and Eve (and, specifically, the prelapsarian Adam and Eve) as the heroes of his epic leads Addison to correct Aristotle even as he elsewhere takes him as a model of criticism. While the *Poetics* cautions "that a Person of an absolute and consummate Virtue should never be introduced in Tragedy," Addison observes that this rule no longer applies: it "cannot be supported to quadrate exactly with the Heroic Poems which have been made since his Time." The rule certainly does not "quadrate" with the case of our biblical ancestors, who must be understood as both characters in an epic and, at the same time, avatars of our own fall into sin: "Though the Persons who fall into Misfortune [that is, Adam and Eve] are of the most perfect and consummate Virtue, it is not to be considered as what may possibly be, but what actually is our own Case." Their case, then, can be understood as a conjectural account of our own, an explanatory narrative that helps us understand the condition of our own fallen state.

Addison's move to validate the conjectural has significant implications for the novel, which similarly asserts fiction's priority to history.[7] Gallagher captures this succinctly: the novel depends on the possibility of "a nonreferentiality that could be seen as a greater referentiality."[8] In other words, the novel's willingness to invest in characters that do not correspond to actual persons results in figures that can appear both more ambitious and more meaningful than actual persons ever could. Gallagher likewise turns to Aristotle, who asserts the superiority of poetry over history in just these terms: "[History] relates what has happened, [poetry] what may happen. Poetry, therefore, is a more philosophical and a higher thing than history: for poetry tends to express the universal, history the particular."[9] Like Addison, I would dare to adjust Aristotle a bit: Clarissa attempts to understand not what *has* happened, but what *should* happen, and in so doing effaces the particularity of her own life by viewing it through the lens of universal applicability. While theorists of the novel have for some time now emphasized the genre's privileging of probability over facticity, the microcosmic recapitulation of this dynamic *within* Richardson's novel (the logical path of Clarissa's story as prioritized over the experiential development and conversion plots of Anna and Belford) has gone unobserved.

Of course, the lingering fascination with narratives of origins that Addison underscores was not limited to the eighteenth century's renewed interest in Milton's epic. In tracing this aesthetic line, I find myself challenging Ian Watt's rejection of the longer history of newness and originality in *The Rise of the Novel*. "The term 'original,' which in the Middle Ages had meant 'having existed from the first' came to mean 'underived, independent, first-hand,'" Watt writes, overstating this "semantic reversal" to emphasize the significance of empiricism to the novel.[10] Enlightenment writers of philosophical or conjectural history (Adam Smith, Johann Gottfried von Herder, and Bernard Mandeville among them) believed that the narrative recreation of original conditions could be as, if not more, helpful in explaining our present circumstances than a narrative of the historical events that actually produced those circumstances.[11] As Dugald Stewart would later explain in the work that gave the form of conjectural history its name, "In most cases it is of more importance to ascertain the progress that is most simple, than the progress that is most agreeable to fact."[12] This aim to produce the most "simple," or natural, account made conjectural history a particularly unhistorical form of history, but one that was clearly invested in considering why things are the way they are and what it would mean for them to be otherwise.[13] This aim makes conjectural history particularly important to the emergence of the novel form, especially as the novel understands itself to be taking a consonant approach with respect to history.

Conjectural history places great emphasis on the unity of historical unfolding, on the inevitability of endings as they are contained within their beginnings.[14] The belief in the explanatory power of origin stories suggests why conjectural histories so often narrate prehistorical moments (like the emergence of a certain social practice or condition) rather than counterfactual events (say, the defeat of Cromwell in the English Civil War).[15] Thus, Jean-Jacques Rousseau famously begins his Second Discourse, "Discourse on the Origin of Inequality" (1754), with a speculative reconstruction of the origin of social inequality: "The first man, who, after enclosing a piece of ground, took it into his head to say, 'This is mine,' and found people simple enough to believe him, was the true founder of civil society."[16] The form of conjectural history does not pretend to offer a historically accurate explanation of prehistory, not simply because such an account is impossible but because, more importantly, conjectural histories ground themselves not in the reliability of testimony but in logical necessity. As Rousseau puts it, his project is "to know accurately a state which no longer exists, which perhaps never did exist, which probably never will exist, and about which it is nevertheless necessary to have exact Notions in order accurately to judge of our present state."[17] They provide hypothetical narratives that proceed according to a deductive logic.[18]

While some conjectural histories, like Herder's *Ideas for a Philosophy of the History of Mankind* (1785), were, like *Paradise Lost*, reconceptions of Genesis,

Rousseau explains that he is not discussing early man in Eden but is instead exploring "hypothetical and conditional reasonings, fitter to illustrate the nature of things, than to show their true origin."[19] There are at least two reasons for this reorientation. First, as Rousseau points out, the biblical account of humanity's origins does not actually presume a state of nature but rather introduces Adam as already preprogrammed, as it were, with "instructions and precepts."[20] In other words, rather than recreating the conditions of Eden as Milton does, Rousseau produces an even *more* original state. Second, it is simply impossible to consider the foundation of society through an origin story where society is absent. The innocence of Adam and Eve is not relational but absolute, for there are no mortal beings with which to compare them and their fault incurs a judgment that is not mediated through a social world (the company of angels notwithstanding). The beginning of the Second Discourse, then, is both a beginning (of civil society) and an end (of the state of nature). This is why, for Rousseau, radical innocence is significantly located not in his hypothetical "first man" but in those over whom he suddenly gains power, those "simple enough to believe him" when he not only invents but seizes property. Here, the essay's focus on the introduction of society—on, as the title makes clear, the "Origin of Inequality"—requires that inexperience play a supporting rather than a leading role. Society brings with it corruption; however, that corruption can be understood only in terms of the natural state that it supplants.

Clarissa, the novel central to Rousseau's thought, similarly works to understand society through a comparison to the natural, but in Richardson's novel it is that natural state—in the form of Clarissa herself—that takes center stage.[21] Like Addison, Richardson privileges the "highest innocence and perfection" that this state represents. While it may seem perverse to read *Clarissa* (a novel composed of a proliferation of testimony) alongside a genre that questions the necessity of testimony in the production of truth, it is nevertheless clear that conjectural histories—including, in Addison's reading, Milton's—provide a highly relevant cultural touchstone as they accord a logical and psychological authority even to characters who have not had much, or indeed *any*, experience of the world.[22] It may seem a stretch even to claim that conjectural histories contain characters—rather than, say, agents, figures, or even variables—as these texts are generally read as offering insight into the far larger movements of civilization. Even so, these movements are narrated through a tight focus on individual actors, however hypothetical or algebraic. *What would someone do in this situation?* they ask. *How would a person respond to this stimulus?* And, in asking these questions, conjectural history gets to the heart of how we think about literary character; these unhistorical histories have much to tell us about how we read fiction.[23]

Recent scholarship has connected the form of conjectural history to the bildungsroman, as each genre centrally considers the process of development.[24] Such a comparison recognizes, as Jean Starobinski has observed, that for Rousseau "historical distance is reduced to mere interior distance"; the path of civilization is rendered in the microcosm of the individual life.[25] But it is misleading to see narrative produced by conjectural history as resembling the sort we associate with *Bildung*: conjectural narrative is not a matter of inculcation nor of accommodation to society but rather, as we will soon see in the case of Clarissa, about logical deduction. With respect to the novel, conjectural history more powerfully illuminates the choice to begin at the beginning. That is, each individual need not be literally present at creation to have a sensibility that is open to the world in the way that such a lack of experience makes available. *Clarissa* operates by putting these two modes—the conjectural and the chronological, the literary and the historical, the anti-empirical and the empirical, the plot of inexperience and the plot of development—into (literal) correspondence with one another. These two modes pose questions in competing ways, and so we can understand the difference between Clarissa and Anna Howe—the novice and the ingénue—not as a trivial characterological difference, not as mere personality, but as a concern at the heart of the novel's form. While the rich history of critical responses to *Clarissa* has tended, understandably, to center on the dynamic relationship between Clarissa and Lovelace, my analysis will instead elevate the mutual constitution of Clarissa and Anna, even to the point of overcorrecting this tendency. Only here, I contend, can we see the specificity of Richardson's characterization of the two young women and their polar responses to plot.

The Novice and the Ingénue

"My mamma, and all of us, like the rest of the world, talk of nobody but you on this occasion," Anna Howe writes in the first letter of *Clarissa* (40; 1:3). While it is Clarissa who has become the topic of public conversation, Clarissa whose name seems to be in the air, it is her friend Anna who lets the reader know this. In the immediate aftermath of the duel between Lovelace and Clarissa's brother James that catalyzes the novel's action, Anna has spoken to no fewer than five correspondents who quickly grow in her account into "some people," "every-body," indeed, "the world" (39–40; 1:2–3). Here, as in the remainder of the novel, Anna is Clarissa's contact with that outside world, as well as her representative in it. She is the guarantor of Clarissa's character even with those whom Clar-issa has never met. Accordingly, Anna's aunt Harman ("a stranger to [Clarissa] personally")—who is bold enough to request a personal copy of Clarissa's grand-father's will—is not only a handy surrogate for the reader, who requires expo-sition quickly as the novel begins in medias res, she is also synecdochic for the widening social circle that has designated Clarissa as its center (41; 1:4). With this ever-expanding audience in mind, Anna expressly requests Clarissa's me-ticulous account—of not only her situation but also her thoughts and feelings about that situation—and that account must pass through Anna to be intelli-gible to others.[26]

Anna's Aunt Harman remains little more than an expository device to allow Richardson to introduce material that is already known to Anna but yet un-known to the reader; it is clear that she cannot take Anna's place as Clarissa's chief correspondent.[27] Nor, it seems, could a comparable figure closer to Clar-issa's domestic circle, such as, for example, her often-sympathetic Aunt Hervey. It would seem that it is neither the length of Anna's tenure in the social world nor the nature of her reputation in it that qualifies her to fill this role. On the contrary, the fact that Anna is herself only just entering society seems not to diminish but rather to strengthen her ties to it—both practically, as her eligi-bility leaves her open to calls from multiple suitors (and, by extension, a larger circle of acquaintance, or social network), and also conceptually, as the extreme social pressures on a young woman can appear to force out all other concerns until only the social remains, a concentrated distillate of modern life. The novel suggests that the very condition of eligibility accords Anna a life that is pre-dominantly public, as the very imminence of marriage places her however tem-porarily between families and thus between private lives. But it is also Anna's position at the cusp of her social existence that makes her precise status with respect to the social so ambivalent. She appears at times to be an expert—as she does here, in her orchestration of the town's gossip and broadcasting of reliable news—and, more often, to be an ingénue—as in her sometimes sulky argu-ments with her mother or her wounded recounting of a failed love affair. In one of her early disagreements with her mother about what options are available to Clarissa, Anna highlights the centrality of her own youth and inexperience to the process of moral deliberation. Mrs. Howe wonders to Anna why, if Clarissa really has no love interest, she cannot simply marry the man her parents have chosen. "Very well, my mamma, thought I!" Anna writes to Clarissa with characteristic fervor. "Now may you ask this. At FORTY, you may—But what would you have said at EIGHTEEN is the question!" (245; 2:75). Anna establishes, even in this moment of pique, a concern that remains at the center of *Clarissa*: the need to understand the perspective of a young woman suspended at the moment of entering the world—and the distance of that perspective from one of mature adulthood.

That Anna is both constitutively a social being and, at the same time, often naïve, underscores the embeddedness of the very concept of naïveté in a social context. Anna is naïve only in relation to a set of social precepts she has yet to fully master. Naïveté denotes, as Anna's case reminds us, not a lack of knowledge generally but a lack of worldly sophistication specifically. Furthermore, in Anna's case, the term contains within it the germ of its own eradication: her naïveté marks her as susceptible to social education, suggesting her ongoing acquisition of such knowledge. However severe Anna's social ignorance may strike us, the very fact that she shuttles among social actors with such regularity, if not yet facility, tells us that we can rest assured that her inexperience is temporary.

Richardson—author of both a conduct book for young men, *The Apprentice's Vade Mecum* (1734), and a letter-writing manual for the socially incompetent, *Familiar Letters on Important Occasions* (1741)—is inarguably invested in the liminal state of adolescence. Not surprisingly, when writing the preface to the first two published volumes of *Clarissa*, he contrasts what he sees as the narrative requirements of young and more mature readers. Responding to the proposal of a reader who had urged him to shorten his increasingly lengthy novel, Richardson protests that the parts proposed for excision were

> some of the most natural in the whole collection, and no less instructive, especially to youth, which might be a consideration perhaps overlooked by a gentleman of the adviser's great knowledge and experience. For . . . there is a period in human life in which, youthful activity ceasing and hope contenting itself to look from its own domestic wicket upon bounded prospects, the half-tired mind aims at little more than amusement—and with reason; for what in the instructive way can appear either new or needful to one who has happily got over those dangerous situations which call for advice and cautions, and who has filled up his measures of knowledge to the top? (36).[28]

This reader, Richardson points out, has already successfully negotiated the business of his life such that he no longer requires instruction; his "prospects" no longer appear endless but are "bounded," his path determined. He is now in a position to read at leisure—and for "amusement" alone—but others will need to know about the potential dangers of the world to reach a position of such security and luxury. The anecdote is significant not only as justification for Richardson's decision to leave his manuscript unabridged but also because he seems to be warning the majority of his readers that they are not in the same position as this "gentleman . . . [of] knowledge, judgement, and experience" (35). Richardson's unnamed correspondent is not, we can plainly infer, his ideal one, but nor is he representative of the typical or common reader Richardson imagines approaching his text. That is, we should hear in Richardson's words the echo of Johnson's suggestion that novel readers are "the young, the ignorant, and the idle."[29] Furthermore, Richardson makes this resonance explicit in a letter to another early reader, his friend and advisor Aaron Hill: "[Clarissa is] principally suitable to the Years and Capacities of Persons under Twenty of the one Sex, and under Thirty of the other."[30] He projects, that is, a young adult audience. Such readers must not be so quick to assume that the decisions they face are straightforward ones. They cannot be as quick as this reader to excise the instructional in favor of the more amusing, the more sensational, "affecting story" (36).

This is how we tend to think of eighteenth-century fiction, as depicting experiences from which readers may learn vicariously, such that even the most inexperienced reader may become experienced in absentia, from the comfort of their own drawing rooms. Yet, at the same time, the length of this anecdote in Richardson's short preface threatens to obscure the fact that the bulk of *Clarissa* is not ultimately the social handbook that the preface promises. The "dangerous situations" of contemporary social life (presumably synonymous with J. Paul Hunter's "career [and] marriage") are in fact so marginal in the novel that this reader could conceivably propose their exclusion.[31] That Richardson rejects such a proposal should not negate the force of its plausibility. While Richardson insists that the subplot of Clarissa is "no less instructional" than Clarissa's own, he effectively admits, in his reference to her "affecting story," that Clarissa's own narrative is not instructional at all—or, at least, not in the same sense of providing a manual for individual development. In fact, Clarissa's exemplarity is remarkable, even within the diegesis of the novel, for its impracticality. As critics have often noted, exemplarity implies both that the exemplar is representative—an achievable model for action—and also that she represents an unattainable ideal.[32] That ideal is motivated by an intensity of conflict unlikely to be faced by most novel readers. As Anna Laetitia Barbauld drily notes, "Least of all will a course of novels prepare a young lady for the neglect and tedium of life which she is perhaps doomed to encounter. . . . [S]he has been instructed how to behave with the utmost propriety when . . . locked up by a cruel parent, like *Clarissa*; but she is not prepared for indifference and neglect."[33] And yet it is precisely the extremity of Clarissa's situation throughout the novel that makes her story so "affecting," over and above the quotidian scenarios recounted in Richardson's more clearly practical conduct writing.

Perhaps this is why in much of *Clarissa*'s influence on the later development of the novel in English, we can see Anna's legacy with greater clarity than we can see Clarissa's. Anna's narrative, that of the headstrong young woman resisting an overbearing mother's insistence on a dull prospective husband, would be entirely at home, for example, in an Austen novel—if, that is, she were the heroine.[34] The fact that Anna is not the heroine should lead us to consider how and why *Clarissa* fits the *Bildung* model only in its subplot, with respect to its subordinate character. When even so central a text as *Clarissa* relegates the familiar narrative of youth surmounted (the story that will become the bildungsroman), to its margins, it is clear that another model of character becomes necessary. This subplot serves as the frame for an altogether more radical understanding of the new or novel protagonist—one that highlights the impact "a young lady's entrance into the world" has on that world, rather than the impact the world has on the young lady.[35]

The divergence of Anna and Clarissa's varieties of inexperience is less clear in the novel's early pages. Everything about the novel's beginning suggests that Clarissa and Anna are in analogous social positions; after all, Clarissa's story is likewise, as the novel's subtitle suggests, that of a "young lady."[36] Like Anna, Clarissa has recently found herself entangled in the intricacies of courtship; both are negotiating between their own desires and those of their families. That Anna seems more confident in her early choices seems merely to be a difference of personality; that she is more acquainted with social convention seems to suggest that she is simply adept where Clarissa is, perhaps even temporarily, rather inept. But the precise nature of Clarissa's newness suggests that she and Anna cannot be read as functioning in equivalent social states or even on the same social continuum. As we shall see, the remainder of the novel produces an account of Clarissa that cannot be understood through the same paradigm of naïveté we might apply to Anna. Instead it might lead us, in applying the period aesthetic of novelty to an individual life, to think of her as a novice. The novel polarizes Clarissa and Anna's experiences so as to render ironic Anna's early understanding of who Clarissa is and how she operates.

That Clarissa is not embarking on this youthful journey with her is something Anna registers only incompletely, if at all, until the end of the novel. While Clarissa's slow departure from the mortal world by the novel's end is duly famous, it is important to note just how early she establishes her isolation from society, long before we find her alone in a garret, writing letters atop her coffin. "Everybody pities you," Anna writes in that first letter. "So steady, so uniform in your conduct, so desirous, as you always said, of sliding through life to the end of it unnoted" (39–40; 1:2–3). Everyone has noted, that is, that Clarissa would like to go unnoted. It is a pity—as Anna's tense suggests ("you always said")—that she can no longer expect such a thing. Or, perhaps, it is a pity that she ever expected it, that she ever had the nerve to resist that "everybody," that she ever dared to "slide." Just as Anna's eligibility makes her life appear more public, Clarissa's appeal to remain single is an attempt at securing her privacy. Clarissa crucially sees herself as having no part in the social world. In this sense, the novice departs significantly from the character of the socially determined ingénue, despite the formal resemblance of the two roles. Anna's resistance to this life outside of the social—or, more accurately, her ignorance that such a possibility might exist—is registered in her repeated insistence that Clarissa has (despite or even because of her desire to go "unnoted") led a life so captivating that she has commanded the attention of the social world even when she has most actively shunned it. That Clarissa's merit is recognized even when she shuns society becomes increasingly significant as the novel goes on. Clarissa's absence from the wider world is figured insistently throughout the novel: first as an eccentric desire to maintain a private life, then as punishment for questioning her family's wishes, and finally as the entrapment that culminates with her death.

Just as insistent is novel's claim that this seclusion paradoxically magnifies Clarissa's social influence. According to Anna, it is precisely Clarissa's excellence that has forced her into the public eye, her "distinguished merits [that] have made her the public care" (39; 1:1). She continues: "You see what you draw upon yourself by excelling all your sex" (40; 1:4). And, of course, Anna's request for a complete account of Clarissa's situation—written with a general audience in mind and supported by documentary evidence—implicitly validates the claims of others upon Clarissa's actions. "Your concerns are my concerns," she writes, but they are also, in this dissemination of the story, the concerns of "every in-dividual . . . [who] seems to think you answerable to her" (40; 1:4). Clarissa's cultivation of a private life, long before it becomes a repudiation of the social, makes her a particularly compelling figure. Without gaining experience in the world, then, she nevertheless circulates in it, as her desires—even her desire for privacy—are taken on by an increasingly larger social circle. Clarissa responds to such social claims not with rejection but with excavation. She attempts to locate what is beneath or, more often, *before* the social, so as to ground her ac-tions upon what she believes to be a more solid foundation. This foundation is not only, as we might expect, a moral one; it is also crucially narrative in nature. Clarissa continually attempts to locate a story other than the one she finds herself in, a story that will offer a better explanation of her own actions, sometimes even before she has acted.[37]

Narrating Inexperience

Clarissa's conjecturalism is not limited, then, to her peculiarly abstract state-ments but extends to her very way of being in the world. Take the moment, at roughly the middle point of Richardson's novel, when the reader is presented with a letter that threatens to bring its narrative to a premature end. Anna writes to Clarissa to inform her that she—though believing herself to be living in a respectable boarding house—has all the while been living in a brothel. "My dear," Anna writes, "you are certainly in a devilish house!—Be assured that the woman [who runs it] is one of the vilest women!—nor does she go to you by her right name—Very true—her name is *not* Sinclair—nor is the street she lives in, Dover Street" (744; 5:32). Anna's news is punctuated by breathless dashes and significant exclamation points, but this news comes as no surprise to the reader. What Richardson calls the novel's "double yet separate" correspondence renders the narrative multiply focalized, alternating between Clarissa's account and Lovelace's version of those same events (35). Because of our open access to Lovelace's correspondence, the reader knows that Clarissa has been in danger, has been able to confirm her suspicions when they have emerged, and has, no doubt, been continually frustrated by her inability to see where she is and in whose care she finds herself. What Fanny Hill—an ingénue placed in nearly the same situation—figures out in a matter of days, Clarissa takes months to dis-cover (and even then only with considerable assistance).[38] The particular case of Sinclair's (bawdy) house is perhaps most striking because Clarissa's resistance to the reality of vice takes a disturbingly literal form: her moral blind spot renders her unable to see what is physically all around her, to recognize her surroundings for what they are. We might go as far as to say that Clarissa's inexperience compromises even her registration of empirical reality.

Anna's warning concretizes Clarissa's characteristic inexperience, which is reinforced spatially by her consistent physical isolation (first imprisoned by her parents, later by Lovelace). Notoriously, Watt goes even further, suggesting that Clarissa is not only ignorant of the world but of herself as well: "We are fully entitled to suspect Clarissa herself of not knowing her own feelings."[39] While I am more willing than Watt to credit Clarissa's protestations against her persecutor, it is nevertheless true that Clarissa is granted a severely limited epistemology. Indeed, this remains true even after the moment I am dilating here, as Anna's admonitory letter is unable to provide Clarissa with the moment of comprehension that the reader has longed for. The letter is intercepted by Lovelace and rewritten by him in order to remove the warnings that might otherwise save Clarissa from the novel's devastating climactic assault. Moreover, the letter's presence in the novel is mediated by Lovelace's snide commentary on Anna's warning, complete with indexical hands in the margins that point tauntingly at Anna's expressions of apprehension. The letter cannot enlighten Clarissa, but it *can* highlight for the reader just how misguided she has been. Anna acknowledges that she and Clarissa have both been "led . . . on— like fools, like tame fools on a string," but even she registers disbelief that Clarissa has been unable to figure things out on her own: "Did you never go out by yourself, and discharge the coach or chair, and return by another coach or chair? If you did . . . you would never have found your way to the vile house, either by the woman's name, *Sinclair*, or by the street's name" (744; 5:32). Though Anna says that both she and Clarissa have been fools, there is a matter-of-factness to Anna's tone, a sensibleness to her sensibility, that rends asunder the union posited by that identification. Maybe *she* would have gone out by herself—*of course* she would have—but Clarissa did not.

Anna's question nevertheless conjures a scenario wherein Clarissa might have easily determined the truth of her situation, just as the inclusion of Anna's letter in Richardson's narrative proposes a scenario wherein that letter reaches its intended recipient and serves its intended revelatory function. We can quite easily classify both scenarios of disclosure as counterfactual, as only suggesting the idea of Clarissa's successful evasion of Lovelace's further deception, before foreclosing the reality of that escape. More difficult, I think, is the question of how we determine the status of the narrative that is focalized through Clarissa at this moment, and at most others, in the text. How, in other words, might we consider Clarissa's *false* understanding of her situation as a narrative in its own right?

Narrative theory has taken seriously just this kind of question. Gerald Prince's introduction of the category of the "disnarrated" and Robyn Warhol's further elaboration of the category have considerably expanded the possibilities for analyzing complex narratives by drawing attention to what Prince calls "those elements in a narrative which explicitly consider and refer to what does *not* take place (but could have)."[40] This category, however, can seem more helpful in understanding a *moment* of narrative foreclosure rather than a protracted parallel account. Indeed, Prince's local examples tend to focus on the sentence level—such as Anna's "Did you never ... ? If you had ... you would ..."— rather than on what does not take place again and again *consistently* or, in other words, on entire states of being or knowing that are unrealized. Marie-Laure Ryan and Hilary Dannenberg have promoted the applicability of "possible worlds" theory to the analysis of complex narratives, considering extended counterfactual alternatives as key components in a narrative's dynamic orchestration of temporal possibilities rather than as mere diversions from what previous narrative theory might have considered the "actual story."[41]

Clarissa provides an ideal site for this valuable work, but it also suggests certain intriguing complications. First, it is important to note the ways in which the epistolary novel's juggling of perspectives offers a significantly different model for ontological plotting than, say, the third-person realist novel. This is because the protracted alternative world (here, Clarissa's naïve complacency) is in this case repeatedly interrupted by a narrative that is understood from early on as having ontological priority (Lovelace's revelation of his "plot").[42] Richardson's novel oscillates for hundreds of pages between Clarissa's account of her experience and Lovelace's falsification of that account through his explanation of how he has deceived her. Here, epistolarity gives Dannenberg's concept of "temporal orchestration" a particularly syncopated rhythm.[43] At the same time, however, Richardson ensures that even the reader who is most irritated by Clarissa's myopia is unable to detach completely from her plot of inexperience, even when Clarissa is herself finally disabused of her false understanding. Consider the fact that even Anna's warning letter does not actually correct Clarissa's misconception; it is only able to negate it: Mrs. Sinclair is *not* this woman's name. Dover Street is *not* the address of this establishment. Anna is unable to offer a positive, superior account. Furthermore, Richardson himself refuses to provide such an account: the paratextual dramatis personae that prefaces the novel lists Sinclair as "the pretended name of a private brothel keeper in London" but refrains from revealing the identity behind that alias. Sinclair is even given an assumed Christian name at one point in the novel—it is, no surprise here, Magdalen—but her true identity is never revealed, not in Lovelace's correspondence and not even during the narration of her protracted and gruesome death. Clarissa's perspective—however partial—is permitted, even encouraged, to linger.

Unless we acknowledge the capaciousness of Clarissa's credulity, it can seem like a straightforward example of dramatic irony: the reader has information that the protagonist does not. It *is* that, of course. As Ralph Rader compellingly argued of *Pamela*, the reader's registration that there is a plot guiding a character's actions—a plot of which the character is unaware—is central to the emergence of the novel as a genre.[44] The space between these strata of knowledge creates both suspense (fear for what will happen to the character) and, in some cases, distance (contempt for the character's ignorance). Yet, as I have suggested, Richardson encourages the reader to realize that his supposedly superior knowledge is rarely itself complete. As a result, even so astute a reader as Terry Castle, who repeatedly references Clarissa's "ponderous naïveté," must admit that we as readers are no more knowledgeable about the actual location of Mrs. Sinclair's brothel (which is called the house on Dover Street but which cannot be found there) than we are about Mrs. Sinclair's real name. "Indeed," Castle writes with notable chagrin, "I have referred to Sinclair's brothel as 'the house on Dover-Street.'"[45]

Traditionally, narrative theory has held that it is the movement *away* from a state of ignorance or immaturity that holds narrative potential; this assumption is behind D. A. Miller's suggestion that naïveté is an especially "narratable" epistemological position.[46] This is tantamount to a narratological truism: narrative is generated out of moments of disequilibrium that must find closure. Like Miller, most narrative theorists have suggested that inexperience is essentially precarious; hence literary criticism's time-honored focus on moments or arcs of education or enlightenment: *Bildung*, epiphany, anagnorisis, the fall. Rather than elevate Clarissa steadily to a position of comparative maturity or understanding, however, Richardson's novel suspends her in the condition of inexperience, suggesting that she possesses a wisdom superior to worldly knowledge and, moreover, that she has possessed it from the novel's beginning. As

Fanny Hill's example confirms, *Clarissa* underscores the fact that educability is not an inarguably desirable characteristic. This privileging is an instance not only of didactic caution or conservatism but also, I want to stress, of narrative experimentation.[47]

Although Clarissa is unable to assess adequately the motivations of the malevolent characters with whom she comes in contact, she is surprisingly capable of identifying inexperience in others. Alex Woloch has argued that Austen's characters "get continually contrasted, juxtaposed, [and] related to others," creating the framework by which the novels can be understood and, crucially, the matrix in which the protagonist can be identified.[48] This principle is certainly at play in Richardson's novel, particularly in the ways Clarissa is set alongside other young or gullible women. The comparison between Clarissa and Anna is only the most protracted of these pairings. Consider a moment that is easier to overlook, when Anna tells Clarissa at the novel's beginning of the young girl that Lovelace is wooing in the next town over. Clarissa explodes in response:

> Never talk of innocence, of simplicity, and this unhappy girl, together! Must she not know, that such a man as that, dignified in every aspect; and no disguise able to conceal his being of condition; must mean too much, when he places her at the upper end of his table, and calls her by such tender names? Would a girl, modest as simple, *above seventeen*, be set a singing at the pleasure of such a man as that? A stranger, and professedly in disguise!—Would her father and grandmother, if honest people, and careful of their simple girl, permit such freedoms? (285; 2:156, emphasis added)

"Must she not know?" The rhetorical charge with which Clarissa attacks the question of Rosebud's age might tempt us to forget that Clarissa is herself only eighteen.[49] The subsequent emergence of the fact that Lovelace has been crafting and circulating Rosebud's story in order to inspire Clarissa's jealousy further levels the two women, marking both as objects of manipulation. Later, a similar juxtaposition is effected when Lovelace convinces a woman (Widow Bevis) to impersonate Clarissa in order to intercept an important letter from Anna. After belatedly discovering the plot, Clarissa writes to Anna:

> Your messenger has now indeed seen me. I talked with him on the imposture put upon him at Hampstead: and am sorry to have reason to say that had not the poor man been very *simple*, and very *self-sufficient* [i.e., conceited], he had not been so grossly deluded. Mrs Bevis has the same plea to make for herself. A

good-natured, thoughtless woman; not used to converse with so vile and so spe-
cious a deceiver as him who made his advantage of both these shallow creatures.
(1021; 6:193)

Clarissa has, of course, herself been duped by Lovelace at every turn. The final
sentence of this passage could pass as a description of Clarissa herself. Clarissa
pointedly distances herself from these inexperienced characters at the moment
she seems most to resemble them. The resemblance is often—as with Widow
Bevis's impersonation—a literal transposition of identity. Clarissa herself impersonates simple figures—a rustic dairymaid in the dairy house her grand-
father has deeded her; a servant, Mabel, when she finally escapes Mrs. Sinclair's—
and in doing so seems not to stress the interchangeability of herself with these
figures but instead to emphasize the contrast that makes such a masquerade so
striking.[50] Clarissa's proximity to and, at the same time, distance from these
figures might suggest a lack of self-awareness on her part but I would caution
against this interpretation. Instead, I contend that the distinctions the novel
leads us to make among its simple characters encourages us to make finer dis-
cernments about the nature—and natures—of simplicity than we might otherwise be prepared to make.

   This string of encounters brings us to Clarissa's rape, which would seem to
challenge the account I have produced here so far. Surely if we are to find the
obliteration of the universal, the intrusion of experiential eventfulness, or the
movement out of ignorance, it would be in Clarissa's response to her sexual
violation. Dorothy Van Ghent infamously claimed that the rape of Clarissa was
"a singularly thin and unrewarding piece of action—the deflowering of a young
lady—and one which scarcely seems to deserve the universal uproar it pro-
vokes in the book," suggesting that it does not provide the necessary objective
correlative for her subsequent despair and death.[51] While I sympathize with
critics who fault Van Ghent for her callousness here, I nonetheless think it is
important to affirm that the rape does not represent a narrative center for the
novel but rather an aporia, the absence of experience. In fact, I want to propose
that the violation at the heart of the novel is *not* the physical penetration of rape
but the drugging that robs Clarissa of her consciousness, and, furthermore,
that this act is consistent with and even the pinnacle of the inexperience with
which she is associated throughout.[52] Clarissa is simply unable to have access
to what has happened to her. Or, to adopt the language of empiricism, her inability to *sense* what happens renders her unable to *produce knowledge* of it.[53]

This violation must be understood as consistent with the rest of the novel, which has time and again isolated Clarissa from experience.[54] That Clarissa's isolation from experience marks both the depth of her subjection and the foundation of her moral authority is the tragedy of the novel.

As the novel progresses, Clarissa's inexperience is figured in increasingly abstract terms. The drugging that occasions her rape becomes inexperience par excellence, and its aftermath is signaled by the white damask gown she refuses to remove for the remainder of the novel—a sartorial blank sheet of white paper. The empirical fact that Clarissa is raped while unconscious points to a deep principle of the organization of her life. Castle calls Clarissa's rape "epiphanic," and claims, "For the real reader, witnessing her extreme, attenuated demise, it is as if the heroine's naïveté were replaced by awareness—by melancholic recognition, finally, of deceit."[55] Castle's prevarication here ("it is as if") is again telling, for it is ultimately unsatisfying to identify Clarissa's rape as a moment of enlightenment. This is not only because it is never really clear exactly what Clarissa would learn (or how the rape itself would teach her) but also because the reading of the rape as epiphanic—or even as the decisive moment in a slower development of knowledge—understands Clarissa's narrative to be historical rather than conjectural.[56]

Clarissa's protracted "long time a-dying" can be understood, then, as the experience of longing, of the sort Susan Stewart writes about so powerfully: "The location of desire, or, more particularly, the direction of force in the desiring narrative, is always a future-past, a deferment of experience in the direction of origin and thus eschaton, the point where narrative begins/ends."[57] Clarissa's willing of death collapses ends and beginnings together until we can understand Clarissa's death to be another sort of origin, a moment outside of narrative time and apart from the appeals of history and development.[58] The sheer volume of her correspondence, which continues to proliferate after her rape (and even, uncannily, after her death), aims in part to substitute for the experience she lacks. Returning again and again to her own responses and motivations, Clarissa seems to expect that she will turn up new information, like a detective tirelessly reviewing a case in search of clues. But instead of producing the experience that would endow her with this knowledge, Clarissa's incessant writing instead produces, to paraphrase Frances Ferguson, the *representation* of experience rather than experience itself.[59] As my final section will show, the novel's ending supplements this pursuit in its attempt to fabricate through eulogy the impression of development.

Fabricating *Bildung*

Anna's final letter in *Clarissa* provides Belford, Clarissa's executor and Lovelace's interlocutor, with the "character" of Clarissa that he has requested, a description of her life that he hopes will help him understand how she possibly could have amassed so many uncanny perfections in her short lifetime. Prefacing the letter, Anna makes a distinction between two kinds of accounts that she might give: "I suppose you intend [for me] to give a character of her at those years when she was qualified to be an example to other young ladies, rather than a history of her life" (1466; 8:196). Anna—rightly, the reader gathers— assumes that Belford wants a report of Clarissa's everyday adult life, one that he has not been privy to, having encountered her story only during its tragic dénouement. Accordingly, Anna provides a meticulous hour-by-hour description of a day in the life of Clarissa Harlowe. The letter takes the already foreshortened "history of a young lady" that Richardson offers his readers and shortens it further, from roughly a calendar year to a single day. It should come as no surprise at this point in the novel that, by Anna's account (itself really just a glowing review of Clarissa's daily logbook), her friend is morally impeccable: charitable and talented, the ultimate conversationalist and correspondent, with excellent spelling for good measure.

But if the reader, like Belford, wants this account to somehow account *for* Clarissa, to explain her perfections rather than enumerate them, she is likely to remain unsatisfied. Nor is Anna's letter etiological in the sense of determining why Clarissa has met the end she has. The letter does, however, characterize Clarissa herself as having started something. While Belford has not mentioned a wider audience for this text—he presumably wants only to satisfy his own curiosity and to cement his burgeoning moral reformation—Anna suggests that the letter will supply an entirely suitable "example to other young ladies." However, this example is by no means a straightforward one. Clarissa's short life has already led Anna and Belford to examine their own more conventional narratives: Anna's, that of the headstrong young woman approaching sexual maturity and marriage, and Belford's, that of the reformed rake or the convert. Both had taken seriously the project of entering society only to see that project nullified by Clarissa's aberrant example. Thus, when we reach the end of Anna's own life story in the novel's conclusion, the trajectory of her route through Clarissa's means that her conventional comedic ending can be registered only with ambivalence: "Miss HOWE was not to be persuaded to quit her mourning for her dear friend, until six months were fully expired: and then she made her Mr HICKMAN one of the happiest men in the world. A woman of her fine sense and understanding, married to a man of virtue and good-nature . . . could not do otherwise" (1491; 8:272). Rather than conveying the certainty of a subjective compulsion, that "could not do otherwise" carries the weight of resignation and also of the social compulsion that Anna seemed previously to control and even invite.

That this concluding epilogue is "said to have been written by Mr Belford" should seem entirely appropriate. Perhaps even more so than Anna, he has reached the end of a narrative the very possibility of which the novel calls into question. Since Richardson has throughout *Clarissa* (and its paratextual material) emphasized the impossibility of the genuinely reformed rake, Belford becomes a shadowy figure whose existence cannot be directly acknowledged without doing damage to the moral force of the novel itself. His development, his *Bildung*, is both necessary and highly inconvenient. As Richardson puts it in his preface, Belford "actually reform[s]" (35). Yet in that same short preface, Richardson warns against "that dangerous but too commonly received notion, *that a reformed rake makes the best husband*" (36), a warning that might lead us to place a bit more pressure on the surprise contained in that "actually."

Once it is clear that the novel itself contains the undoing of its own avowed precepts, it should come as no surprise that the project of moral instruction generated within the diegesis also unravels. Anna tries in her long letter to Belford—with dubious success—to recreate out of the material of Clarissa's life a new conduct book, one that does not advise its reader on courtship, motherhood, or any other supposedly determining experience. Clarissa's short life threatens to collapse the very possibility of ordering one's life sequentially, of using milestones to make meaning. Consequently, the model of authority that Clarissa's life proposes is one based on ignorance and innocence rather than wisdom and experience. Her inexperience, by the novel's end, is clearly a model for living an authentic life rather than a stage to grow out of. Without quite recognizing this crucial difference, Anna is in effect recreating the comical scene she earlier recounts, wherein Clarissa impersonates through writing an "anonymous elderly lady" to assist a friend (246; 2:78). Anna's attempt to fashion Clarissa's story into one of experience and wisdom is not only unlikely to be effective, it also rings false. As Anna's mother asks upon hearing of Clarissa's "personation" plot, if Clarissa "at her time of life, could so well assume the character of one of riper years," how can we excuse her "if she should rush into any fatal mistake herself?" (247; 2:79–80). Clarissa's ability to feign maturity does not save her from error any more than Anna's careful editing of Clarissa's story convincingly makes it into a bildungsroman.

Recall that when Anna chooses to write a cross section of Clarissa's life, she contrasts it to a diachronic "history," one that would presumably begin at the beginning, with Clarissa's "wonderful . . . *infancy*" (1466; 8:196). A history, Anna implies by comparison, cannot perform the same work of instruction, despite Anna's repeated vows earlier in the novel to gather together Clarissa's letters and writings for just such a purpose. Anna's aversion to history in this moment of mourning lies in the fact that the genre would necessarily require her to move past Clarissa's idyllic early years into the more dynamic events of the previous few months. That is, Anna would have to recount via reduction what has already been recounted for the reader. She would be charged, if following this tack, with giving the survivor's testimony that has been a literary form at least since Horatio's distillation of Hamlet's life at the end of Shakespeare's play.[60] Instead, by closely following her source material (Clarissa's memoranda), Anna is able to stop where Clarissa stops, at the fateful day of her departure from her father's house. In fact, Anna quotes Clarissa's apocalyptic memorandum verbatim:

APRIL 10. The account concluded!—
And with it, all my worldly hopes and prospects!!! (1472; 8:322)

Ending where she does, Anna stresses Clarissa's loss of everything "worldly," even though the worldly seems otherwise to be of little interest to Clarissa. *What "worldly hopes and prospects"?* we might be tempted to ask. It is fitting that this note enters the novel not via Clarissa herself but through Anna's repetition and appropriation of it. In fact, the absurdity of this final memorandum (with its ludicrous hyperbolization of writing-to-the-moment) does suggest the (admittedly speculative) possibility that Anna has fabricated it. This would surely help to explain the emphasis on the worldly, which seems otherwise out of character for Clarissa.[61]

Leaving aside the sheer absurdity that Clarissa would have actually been able to produce this final record of an "account concluded" (presumably bringing her daybook with her to her fateful meeting with Lovelace), it seems important to note that Clarissa continually attempts, as Anna does here, to suspend her life story at a previous moment in time. This is most clear in her repeated insistence that her life ended on April 10, not only in this instance but also in her decision to use that date as her date of death when having her coffin engraved. The date marks the beginning of her plot but the end of her life. Yet it should be noted that Clarissa's impulse to project backward is present even before the gravity of her situation is clear. In her *very first letter* of the novel, Clarissa writes to Anna, "I have sometimes wished that it had pleased God to have taken me in my last fever" (41; 1:5).[62] Clarissa's willful avoidance of change—we might justly call it an avoidance of maturation—is to be taken by the reader not as a result of her fateful decision to leave her father's house, as is often suggested, but as constitutive, as characteristic. Clarissa's *being dead* is then spread out over the length of the novel's *longue durée*, carrying more significance than the moment of her death. As I have shown, we might extend her protracted death-bed scene not only back to her escape from her family home but back further still beyond the parameters of the novel. Clarissa's conjectural logic renders even her own death a beginning. Rader has convincingly argued that Richardson is able to give the impression that Clarissa has indeed received her celestial reward by presenting her letters to family after her death (and thus seemingly from beyond the grave): "By presenting posthumously Clarissa's long will and a number of her letters to various persons, Richardson achieved the wonderful effect of giving Clarissa's afterlife a seemingly concrete manifestation, whereas if her voice had ceased at her death, the effect would have been far different."[63] It is possible to take Rader's argument a drastic step further. In her repeated insistence that the time of her death (that is, time she *should* have died) has already passed, Clarissa gives the impression that *all* of her correspondence is posthumous; her stasis is a rigor mortis. As Ann Kibbie puts it in her brilliant reading of *Clarissa*'s Gothic potential, "Clarissa asserts that she has, in effect, been dead all along, a ghost haunting her own story."[64]

Then again, given Clarissa's propensity to renounce not just the material world but the social world specifically, it might be even more appropriate to think of Clarissa not as prematurely deceased but as *civilly* dead. As Kibbie also points out, those entering a religious order were once considered to be entering a state of so-called civil death.[65] During this transition, they would compose and carry out their wills, becoming legally recognized as having died. As William Blackstone mordantly notes, "The genius of the English laws would not suffer those persons to enjoy the benefits of society, who secluded themselves from it, and refused to submit to its regulations."[66] Clarissa does not, of course, enter a religious order and thus cannot be considered a "novice" in the church sense. Although convents are no longer extant in England when Clarissa is living, this does not stop Clarissa from identifying novitiation as an ingenious solution to her situation: "Were ours a Roman Catholic family, how much happier for me, that they thought a nunnery would answer all their views!—" (83; 1:84). Note, again, just how early in the novel Clarissa expresses this wish to remove herself from society. In turning a blind eye to her family's pecuniary ambitions, Clarissa suggests that her family (or, perhaps, that conjectural version of her family she proposed to Anna) would agree to such a solution. Such an alternative would seem to provide the perfect resolution to her own foreclosure of society and its claims upon her. Imagining such an alternative where she can remain living without inhabiting the social world is, for Clarissa, strictly a fantasy. To be Catholic would be, for one of Clarissa's markedly Protestant constitution, to be someone else entirely.[67] Perhaps more importantly, to be Catholic would mean living in the past, or at least in a counterfactual present, as England's convents had been disbanded for more than two hundred years.[68] And, as my discussion of conjectural history (and Clarissa's own use of the subjunctive) should suggest, going back two hundred years is still not going back far enough; it would be impossible to go far enough back in historical time to adequately undo the social problem Clarissa faces here.

The difference, then, between Clarissa and Anna centers on this fundamental difference between conjecture and history, inexperience and experience. Anna herself settles on the difference between herself and Clarissa with an eerie observation: "I am fitter for *this* world than you, you for the *next* than me— that's the difference" (69; 1:58). Her tone is light here, and she intends her remark to be trivial. Clarissa is quite simply a better person, certainly a more obedient daughter, but the difference is so slight for Anna that she can say just one paragraph earlier, "You are me" (69; 1:58). However, as I have suggested throughout, Anna is more astute when she recognizes Clarissa's alterity. Where she errs is in locating Clarissa's prowess in the "next" world rather than a speculative one: another world entirely. Clarissa's logic is one of deduction, not projection, where even her death can be conjecturally derived—a fact that the historical, factual world is only belatedly catching up to as it insists that her preparations for death indicate overreaction, depression, or hysteria.

Seeming at last to recognize this, Anna suggests in writing to Belford that Clarissa's history, with its necessary structure of cause and effect, gets complicated in a way that her memoranda never do. Clarissa's meticulous method of recording her moral debits and credits ensures that any momentary failing can be straightforwardly repaired. Not enough reading to the industrious poor in a given week can be easily recompensed the next; Clarissa's life remains virtuous through the balancing of her moral checkbook.[69] But what Watt calls "ridiculous"—this "systematic apportionment of [Clarissa's] time"—is only absurd if we expect it to be real, to be a historical account.[70] The flatness of such a quantitative understanding of Clarissa's life is more than offset by benefits of a clear communication of her unambiguous perfection.

However timeless Anna wants Clarissa's "character" to appear, it nevertheless reaches the reader at the end of Richardson's long novel, written as it is after Clarissa's life is over. It is thus implicated in the narrative expectations even a mid-eighteenth-century reader has about what happens at the end of a novel. Though the epistolary eulogy paints a picture of a prelapsarian (and pre-diegetic) Clarissa, its effect is one of conclusion, as if it instead depicts the point that Clarissa has *reached* after overcoming such hardships as she has had to endure, learning from her own mistakes and those of others. But it is crucial to see how the anachronistic finality of the letter creates merely the false impression of a bildungsroman. Clarissa was never in a position to *learn* the lessons she embodied; she seems instead preternaturally equipped with them from the outset. In this sense, Anna need not have chosen between a list of Clarissa's perfections and an account that begins with her "wonderful infancy," for the two are one and the same.

If the novel does not depend on a model of development, then there is a way in which the end can be seen as simply replicating the beginning, even if, by the novel's end, its heroine is dead. This compression at the heart of *Clarissa* renders the novel at once both an exemplary and a cautionary tale, meaning that it can effectively be neither. The two plots cancel one another out, and the moral point Richardson wants to make in his preface and postscript to the novel would seem to dissolve. And yet, oddly enough, the novel's didactic power appears to be undiminished by its attendant formal problem. This is because the novel's ending creates an illusion that unravels the contradiction at the core of its form. By leaving the reader with the uneasy sense that the novel *is*, in fact, a bildungsroman, that Clarissa has acquired the perfection that the novel otherwise leads us to believe she was born with, the reader is able to understand virtue as a process, as developmental rather than intrinsic. But this sense—a "relationship remembered against relationship forgot"—is ultimately just an illusion, one that threatens to obscure Clarissa's conjectural history and to deny the dependence of the novel on the figure of the novice.

CHAPTER 2

When Experience Matters (and When It Doesn't)

Tom Jones and the Rake's Regress

This will . . . afford a reason why many simple and innocent characters
are so generally misunderstood and misrepresented.

—HENRY FIELDING, *Tom Jones*

In the previous chapter, I argued that Clarissa Harlowe's conjectural narrative
skims like a stone over the facts of her empirical existence, only infrequently
making contact with the realities of her situation but, in doing so, securing her
status as a moral exemplar untainted by the world. I connected this narrative
maneuver to the philosophical genre of conjectural history, which, in the hands
of a writer like Rousseau, likewise proceeds according to a deductive logic rather
than a verifiable, historical path. While Clarissa's sympathetic fellows, Anna and
Belford, take great pains to craft and present her story according to the model
of a plot of development (a plot they themselves follow), Clarissa's story is not one
of maturation through social accommodation but rather one of self-preservation
through social withdrawal. She figures not character development but character integrity. Operating outside, or, perhaps better, alongside, the protocols we
may otherwise expect of realist narrative and characterization—wherein narrative incident produces a corresponding change in character—*Clarissa* atten-
uates plot even as its pages proliferate. I turn in this chapter from Samuel Richardson to Henry Fielding, to consider what happens when the inexperienced
protagonist is located not in an effectively plotless novel like *Clarissa* but in-

stead in one that has been considered to have a "perfect plot."[1] The comparison of Richardson to Fielding is a time-honored one, but in demonstrating that *Tom Jones* and *Clarissa* address the same central problem—namely, whether experience can be understood to shape character—I tend to challenge the opposition between Richardson and Fielding that has long dominated work on the early novel. Indeed, I paint a far more sentimental (which is to say a far more Richardsonian) picture of Fielding's novel than readers might expect.[2]

Critical attention to Fielding's well-made plot has often drawn attention away from the novel's depiction of Tom as a character. Indeed, the pleasures of the novel's plot are often read as a kind of consolation for the deficiencies of its characterization. (Deficiency, here, usually means stability.) And yet, as I have argued, character consistency holds its own conceptual complexities and narrative possibilities, as Fielding himself was well aware. Writing about the internal probability expected of drama, Fielding compresses into the term "Conservation of Character" both the author's skill at managing character consistency over time and the stability of character as ethos—what Claude Rawson calls "a willed truth to self, stubbornly adhered to."[3] This chapter centers on the ways that Tom Jones, as loveable rake, evinces both consistency of character (in his steadfast, even doltish, goodness) and a kaleidoscopic multiplicity of identities (as he is perceived by those around him, who cannot quite place him or make him out). This contradiction reaches a head by the novel's finale not in the hanging the reader is promised but rather in a marriage. In marrying Tom, Sophia Western must recognize his stable goodness and must herself cultivate inexperience: acting as if she did not witness Tom's history and as if she did not fear that that history may influence his (their) future. Sophia's difficult embrace of risk corresponds to the larger, and less conflicted, social amnesia with which the public greets Tom's sophomoric exploits, which he gets both to experience and to have stricken from the proverbial record. This chapter, then, is something of an outlier in its treatment of novice masculinity, but, at the same time, it sustains an investment in the difficult ethical choices young women confront by training equivalent attention on Sophia's role in establishing Tom's character alongside her own.

Perhaps the clearest way to think about how Tom can have his experiential cake and eat it too is with respect to the novel's treatment of sex. Tom does not just have premarital sex and get away with it (which would not seem that surprising given the powerful and enduring sexual double standard Fielding celebrates); he, more surprisingly, engages in carnal acts without appearing to acquire carnal knowledge. How can Tom Jones have so much sex and still seem so unknowing?[4] Tom's erotic exploits, though only obliquely narrated, were central to the novel's notoriety upon its publication and continue to contribute to its popular appeal. (Let us not forget that the novel is responsible for the stage name of its Welsh Sex Bomb namesake, whose agent attempted to capitalize on the popularity of the raunchy 1963 adaptation.) But to picture Tom as winking, as it were, to the reader (as Albert Finney does when playing him, breaking the fourth wall), is to overlook just how innocently, how unabashedly, he tumbles in those sheets and hay bales and bushes.

Like *Clarissa*, though in a markedly different tenor, *Tom Jones* belies the commonplace that with the loss of virginity comes the mantel of experience. Take the narrator's description of the aftermath of Tom's first sexual encounter:

> Molly so well played her part [in seducing Tom while appearing to be herself seduced], that Jones attributed the conquest entirely to himself, and considered the young woman as one who had yielded to the violent attacks of his passion. He likewise imputed her yielding to the ungovernable force of her love towards him; and this the reader will allow to have been a very natural and probable supposition, as we have more than once mentioned the uncommon comeliness of his person: and, indeed, he was one of the handsomest young fellows in the world. . . .
>
> He considered this poor girl as one whose happiness or misery he had caused to be dependent on himself. Her beauty was still the object of desire, though greater beauty, or a fresher object, might have been more so; but the little abatement which fruition had occasioned to this was highly overbalanced by the considerations of the affection which she visibly bore him, and of the situation into which he had brought her. The former of these created gratitude, the latter compassion; and both, together with his desire for her person, raised in him a passion which might, without any great violence to the word, be called love; though, perhaps, it was at first not very judiciously placed.[5]

Believing himself to have conquered Molly is only one of several misapprehensions Tom arrives at after his first sexual experience. Rather than revealing the world as it is, sex only leaves Tom more deluded, if, as the narrator seems to stress, understandably so. This may come as a surprise. We tend to think of carnal knowledge *as* knowledge, sexual experience *as* experience. As Eve Sedgwick puts it, "Cognition itself, sexuality itself, and transgression itself have always been ready in Western culture to be magnetized into an unyielding though not an unfissured alignment with one another."[6] But Fielding's novel, by contrast, supports a notion just as abiding and as powerful as the perennial conjuncture of carnality and epistemology: the idea that having sex keeps us, indeed, *makes* us stupid.[7] Indeed, sex does not lead to worldliness in Tom's case. On the contrary, after having sex with Molly Seagrim (both that first time and after many, many implied repetitions) Tom's ignorances only multiply: He believes himself to have corrupted her. He believes that he loves her. He believes that she loves him. He believes that he is her only partner. He believes he is the father of her unborn child. Tom may know a thing or two about sex but to call him knowing would be to inflict far more violence on that word than would Tom's use of the word "love."

In his sexual (in)experience, Tom may resemble a rake, but he is never a very good one. We might think of him not as rakish but as rake-*ish*; the resemblance is only ever approximate. After all, compared to Molly's first lover—who had "reduced several women to a state of utter profligacy, had broke the hearts of some, and had the honour of occasioning the violent death of one poor girl, who had either drowned herself, or, what was rather more probable, had been drowned by him" (188)—Tom is a veritable vicar.[8] Tiffany Potter argues that Tom is "the archetypical Georgian [as opposed to Restoration] libertine," embracing the philosophical tenets of libertine philosophy "but manifest[ing] them less aggressively."[9] I would recast this; Tom's rake-ishness is a matter not simply of degree but of mode, more a sympathetic send-up of libertinism than simply a milder version. Tom's bathetic brand of the Restoration figure may not leave a rake wake of fallen (and even dead) women, but it nevertheless exposes the logic by which more extreme crimes are likewise excused and their perpetrators exonerated. Tom is a novice who operates according to a rakish logic of cathartic experience, one that imagines experience to be something you get out of your system rather than something that makes you who you are. To designate Tom in this way is to recognize the fundamentally presentist orientation of libertinism. "Our sphere of action is life's happiness," Rochester writes in "A Satyr against Reason and Mankind," "And he that thinks beyond, thinks like an ass."[10] To focus on "life's happiness" is not just to embrace a scandalous materialism (to reject the prospect of an *after*life), it is also to reject the logic of consequence as such, to find foolish the very idea that experience accumulates.

Profiting from such a logic, divested of his poor decisions, our final Tom is an inexperienced Tom: seemingly younger, aging in reverse, the beneficiary of a system that creates good men by categorizing their experiences as boyish.

Natalia Cecire refers to this gendered quality as "puerility"—capturing a way of being in the world that is "not just childish, but *boyish*, for a particular notion of what a 'boy' is. Puerility makes everything into a game, even things that are not games, even things that *must not be* games."[11] By the end of *Tom Jones*, Fielding has re-narrated his friend William Hogarth's *Rake's Progress* series, only in reverse. Tom begins his life in disrepute—as good as dead, the narrator assures us—and ends with his inheritance, never squandered because it was not bestowed in time for youth's profligacies to take their effects. While Hogarth's print series are quite pointedly cautionary, Fielding's novel rewards Tom's virtue as it frees him from his experiences, suggesting another moral altogether: men can get away with just about everything, perhaps even murder, so long as men will be boys.

Mixed Character and the Pamela Problem

If what I am calling Tom's rake-ishness suggests a parodic or evacuated version of a common eighteenth-century type (the libertine that conduct books so often warned both young men and women to avoid), we may also think of that type as a rearticulation of Samuel Johnson's famous suspicion of Fielding's method of characterization. Johnson's polemic against so-called mixed character excoriates writers who "mingle good and bad qualities in their principal personages," coaxing the reader into forgetting what was so bad about those bad qualities to begin with.[12] While such a combination of characteristics may be common in real life, Johnson concedes, realist art must be selective if it is to maintain its didactic utility: "If the world be promiscuously described," Johnson writes, "I cannot see of what use it can be to read the account."[13] Though Johnson could as easily be speaking of an alluring villain like Richardson's Lovelace in this essay, he is almost certainly taking aim at the dashing Tom Jones: so loveable that readers may be tempted to forget or at least forgive certain transgressions—to forget, for example, that Tom finds his calling, for a rather lengthy episode in the novel, as a gigolo.

While Johnson's fear of moral ambiguity may strike us now as antiquated (where he sees inconsistency, we are likely to see complexity), his additional claims that Fielding's characters were superficial—mere "characters of manners" compared to the deep psychological renderings of Richardson—have retained more critical currency, not least because these claims were endorsed by Ian Watt's still widely influential theory of the novel.[14] These two complaints are, however, more closely connected than the critical tradition might have us think, and the substance of Fielding's critique of exemplarity lies at their intersection. These debates tend to be kept distinct in part because they appear to contradict each other in their assessments of the value of early realism. In the first, Johnson appears to prefer the perfect exemplarity of Richardson's protagonists to Fielding's more verisimilar depiction of the individual as well meaning but inevitably flawed. (In other words, Johnson wants more Clarissas.) In the second, however, Johnson appears instead to align Richardson with a mastery of naturalistic psychology; in fact, as Boswell reports, Johnson explicitly contrasts Fielding's "characters of manners" with Richardson's "characters of *nature*, where a [reader] must dive into the recesses of the human heart" to understand them effectively.[15] While Johnson is being evaluatively consistent (that is, Richardson in both cases comes out on top), the conceptual interference between these assessments produces a blurrier picture of the Richardson/Fielding debate, and thus of the early novel, than we might expect. It is simply impossible to line up the accounts of realism here. Exemplarity works across Johnson's assessments by selecting the good until it would seem to verge upon, even tumble headlong into, the too-good-to-be-true.

In what follows, I will consider Fielding's apprehension of and response to this problem. Through Tom, Fielding demonstrates how certain social narratives fabricate exemplarity by designating particular experiences as irrelevant to identity. Thus Tom, once his class status is revealed, is rendered *in*experienced by unanimous agreement of the very society that embraces him; the erasure of Tom's experiences in the construction of his final character identity reveals the extent to which political considerations are caught up in character's social construction.[16] At the same time, the activation of this very social construction by Sophia's trusting acceptance of Tom's hand further complicates the understanding of character with which Fielding leaves us, stressing the place of intimacy in an otherwise large-scale, systemic process.

Despite the apparent contradiction of Johnson's two statements, both critiques of Fielding ultimately hinge on accounts of how a character's experience in the world should or should not be represented in the new form of the novel. Both recognize Richardson and Fielding as having fundamentally different understandings of how characters should encounter and respond to plot, specifically in terms of how isolated a protagonist can or should be from the workings of plot, understood as the literary depiction of experience. Attention to this issue raises central questions for how we encounter Fielding's novel: What does it mean for a character like Tom to reform over the course of the novel, or, to put it differently, when might the reader find reform to be credible? How is Tom's reformation related to his treatment of others; that is, how is *being* good related to *doing* good? And what does it mean to suggest, as Watt does, that a character like Sophia acts *out of character* at the novel's conclusion, when she chooses to accept Tom's hand in marriage against her better judgment?[17] These questions are, as I hope to demonstrate, closely connected, as Sophia's acceptance of Tom both coincides with his reformation and validates his latent potential to do good in the world. Though this chapter necessarily traces the ways in which Tom's character identity is formed and unformed in Fielding's novel, my ultimate emphasis will be on the complex operations—both formal and political—of Sophia's recognition of that character.

Sophia has long been read as an allegorical representation of virtue or, as critics have long pointed out, of the virtuous "wisdom" that her name etymologically evokes. We might recall Martin C. Battestin's succinct conclusion: "Ultimately, [Sophia's] true identity is ideal, an abstraction."[18] Such a reading tends to view *Tom Jones* as, on the one hand, lingering in the world of romance, and, on the other, offering a variation on the *Bildung* narrative.[19] That is, by such an account, Tom learns from the trials of the novel's plot so that he may earn wisdom by its conclusion; this achievement, Tom's coming of age as a virtuous adult and model citizen, is represented allegorically through his union with Sophia. But seeing Tom's experiences as formative in this way requires taking too seriously the insistent *mock*-heroic nature of Fielding's representation of experience in the world. As we will see, Fielding again and again points to cases in which experience does *not* produce the individual but instead falls away disregarded and undone, not constitutive of but irrelevant to identity.

In contrast to the romantic reading of Sophia, I will demonstrate Sophia's swerve away from allegory in her pointedly *unwise* decision to accept Tom's hand in marriage at the novel's end. This decision is less a moment in which Sophia acts *out* of character than one that reveals the trajectory of her character. It is this moment, which we might read as a devolution or regression for Sophia, that most vividly indicates Fielding's interest in the production of inexperience. Unlike most heroines of eighteenth-century fiction, Sophia, we should remember, finds herself in public circulation throughout the novel: in carriages and country inns, from the rural hunt to London society. This circulation grants Sophia the unparalleled ability to read her own society symptomatically, to understand its operations, and to exploit them as she sees fit.[20] Sophia's choice

of Tom endorses society's blanket pardon of the youthful indiscretions of gentlemen, with her recognition that this is a social act indicated by the fact that she
allows her own decision to be activated by her father's. Sophia's self-interested
expression of love coincides with the social unraveling of Tom's rakish past, an
opportune concurrence that undermines his experience along with her own.

Sophia's choice to consider Tom's past as cathartic rather than constitutive
is a choice to reject the rival paradigm in which past experience is considered
to be a sufficient, even a necessary, guide for correct future action. To put it in
the language of the novel, Sophia chooses to reject "prudence," which would
encourage her to avoid a relationship with Tom in light of his past actions and
her own past heartache.[21] Sophia's salvation as a character also comes to produce Tom's own since she does not recognize Tom as having changed so much
as she acknowledges that he has retained certain qualities that he has possessed
all along (namely: largeheartedness, generosity, and the very credulous faith that
Sophia herself exhibits in this moment). Sophia's acceptance, then, makes clear
that the novel does not in fact operate on the model of *Bildung*, in which character is gradually produced by experience. Instead, we might think of the narrative as producing a multiplicity of Toms that are superimposed upon one
another as the novel progresses and out of which common, defining features
must be discerned. Sophia's task at the novel's conclusion, in other words, is to
bring Tom's essential character into focus. In doing so, she sifts through and
discards those qualities contingent upon his experiences, and her acceptance
of him erases those contingencies. The novel's picaresque plot does not merely
get cleared up, exposed as a simple misunderstanding; it is instead revealed
as having been a kind of illusion, an alternative reality that is not permitted
to come to fruition. Fielding thus stresses a theory of character that does not
resolve plot into a series of occasions for characters to act in such a way as to
prove their character but that is instead one in which plot is, however perfect,
in the end subordinated to and dependent on fundamental character identity.

The denouement that reveals Tom's parentage suggests an identity both as
an individual and as a member of society, but, as Tom himself makes explicit,
Tom's identity is fixed only through Sophia's acceptance, her ratification of his
new identity. This sudden—and belated—production of character is, as we will
see, the trick of the novel's famously perfect plot. But first, to explain further
how that trick works, it will be necessary to recognize that this plot is to a significant degree appropriated from the text that Fielding so notoriously derided:
Richardson's *Pamela: Or, Virtue Rewarded* (1740). Critics have long recognized

that the rivalry between Richardson and Fielding energized the development of the early English novel.[22] Our understanding of this connection has focused primarily on Fielding's most explicit and immediate volleys in the anti-Pamelist backlash that followed Richardson's publication of *Pamela* in 1740: *An Apology for the Life of Mrs. Shamela Andrews* (1741) and *Joseph Andrews* (1742). Richardson, in depicting a servant girl whose unerring virtue earns her not only the love of a rakish gentleman but also, through their marriage, a place in his social class, prompted a crisis in the reception of naïve virtue that is inextricably linked to the emerging dominance of fictionality as a mode of expression.[23] The novel raised a series of questions at the intersection of epistemology and ethics: Could the reader believe Pamela's account? How might the reader know whether to believe her? Does a belief in naïve virtue make the reader herself laughably—even perhaps tragically—naïve?[24]

As I will discuss in more detail below, Richardson would himself come to fear that *Pamela* had encouraged such excessive credulity in its readers, particularly regarding the risky notion that the reformed rake makes the best husband. This commonplace rested on what I have been referring to as a model of "cathartic experience": the idea that young men needed to have certain kinds of experiences in order to get those experiences out of their systems. Experiences were, in this line of thought, purgative; rakishness was, then, not constitutive of identity or even characteristic of a certain type of person but was instead a phase that a man was expected to move out of eventually. The daunting task for young women, it follows, was to determine that a man was ready to leave those days behind him, or, more often, to convince him that he was ready to do so. The popular cathexis onto Pamela notwithstanding, reactions against Richardson were often more vocally concerned with the dangers Pamela's example posed *for those men*. This anxiety is unambiguous in the title page description of Eliza Haywood's contribution to the debate, *Anti-Pamela* (1741): "A Narrative which has really its Foundation in Truth and Nature; and at the same time that it entertains, by a vast variety of surprizing Incidents, arms against a partial Credulity, by shewing the Mischiefs that frequently arise from a too sudden Admiration. Publish'd as a necessary Caution to all Young Gentlemen."[25] Like Richardson himself, Haywood claims that her story will both delight and instruct, but the instruction here is in hardening men against affection, as affection tends toward gullibility. Here, Haywood is parodying Richardson's own title page for *Pamela*, as she does when she changes the subtitle *Virtue Rewarded* into her own *Feign'd Virtue Detected*.[26] Haywood's subtitle reminds us that the fashionable critique of Pamela—unlike later critiques of Clarissa—was founded not on a charge that she was *too* virtuous but that she was not virtuous *enough*. The implication is that Richardson's novel might lead men to marry ruthless, deceitful women; by this logic, the problem inherent in naïve virtue is that it too readily resembles its opposite: cunning deception.[27] It is simply impossible to know, according to this logic, whether a young woman is virtuous or devious, as the signs of virtue are dangerously overdetermined signifiers.

The reference to "too sudden admiration" in Haywood's warning suggests that the solution to this problem might be as simple as protracting the period of courtship. Indeed, this "truth-will-out" model was a common recommendation in anti-Pamelist literature. As another critic ventured, "At least, [Pamela] might have made her Admirer wait a few Years, before she concluded the Match." He goes on to suggest that this solution would not only certify Pamela's value but would also help her to "avoi[d] the Censure now pas'd upon her."[28] (It is amusing here to follow the logic, which suggests that feigning virtue is so laborious that, over time, the deceiver will just give up out of exhaustion.) Beyond pointing out the relatively straightforward problem of deceptive appearances, Haywood's admonition captures the concern that a man might—without due time and reflection—mistake a purgative (and thus nonbinding) experience for a commitment that would be formative of his character. The anxiety of Haywood's preface, in other words, is the anxiety that young men might not be able to distance themselves as much from their experiences as the cathartic model presumed (and promised).

In his own response, Fielding exaggerates the problem of speed not only by making the text of *Shamela* very brief but also by highlighting the impression that Shamela's marriage to Squire Booby is impending from the very beginning: "I don't doubt that you will shortly be my Mistress," Mrs. Jewkes tells Shamela early in the account, "I am convinced you will shortly be my Mistress" (258, 259). "Mrs. Jewkes . . . assures me that I shall shortly be Mistress of the Family," Shamela confidently reports to her mother (260). Published a few months before Haywood's story, Fielding's burlesque was the first and certainly the most famous public response to Richardson's novel and is generally credited with stemming the initial tide of popular support for Richardson, encouraging readers to respond with skepticism to Pamela's claims to virtuous humility. Fielding contorted Pamela's virtue into Shamela's "vartue"—a term he first coined in his farce *Rape upon Rape* (1730) to designate the calculated display of a virtuous appearance for ambitious or otherwise immoral ends.[29] In his next volley, *Joseph Andrews,* Fielding charted the story of Pamela's purported brother Joseph—like his famous sister the chaste victim of untoward advances from his employer—and in so doing considered the requirements for and limits of masculine virtue. (Indeed, the ideological thrust and running gag of *Joseph Andrews* is that a male paragon—or a chaste one, at any rate—is a mythical beast.) These contributions to the media event following *Pamela*'s publication not only indicated the multiplicity of contemporary perspectives on social issues, they also galvanized the emergence of the novel form.[30] In *Joseph Andrews,* especially, Fielding appeared to consider with more rigor what his "new Province of Writing" would be in its own right and not only in contradistinction to Richardson's "new species of writing."[31]

Part of what I want to demonstrate in this chapter is that the dispute between Fielding and Richardson runs even deeper than this brief outline suggests. True, critics have considered how *Tom Jones* bears a tense relationship with *Clarissa,* not only because the novels were published almost concurrently but also because Fielding came to express admiration for Richardson's second novel.[32] But it is not clear that Fielding had more than a general familiarity with *Clarissa* when beginning to compose *Tom Jones,* and the similarities between the two texts remain relatively superficial.[33] Indeed, one problem with too closely aligning *Tom Jones* with *Clarissa* is that it is all too easy to line up characters with their counterparts in ways that turn out to be misleading. Thomas Keymer, for example, in the introduction to his recent Penguin edition of *Tom Jones* writes of the "interpretive chaos" caused by Richardson's dialogic, epistolary form and corrected by Fielding's third-person narrative: "No one could ever read Blifil as the hero of *Tom Jones,* as some readers had demonstrably made a hero of *Clarissa*'s arch-villain, Lovelace."[34] Fair enough. But, Blifil's insidious sadism notwithstanding, we are likely to be struck first by the oddity of the comparison (*Blifil and Lovelace?*) before we can even begin to consider the validity of Keymer's formal claim. That the insipid Blifil is no dangerously charismatic Lovelace would surely be clear even in an epistolary account; to work, such a comparison must distort both texts and so leads astray even an exceptional critic like Keymer. Likewise, Sophia's virtue is clearly not burnished through continuous trial in the way that Clarissa's is. Most significantly, Richardson's insistent rejection of the reformed rake plot in *Clarissa* requires him to devote that novel to a consideration of experience as reliably constitutive of libertine identity, hence the acrobatics through which he ensures that the rape is formative for Lovelace but not for Clarissa.

Reading *Tom Jones* as Fielding's most serious engagement with the concerns raised by *Pamela* proves more fruitful. Fielding's thoroughgoing critique of Richardson in his early responses is at once formal, political, social, ethical, religious—from his derision of the gimmickry of Richardson's present-tense epistles to his disapproval of the easy class mobility suggested by Pamela's marriage to Mr. B. However, it is crucial to our understanding of the novel at mid-century that we recognize that *Tom Jones* features a complex, at times vexed, engagement with the very idea of naïve virtue that Fielding had derided in *Shamela* and *Joseph Andrews*. This is made clearest in the novel's sudden, pivotal ending, during which Tom and Sophia enter a marriage that produces their characters by effectively eliminating Tom's past experiences and affirming Sophia's sentimental trust in the Tom who remains. By the end of Richardson's novel, Pamela is essentially vindicated by being shown to be a natural aristocrat, while Mr. B is vindicated by an almost progressive ability to recognize that true aristocracy involves virtue (and perhaps virtue alone). It is here that I want to draw the strongest connection to the plot of *Tom Jones*, a connection that appears simple but that contains significant ramifications for Fielding's project: like Pamela, Sophia reforms a rake; like Mr. B, Tom uses Sophia as a justification for a new life of virtue. Comparing Tom to Mr. B is illuminating because the comparison points to the ways in which the reformed rake forces both the heroine and the reader to make difficult judgments regarding character and, more specifically, character consistency over time. To take the comparison of the novels further, however, going so far as to compare *Sophia* to Mr. B may help us to think about the significance of Sophia's recognition of Tom's worth before the facts of his birth are known. This chiasmus (Sophia as Mr. B; Tom as Pamela) may particularly capture the way that characters appear to precipitate out of Fielding's plot. Though we might see Fielding as cheating in revealing Tom to have been "actually" noble all along (thereby avoiding the class mobility problem raised by Pamela's marriage), the novel repeatedly insists that the socioeconomic facts of Tom's birth are inconsequential to Sophia even as she recognizes their larger social significance. Instead, the novel highlights the noble *simplicity* of Tom's essential nature, a quality in evidence long before Tom's noble *heritage* is revealed.

The Recognition Plot and the Removal of Experience

Near the end of *Tom Jones*, Fielding's hero enjoins Sophia, his estranged sweetheart, to "fly" to him, even though he admits to having treated her badly. Tom's epistolary plea is typical of Fielding's mock-heroic flagging of intense emotion: "Pardon me this presumption," Tom writes (referring here to the presumption that his infidelity would have hurt Sophia), "and pardon me the greater still, if I ask you whether my advice, my assistance, my presence, my absence, my death or my tortures can bring you any relief?" (843). But even as he pleads for Sophia's trust, Tom admits that trusting him would likely be foolish: "If . . . wisdom shall predominate, and, on the most mature reflection, inform you that the sacrifice is too great . . . I conjure you drive me from your thoughts" (844). Tom's hopes are pinned on the likelihood that Sophia's wisdom will not, in this case, win out, that her naïve faith in his love for her will undermine her more rational recognition of his profligacy. When Tom writes to Sophia, begging for her forgiveness, even he suggests that she would be foolish to accept him. However, the novel has already prepared the reader to understand that forgiving Tom at this juncture is precisely what Tom himself would do. Tom's own foolish but noble acts of forgiveness (of Black George and of the highwayman, most memorably) are contrasted favorably not only with Blifil's self-interested machinations but even with the benevolent Allworthy's cautious, (overly) rational judgment. *Tom Jones* again and again suggests that large-hearted impulse (the kind generated by inexperience) is superior to careful deliberation. It is imperative to note the novel's repeated insistence that virtue be put into practice: the superiority of largeheartedness becomes legible as evidence of social superiority. Sophia is tasked, in recognizing Tom's goodness, with taking Tom simultaneously as an object of imitation and of her own generosity.

I want to take seriously Tom's suggestion that Sophia's "wisdom" and "matur[ity]" could lead her to act quite differently and, consequently, could lead to a very different ending and a very different novel. Sophia does exhibit a certain kind of wisdom in that she knows all along what the other characters only belatedly discover: Tom has never really been ignoble. She must nevertheless choose to move forward by acting on the basis of that knowledge even when another kind of wisdom might encourage her to act otherwise. That her culminating act of naïve faith coincides with—and may even be seen as *producing* —what the novel leads us to believe is Tom's own rather overdue coming of age should begin to indicate the curious production of character in Fielding's novel. But before getting to why, exactly, Sophia accepts Tom when she does, it is first necessary to consider how Tom arrives at a position in which he is eligible to propose to Sophia in the first place. So, let us back up for a moment.

The plot of *Tom Jones* hinges on an end that is a beginning. This is not only because the narrative, in traditional comic fashion, takes on a circular shape, closing with the restoration of order and Tom's reinstatement to his original position at Paradise Hall. Though this is true, the novel's narrative is much stranger than this: Tom's path is marked not by the driving forward movement of the bildungsroman plot but instead by the jostling of multiple possible competing paths, each of which carries the potential of being the one that leads Tom to the novel's conclusion. This multiplication of paths not taken in fact works to intensify the sense of the inevitability of the one that is. Consider, for example, Tom's early resolution in book 7 to "seek his fortune at sea" (the path that leads him toward Bristol in the first place), or his competing determination to join the king's forces in fighting rebels in the North. We might regard such possibilities as mere devices—the means of shuttling Tom from point A to point B—but I want to emphasize here just how open Tom's options are at this stage in the novel. That Tom has so many alternatives available to him, so many counterfactual possibilities, is, of course, a condition of his youth and inexperience. Moreover, the uncertainty surrounding his birth means that Tom must make his own way; he is free to chart his own course in a way that a gentleman, obligated in very predictable ways to his family and his social class, cannot and need not be.

Tom's instability is precisely what enables the revelation of the truth of Tom's parentage to provide such a ready solution to the puzzle that is Tom's meandering life. Once the facts of Tom's birth are established in the novel's final book, the intelligence travels quickly and is repeatedly received as the key to Tom's identity. The idea that Tom only comes into being as a character in the novel's final book is perhaps most vivid in the reaction of his future father-in-law, Squire Western. Immediately upon hearing the details of Tom's birth, Western, heretofore suspicious of Tom, runs to him and greets him in friendship: "My old Friend *Tom*, I am glad to see thee with all my Heart. All past must be forgotten. I could not intend any Affront to thee, because, as Allworthy here knows, nay, dost know it thyself, I took thee for another Person" (963). Western characterizes his new impression of Tom, informed by the details of Tom's birth, as the clearing up of a simple case of mistaken identity. Western's prior actions, directed as they were toward the old Tom, cannot be understood as having been directed at this new and improved Tom; there is simply no continuity between the two identities.[35] "I could not intend any affront to *thee*," he seems to stress, whatever the harm he intended to inflict upon that other poor chap. That Tom is an entirely new person would appear to be self-evident: Western knows it; Allworthy knows it; and, moreover, Tom himself knows it.

The additional knowledge of Tom's parentage appears to change everything, but unlike the classical plot of recognition (Aristotle's anagnorisis), new knowledge in this case bends the plot toward the comic rather than the tragic. The disclosure of Tom's true birth in fact *reverses* the more properly Oedipal anagnorisis of mere moments before, when he was erroneously informed that he had "been a-Bed with [his] own Mother" (915). The revelation of what supposedly happened at Upton hurls Tom into depths of self-recrimination. Constitutionally happy-go-lucky, he is momentarily forced to assess the extent to which his carelessness has veered into vice. Many critics—including Battestin—have read this scene as central to the novel's indictment of Tom's careless youth; the idea that Tom matures in this scene requires that his youthful wrongdoing fundamentally constitutes his character even as he comes to regret it.[36] Tom certainly seems to agree with such an assessment: "Fortune will never have done with me, 'till she hath driven me to Distraction. But why do I blame Fortune? I am myself the Cause of all my Misery. All the dreadful Mischiefs which have befallen me, are the Consequences only of my own Folly and Vice" (916). Yet it is crucial to note that this scene of regret, in all its melodramatic intensity, remains momentary, as ephemeral as the very idea that Tom has engaged in incest—an idea quickly disproven and as quickly forgotten. Indeed, Coleridge, in his copy of the novel, wished for more durable contrition—and with it, more *Bildung*: "I can not but think, after frequent reflection, that an additional paragraph, more fully and forcibly unfolding Tom Jones's sense of self-degradation on the discovery of the true character of the relation in which he stood to Lady Bellaston [that is, his occupation as her male consort], and his awakened feeling of the dignity of manly chastity, would have removed in great measure any just objections."[37] Coleridge's proposed revision underscores what I suggested in the introduction: that the educative appeals of *Bildung* are strong because they are clear; the novice threatens to further undermine the already unstable operations of readerly identification.

Narrative theorists have highlighted the ways in which plots of recognition, like that of *Tom Jones*, operate by holding multiple possible narratives in a kind of suspension before designating one of those narratives as the "actual" or ontologically privileged one. These competing narratives correspond to competing diegetic storyworlds. As Hilary Dannenberg puts it, "Recognition thus evokes an experience in which a character is, often traumatically, transferred from a world that he or she has hitherto considered to be actual and thrust into a new alien version of reality."[38] In this case, Tom operates in a world in which he is a low-born foundling until he suddenly finds himself thrust into a world in which he is the son of Bridget Allworthy and thus the blood relative and heir of his beloved guardian. Fielding appears to be far more interested in moments of revelation, like that of Tom's birth, that are not traumatic but joyful, that lead not to social rejection but, on the contrary, to the warm inclusion that rules all prior experience invalid. The question that remains for readers is how to find continuity of character over these shifting worlds—or whether to seek it at all. Dannenberg notes precisely this: "The question of *character identity* within changing ontological constellations [that is, shifting designations of which story-world is actual] is . . . central: multiple versions of identity are experienced *successively* by a character within the recognition plot."[39] Once placed in a new world, is this character recognizably the same one from that other world? Or is this Tom, per Western, "another Person"? One thing is certain: when it comes to the recognition plot, successive identity need not imply developmental or incremental identity. We would be unlikely to say, for example, that Oedipus *becomes*, through experience, parricidal and incestuous. Instead, we see his plot as operating outside of his control and as exerting pressure on his character through a sudden realization of circumstances, rather than through a continuous, educative process. For Squire Western, the solution to the problem of character identity is simple; this Tom is simply not the Tom from that previous world. This Tom is effectively a new acquaintance, and one whom Western would like to get to know better.

Of course, we know that Tom is not the only one who has seemed to be what he is not; the novel's intricate comedic plot depends on dozens of cases of misrecognition and misidentification, including a landlord's belief that Sophia is Jenny Cameron, fugitive mistress of Bonny Prince Charlie. Persons in Fielding, it would seem, have such imprecise and versatile shapes that they can be literally interchangeable. At the same time, Tom still seems to be an exceptional case if only for the extreme fluidity of his identity.[40] Most of the incidents of interchangeability in the novel can be attributed to the anonymity of highway travel or to the bustle of London, a place where, as Joseph Andrews complained to Pamela, "next-door Neighbours don't know one another."[41] And Western's response to this new Tom is self-justifying; he needs a convenient way to explain his own opportunistic change of opinion. Still, that response also introduces the more disconcerting idea that someone could know Tom from birth and still not know who he is. Like Western, the reader has known Tom from infancy; the novel narrates Tom's story from his appearance in Allworthy's bed. But the duration of this acquaintance seems nevertheless inadequate to the task of solidifying Tom's identity. Western's encounter may be striking, then, but it is certainly not singular; again, Tom has been mistaken for a number of other persons over the course of the novel and, in at least one case, for a nonperson (if we consider his ghostly visitation in book 7).[42]

Just as it multiplied the narrative paths at his disposal, Tom's formerly ambiguous class status has seemed to exacerbate this problem of multiple identities: he acts like a gentleman but has no money, leaving those he encounters unable to taxonomize him properly, as if the competing class signifiers only serve to cancel each other out. We can see Fielding's interest in the alignment of behavior and identity in his nonfiction writing as well. As he stresses in *An Enquiry into the Causes of the Late Increase of Robbers* (1751), an essay he published shortly after *Tom Jones*, different kinds of actions—drinking and gambling, for example—have different consequences for the poor and the rich. "Here I must again remind the Reader, that I have only the inferior Part of Mankind under my Consideration," Fielding notes, pausing in his discussion of the evils of gambling. For "the Great, who are beyond the Reach of any, unless capital Laws," such vices simply do not count in the same way; they are not subject to the same social and legal consequences.[43] Accordingly, gentlemen are enjoined to recognize their privilege and to avoid negatively influencing those without that privilege: "We may, I think, reasonably desire of these great Personages, that they keep their favourite Vice to themselves, and not suffer others, whose Birth or Fortune gives them no Title to be above the Terrour of the Laws, or the Censure of the Betters, to share with them in this Privilege."[44] Hence the conundrum facing those unsure of Tom's class: it is unclear whether his vices, such as they are, should be punished or overlooked. Tom's behavior in the world cannot clear up the mystery of his class status precisely because it is his class status that is required to determine the significance of those actions.

We may be reminded of Locke's thought experiment in the *Essay* regarding the prince and the cobbler who trade souls: "Should the Soul of a Prince, carrying with it the consciousness of the Prince's past Life, enter and inform the Body of a Cobler as soon as deserted by his own Soul, every one sees, he would be the same Person with the Prince, *accountable only for the Prince's Actions*: But who would say it was the same Man?" (340; emphasis added). Locke's hypothetical body swap is intended to demonstrate that selfhood resides in the consciousness and not in the physical body. While Tom's case is clearly not a body swap, it similarly raises questions both of consistency of identity and, crucially, consistency of class. As Jonathan Kramnick reminds us, Locke's emphasis on accountability is critical here, and we might say the same of Fielding's writing. Could we justly hold the prince-now-cobbler accountable for the actions committed previously by the cobbler? Should we excuse Tom's youthful transgressions now that we know that he is a gentleman? As Kramnick puts it, "Were there no misdeeds, the question of where such [personal] identity lies might not matter so much" (91).[45] Identity, here, is less an existential than a legal matter. As Tom's heritage becomes clear in these final pages, the problem of how to recognize Tom and his actions becomes more pressing. The details of Tom's birth provide him not only with a new class but also with new rules under which identity operates within that class.

Western suggests in greeting Tom again, as if for the first time, that Tom has only now become knowable. And now that Western knows who Tom is, he knows him to be the man Sophia will marry. That is, Western connects the facts of Tom's birth to the eligibility that those facts authorize: "Come along with me; I'll carry thee to thy Mistress this Moment" (963). Western is not alone in making this connection; in fact, Allworthy has already spoken to Sophia on the same subject. As we will see, however, unlike the other characters, Sophia does *not* understand the news of Tom's parentage as having firmly established his character or, for that matter, as having changed anything at all. When Allworthy reveals the news to her, he is certain that in doing so he is providing the magic words, as it were, that will produce her consent to marriage. He creates suspense by employing the same mistaken identity trope that we have already seen signaled by Western's reaction. He first tells Sophia that he has a nephew "the very opposite" of vile Blifil, who is interested in paying Sophia a visit. "A Nephew of yours! Mr. *Allworthy*," she replies. "It is surely strange, I never heard of him before" (954). Only when she demurs does Allworthy, overcome with the felicity of his act of prestidigitation, tearfully reveal that this nephew is in fact Tom. While surprised by this news, Sophia refuses to entertain Tom's proposals all the same. Sophia, it turns out, is alone in imputing character consistency to Tom, in refusing to see Tom as an entirely new person:

> I shall never receive Mr. *Jones* as one who is to be my Husband.—Upon my Honour I never will. . . . I beg, Mr. *Allworthy*. . . you will not insist on my Reasons. . . .
> I beg I may not be farther press'd; for whatever hath been, my Resolution is now fixed. . . . I do not disown my former Thoughts; but nothing can ever recall them.

At present there is not a Man on Earth whom I would more resolutely reject than Mr. *Jones*. (955–96)

Though she has previously declared that she would prefer "Ruin with [Tom to] the most affluent Fortune with another Man," Sophia objects to Tom at the very moment that her previous condition for marriage—her father's endorsement —has been met (733). The identity that allows Tom to be accepted as a social actor does not yet ensure his elevation to the still social but clearly more inti-mate position of Sophia's husband. Of course, since we know that Sophia *does* ultimately consent to marry Tom, the fact that this news does *not* lead to her consent raises the question of what does. We may be tempted to read Sophia's hesitancy as indicative of Fielding's misogyny. Women are fickle, he seems to suggest, and even a woman who has gone to such unaccountable lengths to follow her lover could, at the moment of crisis, refuse him and rescind the commitment she has as good as made. The speed of the novel's resolution only bolsters this skeptical reading. Still, I want to linger with Sophia's refusal (and ultimate acceptance), taking seriously the turns in her thought that work through the operations of experience and its convenient elimination. I slow down the novel's denouement not to explain away Fielding's misogyny but to relo-cate it: not in the emptiness of Sophia's objection but in the complicity of her acceptance—its activation of a larger cultural exoneration of criminal men. While Fielding no doubt endorses the elevation of Tom in the novel's final pages, I ultimately find cynical the cultural weight he places on Sophia's decision.

Sophia's Recklessness

If Allworthy is "surprized" by Sophia's objection, Mrs. Miller, who similarly visits Sophia to vouch for Tom's worth, is completely bewildered: "Anything so inexorable I never saw. . . . She remains inflexible," she reports to Tom (955, 962). Sophia emphasizes her own steadfastness, her "inexorable" refusal to re-lent ("my resolution is now fixed") in contrast to and defiance of reports of Tom's sudden alteration. Like Mrs. Miller, we might attribute Sophia's contin-ued displeasure with Tom to her memory of a series of possible infractions, her refusal to forget the past that Tom has so suddenly left behind him. (Of course, we may not be as ungenerous as Mrs. Miller when we come to this conclusion.) Tom has, we know, been unfaithful to Sophia from the very beginning of their acquaintance; however, she insists that she is willing to believe Tom's protestations that his "*Heart* was never unfaithful" (732). Sophia has also been offended by Tom's willingness to take liberty with her name "in Inns, among the meanest Vulgar!" (732), but this impediment is revealed to be due to a misunderstanding. (It is the bumbler Partridge who has spoken of Sophia publicly and not Tom.) With such objections explained away, Sophia's continued intransigence, the other characters insist, must be based on yet another misunderstanding, as Tom's newfound social identity would seem otherwise to guarantee his marital felicity. "Perhaps he may have been misrepresented to you, as he was to me," Allworthy suggests (955). Tom's latest identity should, by this shared logic, erase any impediment to his marriage, but Sophia remains unyielding even when confronted with the numerous crimes this Tom did not commit, the numerous people this particular Tom is not. "He is no Murderer, I assure you," Allworthy adds hopefully, if to no avail.

As she explains it, Sophia's chief concern is not one particular indiscretion but instead a general sense of Tom's "Inconstancy," a quality clearly linked to the unreliability of his affections but that also stands as Sophia's articulation of the problem of the multiplicity of Tom's character (972). Tom has proven himself hard to pin down, his name attached not only to the sundry acts he has actually committed but also to numerous exploits that turn out either never to have happened or to have happened to others. Unable to argue away this unreliability of his past, Tom encourages Sophia to decouple that past from their possible future together, to loosen the sense of a causal connection between past and future that would lead her to doubt the felicity of their potential union: "Inconstancy to you! O Sophia! if you can have goodness enough to pardon what is past, do not let any cruel future apprehensions shut your mercy against me" (972). As in his previous letter, Tom encourages Sophia to act without prudence and instead to understand his character as separate from his experiences. His new social identity has suggested that understanding Tom in this way is not only possible but to be expected: Tom has been easily pardoned for the crime of murder not only because it is simply impossible for him to have committed it (murder is not murder when the supposed victim remains alive) but also because "two noble Lords" assure the magistrate that Tom now has friends in high places (964). A pardon for the crime of inconstancy, however, proves to be rather more difficult to obtain.

At the same time that this final proposal scene solidifies the novel's endorsement of Tom's ardent goodness, it highlights the inadequacy of Tom's supposed reformation. This is in part because protestations of reform are not enough to guarantee its continuation. In fact, the very changeability inherent to reform suggests ominously that reform can just as easily lead back to dissolution: if someone can alter so thoroughly once, that is, what ensures that he will not change again? Sophia, in responding to Mrs. Miller's protestations in Tom's favor, figures the problem of reform as a decision between two types of character that Tom may be aligned with. She insists that she is willing to "forgiv[e] many Faults on account of Youth;" in other words, she concedes that a cathartic model of experience may pertain in Tom's case (962). Nevertheless, she "expressed such detestation of the character of a libertine" that Mrs. Miller found herself "absolutely silenced" (962). The question that motivates Sophia's response is whether Tom's transgressions are mere youthful "faults" or components of his "character."

Faced with this challenge, Tom rejects the very idea of the latter possibility, using Sophia's own body as evidence that their union, and not his experience, will be formative, presumptively grounding his identity in her choice of him: "'I will show you [proof], my charming Angel,' cried *Jones*, seizing her Hand, and carrying her to the Glass. 'There, behold it there, in that lovely Figure, in that Face, that Shape, those Eyes, that Mind which shines through those Eyes: Can the Man who shall be in Possession of these be inconstant? Impossible! my *Sophia*: They would fix a *Dorimant*, a Lord *Rochester*.'" (973) We might be reminded here of Nancy Armstrong's sharp observation about *Pamela*: "The more Mr. B persists in his attempts to possess her, the more he subjects his behavior to Pamela's view."[46] Tom makes this dynamic explicit, explaining his plea for Sophia's approval as inextricable from his desire to "possess" her. Sophia's distinction between "faults" and "the character of the libertine," is effectively invalidated by Tom's insistence that Sophia could lead even these two definitive rakes, Dorimant and Rochester (let alone someone only moderately rake-ish like Tom), to leave a life of libertinism behind them, to consider libertinism not as an identity but as a phase. The *Oxford English Dictionary* uses this passage in *Tom Jones* to illustrate the meaning of "fix"—defined here as "to make [someone] constant in attachment," rather than with the later, now more familiar, usage: to mend or correct.[47] But we can almost sense that later definition as implicit in the earlier here. To secure Tom, to hold him in place, is to make him a better Tom. This is not, however, because Tom has learned from his experiences, no matter what he protests, but because fastening Tom in marriage suggests that his troublesome mobility, his inconstancy, his multiple identity, have come to an end. To assent to marriage with Tom is not to recognize his constancy (of which Sophia can see no proof) but to bring that constancy about, to create it.

The irony of the mirror episode is that, in attempting to reduce his multiplicity, to show that he is constant and fixed, Tom effectively multiplies both himself and Sophia in drawing attention to their reflections. What is worse, the mirror scene recalls an earlier scene in the novel, one that immediately preceded Tom's first clumsy proposal of marriage. Remember that Sophia, walking into Lady Bellaston's apartment, sees her reflection alongside what appears to be a statue—a statue that turns out to be Tom. (Talk about unsettling the appearance of fixity!) Here at the novel's end, Sophia signals this memory of Tom's infidelity and recalls the unreliability of the mirror as an emblem of security, and she iterates that prudence should lead her to resist Tom's entreaty: "If I am to judge . . . of the future by the past, my Image will no more remain in your Heart when I am out of your Sight, than it will in this Glass when I am out of the Room" (973). Tom's attempt to prove his worth malfunctions in offering Sophia the last thing she wants to see: yet another Tom whose worth she must adjudicate. At the same time, the setting of the proposal—in a domestic space in Western's country home—seems already to hint at the socioeconomic stability (and thus, we are encouraged to believe, the moral constancy) of Tom's new life, just as his exaggerated comparison of himself to Dorimant and Rochester suggests that he is beginning to see himself as in a class approaching theirs. While she continues to demur, Sophia clearly notes the significance of this difference: "Your Situation, Mr. *Jones*, is now altered, and I assure you I have great Satisfaction in the Alteration" (973).

With this, we reach a gap, as Sophia relents to the engagement just as quickly (as capriciously?) as she had rejected it. Yes, in the end, Sophia does forgive and marry Tom, providing the comic novel with its requisite conjugal conclusion, in an act of approval verging on concession. After an extensive argument with Tom during which she agrees to consider his proposal only on the condition of a long and uneventful courtship, she relents immediately upon her father's subsequent request: "I will obey you.—There is my Hand, Mr. *Jones*. . . . [T]omorrow Morning shall be the Day, Papa, since you will have it so" (975). Sophia's initial insistence upon a protracted term of courtship, a decision endorsed by the skeptical response to *Pamela*, is merely a momentary parenthesis before the immediacy of the plot's resolution, in which all of Sophia's protests against marrying Tom dissolve. As my allusion to the requirements of comedy indicates, we should not be too surprised, as our expectations of the comic plot lead us to believe that everything, including Tom and Sophia's courtship, will turn out all right in the end, just as we believe—again correctly—that we will learn the truth of Tom's parentage and, by extension, his intrinsic worth. So-phia's acceptance of Tom would seem to be, then, an example—perhaps *the* example—that supports the critical commonplace that plot takes priority over character in Fielding's novel. In such a reading, character and plot compete in the zero-sum game of the novel; in the case of Sophia's acceptance of Tom, "the denouement has been given a certain comic life, but at the expense of the reality of emotions involved."[48] That "certain comic life" returns to the idea that these characters function more as media for comic effects and less as windows into consciousness. But to read Sophia's acceptance as a mechanical method for resolving the turns of the plot is to neglect the complex operation by which she must both assert Tom's consistency (as the same good-hearted man he always was) and, at the same time, recognize—in what amounts to an official, repre-sentative capacity—the consequences that come with his newfound identity.

Sophia's concerns about Tom arise from her recognition of the same discon-tinuity that so troubled Johnson: "Oh . . . how is it possible! Can every Thing noble, and every Thing base, be lodged together in the same Bosom?" (732). She confides in Mrs. Miller her concern that Tom's mixed character has led his better qualities to become contaminated: "I once . . . fancied I had discovered great Goodness of Heart in Mr. *Jones*; and for that I own I had a sincere Esteem; but an entire Profligacy of Manners will corrupt the best Heart in the World; and all which a good-natured Libertine can expect is, that we should mix some Grains of Pity with our Contempt and Abhorrence" (962). Her acceptance nev-ertheless indicates her ultimate refusal to see Tom's heart as corrupted or to respond to him with contempt. Coinciding with Tom's new social situation, that acceptance necessarily revalues Tom by privileging the noble over the base and then recategorizes Tom's past experiences in turn. That Sophia consents to see Tom as a reformed rake and, in turn, agrees to marry him as such, is central to our understanding of Fielding's novel just as the problem of the reformed rake is fundamental to the novel at midcentury. Richardson, as I have noted, high-lights, even aggravates, the problem in *Pamela* and then claims to correct it in *Clarissa*. As he writes in the preface to the latter novel, "It is one of the principal views of the publication: to caution . . . children against preferring a man of pleasure to a man of probity, upon that dangerous but too commonly received notion, *that a reformed rake makes the best husband.*"[49] Richardson's implicit lesson in this passage is that people cannot change, that experiences are so fun-damental to identity that they cannot be ignored or even completely forgiven. Sophia's acceptance of Tom reveals a naïve faith—not in the possibility of true reformation but in the constancy of a virtue that can be decoupled from experience. In having Sophia accept Tom, in other words, Fielding endorses a model from Richardson that Richardson himself found dangerous.[50] However, Fielding insists that the reformed rake—in Tom's case, at least—is one who was never really that rakish to begin with. Sophia's erasure of Tom's transgressions launders his story until he resembles the virtuous, inexperienced Pamela more than her rakish seducer. The marriage of Tom and Sophia highlights the extent to which society is active in performing this kind of purification on those it deems qualified. Building a foundation for the socioeconomic observations of his writings like *The Late Increase in Robbers*, Fielding showcases in *Tom Jones* an analysis of social inequality as it plays out in moral and emotional lives, culminating in a large-scale societal judgment reflected in a smaller, interpersonal one.

CHAPTER 3

Simple and Sublime

The Otherworldly of Ann Radcliffe's Gothic

> Her heroines voluntarily expose themselves to situations, which in nature a lonely
> female would certainly have avoided.
>
> —SIR WALTER SCOTT, "Mrs. Radcliffe" in *Lives of the Novelists*

In a footnote to "The Age," a satirical poem published between Ann Radcliffe's
The Romance of the Forest (1791) and Jane Austen's *Northanger Abbey* (1803),
C. J. Pitt winkingly offers readers a cheat sheet for turning Gothic romances
into realist novels and vice versa:

> The conduct of the poet in considering romances and novels separately, may be
> thought singular by those who have the penetration to see that a novel may be
> made of a romance, or a romance of a novel with the greatest ease, by scratching
> out a few terms, and inserting others. Take the following, which may, like ma-
> chinery in factories, greatly accelerate the progress of the divine art.
> From any romance to make a novel.
> Where you find—

A castle, ...	put An horse.
A cavern, ...	A bower.
A groan, ...	A sigh.
A giant, ...	A father.
A blood-stained dagger, ...	A fan.

Howling blasts, ...	Zephyrs.
A knight, ...	A gentleman without whiskers.
A lady who is the heroine, . . .	Need not be changed, being versatile.
Assassins, ...	Killing glances.
A monk, ...	An old steward.
Skeletons, skulls, &c. . . .	Compliments, sentiments, &c.
A lamp, ...	A candle.
A magic book, sprinkled with blood, ...	A letter bedewed with tears.
Mysterious voices, ...	Abstruse words, (easily found in a dictionary).
A secret oath, ...	A tender hint accompanied with naiveté.
A gliding ghost	A usurer, or an attorney.
A witch, ...	An old housekeeper.
A wound, ...	A kiss.
A midnight murder, ...	A marriage.

The same table of course answers for transmuting a novel into a romance.[1]

The stark oppositions of Pitt's handy chart can offer only exaggerations of the conventions that had begun to coagulate in both Gothic and early realist fiction. Already, Horace Walpole had set himself the task in *The Castle of Otranto* (1764) to reconcile ancient and modern romance (that is, in Pitt's terms, romance and the novel); to take just one example, Walpole is perfectly content to populate his castle with both a giant *and* a father, even suggesting that they pose equivalent threats. Likewise troubling the distinction between ancient and modern romance, Pitt's point is that the particulars of each genre are more or less superficial; the essential structure of fiction remains, allowing for transpositions that might speak to a matter more of taste or style than to a deeper significance. While the jokes here are many (my favorite might be the swapping of skulls and sentiments—both known to tumble out of closets?), I want to draw the reader's attention to the variable in Pitt's machine that remains unchanged: the constant of the heroine, who "need not be changed, being versatile." If, as we have seen, a reliable quality of the novice as a character type is precisely that she "need not be changed," this chapter will amend to that observation a claim that Pitt already posited two centuries ago: that the novice is precisely the continuity that links Gothic romance to the novel form. While a long critical tradition holds that the Gothic novel is not novelistic at all, and is thus not subject to that form's epistemological requirements, by now we can see that the Gothic in fact only literalizes the novel's suspension of competing ontologies. If early realism held up for consideration a variety of paths for the novice, Gothic fiction, as a variety of early realism, encouraged these possibilities to haunt the novice, to hover in shadowy corners, to leap out of cupboards long shut. To advance this claim is to challenge a view shared by many critics of Gothic fiction. Markman Ellis, for example, has argued, "The supernatural is categorically an unnovelistic aspect of the gothic—it cannot be reconciled with the empirical observation of the novel."[2] On the contrary, the supernatural elements introduced by the Gothic, rather than revealing the Gothic to be unnovelistic, further highlight a skepticism toward empirical observation that, as this book argues, is central to the early novel's project more generally.

Early realism uses the novice to concentrate the effects of counterfactual thinking, and the Gothic is where we see the most dramatic distance between the novice's counterfactual vision and the grounding objections of the real world. Nowhere is narrative more forcefully haunted than in Gothic fiction. The same narrative procedure we have seen—an empirically privileged "real" narrative overwhelmed by the force of the novice's false but powerful vision of the world —structures the early Gothic novel, and especially the vexed novels of Ann Radcliffe, where the optative creates, in effect, a shadow—even an *ectoplasmic*— realism: one in which the ontologically verifiable world seems, no matter its solidity, always obscured by the sticky film of the fantastical. Recall from my introduction that, for Andrew Miller, the realist novel relies on the optative mood to lasso subjunctive desires (wishes, hopes, longings) to the parallel narratives of actualized experience. The novice, in stressing ideas and beliefs over the real, pulls Miller's "what if" construction into the present, creating an alternate reality in tension with the socially accepted facts. In Radcliffe's hands, the longing inherent to the counterfactual is frequently supplemented, even supplanted, by more insistently suspenseful, sensational iterations of that "what if" formula: "What if [that garment] should conceal the mangled body whose blood has stained it?"[3] "What if . . . some of these ruffians should find out the private staircase, and in the darkness of night steal into my chamber!"[4] These moments do not tend to solicit pathos of the kind Miller is interested in and can even appear comic in comparison, in their conjuring of ever more fanciful scenarios that combine and recombine the elements of Gothic convention. However, they do likewise encourage us to consider the way that the novice encounters the world by speculating about the terms of its operations. For the Gothic novice, the supernatural can indeed seem less alien, more predictable, in comparison to the hostile social world into which she is likewise thrust without due preparation. Indeed, though Radcliffe is associated with the dissolution of Gothic trappings through the device of the explained supernatural, we shall see that the novice's spooky what-if imaginings are repeatedly allowed to remain suspended and uninvestigated.

In this chapter, I focus not on the novice's consideration of counterfactual future possibilities nor on the similarly ubiquitous record of counterfactual pasts viewed with either regret or relief. Instead, I return to depictions of a counterfactual present focalized through the inexperienced protagonist's myopic epistemological stance. In these cases, the counterfactual is not triggered by a decisive moment or recalled by a fleeting memory; it is not wistful. Rather, it is prolonged, explored, *lived* by a protagonist who, in most cases, is not aware that she is seeing the world as it is not. In the case of the Gothic, this inexperienced stance confronts the jostling ontologies—the real and unreal—of the supernatural. I focus on Radcliffe's Gothic because it provides a particularly rich site for understanding the mechanics attendant to the characterization of the novice and to the plotting of *the experience of inexperience*. Such a narrative does not trace the path of development but instead charts a curiously recursive movement from experience to inexperience and back again. Narrative shuttles across the divide of Pitt's twinned lists, offering not a translation between genres but a defiance of genre in service of investigating a more fundamental formal operation.

Validating Walpole's Servants

Before turning to Radcliffe, I want to linger a bit longer with Walpole, whose *Castle of Otranto* inaugurates a close relationship between the Gothic and inexperience that is extended and further complicated by Radcliffe's novels. In both prefaces to *Otranto*—the one attributed to a fictitious translator and the second that bears the author's name—Walpole lays out the generic premises behind his experimental fiction. His aim, as he describes it, is to join ancient and modern romance, in order to leverage fantastical phenomena into heightened psychological response. The author "wished to conduct the mortal agents in his drama according to the rules of probability; in short, to make them think, speak, and act, as it might be supposed mere men and women would do in extraordinary positions."[5] This is to say that Walpole joins realist characterization with romance plotting: borrowing from the emerging novel an interest in characters who respond in verisimilar, predictable ways, then coaxing them to enter a world of spectacular possibility: ghosts, giants, curses. Key to this generic experiment is Walpole's defense of his novel's depiction of domestic servants. "Some persons may perhaps think the characters of the domestics too little serious for the general cast of the story," he writes (4). The concern to which Walpole refers here is at least superficially one of decorum: the tragedy of *Otranto*—however absurd it may seem to us now—does not, according to these projected readers, allow for the levity introduced by the ignorant servants who run about the castle in a panic and stammer out accounts of enormous helmets and swords. Walpole's defense of his minor characters rests largely on the authority of Shakespeare's example: "That great master of nature . . . was the model I copied" (8). Most modern critics have in turn followed Walpole's lead in reading the servants as appropriations of Shakespeare's use of low life for comic relief (think *Hamlet*'s gravedigger or *Macbeth*'s porter) and have been content to pursue them no further.[6]

Though Walpole's description of his project rests on realist protocols of characterization, the domestics would appear at first to pose an exception. Certainly, Walpole reserves his more sustained psychological renderings for his aristocratic protagonists; by comparison, the simplicity of Walpole's domestic characters renders them hardly characters at all. They seem at times to be mere indicators of plot elements, conduits that bring the "real" characters from point A to spectacular point B. This apparent subordination is marked in the text by the servants' silence—their inability to shape, through language, the narratives into which they have just found themselves violently inserted: "The servant . . . said nothing but pointed to the court. . . . The fellow made no answer but continued pointing towards the court-yard" (14–15). No speech, only pointing. It is tempting to regard such pointing as requiring the bare minimum of character, as representing the kind of function Vladimir Propp writes of when he invokes certain characters who could as easily be tea kettles or, in this case perhaps, flashing neon signs.[7] When this servant—whose speechlessness has been provoked by his witnessing of a giant helmet that has thunderously crashed into the castle's courtyard—finally finds his voice, he uses it only to name that object: "Oh! the helmet! the helmet!" In this moment, the servant matters only as an index of the object; man as manicule. Better, he may be indistinct from the very object to which he points. To be rendered speechless by an object is effectively to become an object.

Rather than see these servants as themselves objects, however, I want to suggest instead that Walpole's domestics represent a valid knowledge system, one that need not be continually updated in response to experience in the wider world. As Walpole himself points out, "Many passages essential to the story . . . could not be well brought to light but by [the servants'] naïveté and simplicity" (4). These characteristic markers of inexperience—"naïveté and simplicity"—are granted their own kind of authority in Walpole's text due in no small part to the looming presence of the very objects of superstitious belief that the enlightened world discredits. In other words, these characters are not *themselves* objects but instead are characters *because of* objects. They understand objects with an immediacy that does not require qualification or questioning: they seek no strings, mirrors, or other evidence of prestidigitation. And they testify sincerely because it never occurs to them to worry about whether they will be believed. These characters reveal the solidity of inexperience under the conditions of the Gothic novel; if experience of the unprecedented is impossible, then inexperience poses no liability.

It bears repeating: these characters' sincere and open belief in the supernatural is validated by the novel's fantastical plot, which insists that there really *is* an enormous helmet, a massive sword, even a giant in the castle. Moreover, this belief is validated even though the characters are *not* credited or reevaluated within the diegesis. Prince Manfred, the servants' urbane master, is content to believe neither their reports nor his own impressions, instead launching a futile empirical investigation that relies on sensory experience and yet dismisses empiricism's results: "He gazed without believing his sight. . . . He seemed . . . buried in meditation on the stupendous object. . . . He touched, he examined the fatal casque" (15–16). Experience in the world, the novel seems to suggest, *decreases* the likelihood that one might understand experiences that deviate from the norm, that defy probability. The servants' immediate understanding makes it clear that in *Otranto* it is the epistemological outlook of worldly skeptics who *doubt* the possibility of paranormal activity or diabolical retribution that is faulty, insufficiently capacious. Only on the novel's final page does a broken Manfred—having abandoned his wife and murdered his daughter—begrudgingly surrender to the view his servants have held from the beginning. Refusing to accept documentary proof of his rival's claim to his castle, he retires to a monastery to devote the remainder of his life to belief. The "horrors of these days" at last attest to a "vision" beyond the rational, and Manfred concedes that prayer is the best response to the events he can perhaps never fully come to understand.

Terror, Horror, and Inexperience

Walpole's validation of inexperience in *Otranto* lays the groundwork for Radcliffe's own formal experiments with the extension of inexperience across narrative time. Radcliffe's famous use of the so-called explained supernatural in novels like *The Mysteries of Udolpho* (1794) means that the supernatural is *not* ultimately validated by the plot, as it so fantastically is in Walpole's text. However, Radcliffe's protagonists—the young, inexperienced heroines found in each of her novels—*do* nevertheless represent a privileged, however limited, epistemology. They seem, though repeatedly proven incorrect, nevertheless to *know* something that the more worldly, experienced characters do not (and will never) know. The Gothic novel of the late eighteenth century frequently suggests that those characters closest to nature (as Walpole might put it) display an exceptional understanding of the *super*natural: as if the prefix "super" implies not that which is beyond nature but instead nature to the highest degree. (In this sense, the Gothic might be understood as a haunted pastoral, stocked with spirits instead of sheep.) These natural characters include servants, peasants, and young, inexperienced, provincial or otherwise isolated women.[8]

In *The Castle of Otranto*, the category of inexperience is distributed across two sorts of characters: on the one hand, the domestics (who seem always to encounter the supernatural first and are then to be tasked with notifying those in power of its existence) and, on the other, the noble ingénues, the nearly interchangeable Isabella and Matilda (who, by contrast, are relatively isolated from the supernatural goings-on of the novel, contending instead with the more mundane, which is not to say less dangerous, wickedness of the corrupt patriarch Manfred). Radcliffe's heroines, on the contrary, tend to *unite* these two character functions. They are the characters who witness what they believe to be paranormal phenomena (music with no discernable source, lights seemingly borne by spirits, spectral or macabre objects), and they are also subject to comparatively run-of-the-mill persecution at the hands of unwelcome suitors and oppressive father figures. The narrative logic of Radcliffe's explained supernatural most often requires that these two roles be fulfilled sequentially, with the apparently paranormal activity finally revealed as having natural, if still sinister, causes. That is, in these novels, the perception of the supernatural is proven to be mistaken, a matter of misunderstanding. This clearing away of faulty perceptions renders the heroine's already limited experience (that is, her experience of the supernatural) negative, empty. But what is left—the heroine's inexperience—holds persistent value. I have shown how Walpole's servants are content with first impressions, oblivious to any need for further authentication or investigation; Radcliffe's narratives do tend to provide the reader with a second glance that undermines the first. But while later novels, such as Austen's *Northanger Abbey*, would become much more concerned with how those second impressions effect development in characters who are forced then to reconcile the two dissimilar accounts, Radcliffe takes an altogether different approach, suspending the supernatural alongside the real rather than subordinating it. In her novels, second impressions of objects (and of other characters), do not alter our understanding of the heroine but instead reinforce our sense that she does not require development, since she is right about what matters more fundamentally.

The most well-known example of this procedure is the incident of the figure behind the black veil in *The Mysteries of Udolpho* (1794): the heroine of that novel, Emily St. Aubert, encounters a sight so horrible that it haunts her (and the reader) for several hundred pages. At first glance, about a third of the way into the novel, we do not know exactly what the object is, nor even what Emily believes it to be. While the narrator provides a description of Emily's reaction, we are not focalized through her, and so we are deprived of her sensations. That is, we do not occupy her vision even as we, in effect, *see* her encounter with the object:

> With a timid hand, [she] lifted the veil; but instantly let it fall—perceiving that what it had concealed was no picture, and, before she could leave the chamber, she dropped senseless on the floor.
>
> When she recovered her recollection, the remembrance of what she had seen had nearly deprived her of it a second time. She had scarcely strength to remove from the room, and regain her own; and when arrived there, wanted courage to remain alone. Horror occupied her mind, and excluded, for a time, all sense of past, and dread of future misfortune. (*MU*, 248–49)

Whatever Emily's sensory experience of the object may be, its effect is to deprive her of her senses. Like many a Gothic heroine before and after her, Emily immediately faints at the horrid sight, foreclosing any possibility of further empirical investigation. After that first look, she sees the object again but only as a "remembrance" of the first impression. The narration obscures not just the object itself but likewise our registration of Emily's response, softened as it is by vagueness: "The remembrance . . . nearly deprived her of it"—Of what? It is unclear whether Emily is deprived of her memory or her vision. The sketchiness extends through the passage, replicating, perhaps, Emily's hazy consciousness. The narrator here exacerbates through imprecision the distance between Emily's "horror" and what Radcliffe would call the reader's "terror," a distance that will only be furthered when the novel corrects the reader's impression but not Emily's. As Radcliffe explains in the posthumously published essay "On the Supernatural in Poetry" (1826):

> Terror and horror are so far opposite, that the first expands the soul, and awakens the faculties to a high degree of life; the other contracts, freezes, and nearly annihilates them. I apprehend that neither Shakespeare nor Milton by their fictions, nor Mr. Burke by his reasoning, anywhere looked to positive horror as a source of the sublime, though they all agree that terror is a very high one; and where lies the great difference between horror and terror, but in uncertainty and obscurity, that accompany the first, respecting the greater evil.[9]

Terry Castle explains further while glossing this passage of *Udolpho*: "One might argue that Emily feels *horror* because she is in no doubt about the 'dreadful object' she has seen. Since we, as readers, cannot 'see' what she sees, however, our state of mind—theoretically at least—is closer to Radcliffean *terror*, we are free to imagine the worst."[10] The novel's foreclosure of further investigation appears to be merely a reinforcement of Emily's inherent disposition, not an obstacle in the path of a contrary intention. That is, her inability to continue looking is indicative of her belief that she has seen all she needs to see. As Castle puts it, she is in "no doubt"; otherwise, she would look again in the moment when she regains consciousness, which she does not. Marked by an insistent immediacy, her reaction to the object concentrates her consciousness on the present moment, forcing out considerations of the "past" or "future" that might otherwise lead her to further inquiry.

We readers do not know what—or who—is behind the veil, but our speculation about the nature of the horrid object—our "conjecture," to use a favorite word of Radcliffe's—is central to the structure of the novel. We are free to wonder, but our imagination likely credits Emily's reaction; we "imagine the worst" because we trust that Emily's extreme response is warranted. As Austen's Catherine Morland would later exclaim, "Oh! the dreadful black veil! . . . I am sure there must be Laurentina's skeleton behind it."[11] What may begin for the reader as a "terror" that comes from the unknowable becomes, through a combination of prolonged withholding of information and cathexis onto the (seemingly) more knowing heroine, an ersatz knowledge. As Austen rightly surmises, conjecture in *Udolpho* amounts to certainty, no matter Radcliffe's careful distinguishing of horror and terror. The imaginative force of naïve speculation is substituted for empirical investigation. Thus, the novel operates according to the assumption that the reader's speculation will harden into certainty (Catherine's "I am sure") along with Emily's.

Emily never revisits the object, but Radcliffe's narrator ensures that the reader gets a good look behind the veil. The narrator's disclosure of the true nature of that mysterious object comes only at the novel's denouement and threatens to undermine our confidence along with our assessment of Emily herself. However, when this revelation finally comes, it is routed *not* through Emily's consciousness but instead through the narrator's hasty tying up of loose ends. "Had [Emily] dared to look again," the narrator divulges, "her delusion and her fears would have vanished together, and she would have perceived, that the figure before her was not human, but formed of wax" (*MU*, 662). What appeared to Emily to be a rotting corpse is revealed to be instead an elaborate waxen memento mori—not death itself but its sign. Recall Emily's confusion of the object and her "remembrance" of it; fitting, as the memento mori is, of course, itself a prompt to remembrance. This moment of clarification for the reader is lodged in a past conditional that, in providing us with privileged information, ruptures our association with an Emily who did not, in fact, "dar[e] to look again," who did not "perceiv[e]." The Gothic trappings we imagined are displaced from the object itself onto Emily, who continues to emit the aura of that dreadful sight even as we learn that it was a fantasy. In fact, it is unclear whether Emily is *ever* privy to the knowledge the reader receives at that moment. And yet, the narrator does not fault Emily for her lack of curiosity; in fact, the suggestion is that looking twice would have indicated in Emily a relish for the vile object, a perversity almost inhuman. "On such an object," the narrator intones, "it will be readily believed, that no person could endure to look twice" (*MU*, 662).[12] This suggestion that the object does not admit of second glances corroborates Emily even as it undermines the very utility of an object designed for contemplation. So, while readers enjoy the understanding that empirical investigation would bring, this understanding is at the same time tainted by a hint of prurience. That is to say, the narrator's reminder is not, as Ellis and others contend, an "admonishment" of Emily, a "warning against excess sensibility," but rather an endorsement of the ingenuousness indicated by Emily's cursory glance.[13]

The Ethical Sublime

If Emily's indefinite suspension in ignorance corroborates Samuel Taylor Coleridge's complaint that "the curiosity is raised oftener than it is gratified" in Radcliffe's novels, then perhaps we should consider more seriously what curiosity looks like when separated from its gratification.[14] The bathetic movement of the explained supernatural—that is, the letdown we feel when we get to the humdrum bottom of Radcliffe's fantastical phenomena—does not in practice bring about the Enlightenment writ small that we might expect, the a-ha of an achieved knowledge superior to superstition.[15] Quite the reverse, the very inexperience, naïveté, and untutored sensibility that allow for the heroine's supernatural belief in the first place—a constellation of attributes that I take to be synonymous with what Ian Duncan calls "the heroine's romance subjectivity" is, as Duncan argues, "not represented as erroneous and in need of correction, but as a core of spiritual integrity."[16] In other words, the fact that supernatural belief is not validated in Radcliffe does not discredit the heroine. This is both a replication and, at the same time, an inversion of the move in Walpole in which the *proven* existence of supernatural objects does *not* diegetically credit the domestics.[17] Radcliffe works to recuperate this very sensibility, even in the absence of its verifiability. And so, while Duncan sees this uncorrected subjectivity as forming the basis of a female *bildungsroman*, to subscribe to this view would be to suggest that *Bildung* must operate in a curiously recursive fashion, with the heroine learning, then unlearning, again and again.[18] Instead, we might understand this recursivity to be a pointed rejection of *Bildung*, a refusal to instrumentalize these characters' encounters with their worlds. "Spiritual integrity" is also, crucially, character integrity, a solidity that, again, recalls the object without thereby rendering character as object.

In referring here to Radcliffe's episodic recurrences, I am stressing the smaller, more temporary instances of the explained supernatural just as much as those connected to a much longer plot arc—like the figure behind the veil—that have received considerably more critical attention. Radcliffe's episodic structure must continue to produce new events and experiences (which make up its plot), while, at the same time, proving those events to have been irrelevant to character all along. This prolonged recursivity, effecting a kind of stasis in the heroine, has often been understood (just as we saw in Fielding) as manifesting Radcliffe's lack of interest in character and her attendant focus on plot. But the fact that these characters do not (and even refuse to) develop need not indicate that they are failed characterizations. Rather, they represent Radcliffe's insistence upon the validity of untutored reason as moral reason. Experiential knowledge is not cumulative in Radcliffe; it does not lead to something we would call formation. This is in part because experiential knowledge seems always to be negatively constructed, an empty encyclopedia of what does not exist, what cannot happen, what is not to be. By comparison, the knowledge base provided by inexperience appears to offer a positive account, to be capacious and even substantial. Knowledge of the way Gothic worlds work—the ability, say, to predict that something hidden behind a veil must necessarily be macabre—is precisely *not* knowledge of the way the *real* world works. And yet, as we will see, this otherworldly knowledge is nevertheless portable to the "real" one in that its amplification of an innate moral capacity can be applied didactically even if the repetition of specific moral behaviors (that is, the moral exempla of the conduct book) cannot be.

Let us turn to a novel in which the moral thrust of sustained inexperience is considerably clearer. Radcliffe's 1791 *The Romance of the Forest* features a typical Radcliffean heroine, the young and mysterious Adeline, who is taken in by the LaMotte family after she refuses to remain in the convent to which she had been confined her entire life. (The circumstances of this adoption are decidedly peculiar, as the LaMottes, fleeing their Parisian creditors, are forced by highwaymen to take in Adeline upon pain of death.) Seeking a hideout, they inhabit an abandoned abbey. There, they exploit the lore surrounding the abbey, which enables them to hide in what *would* be plain sight, were the abbey not avoided:

> It was reported, that some person was, soon after [the abbey] came to its present possessor, brought secretly to the abbey and confined to these apartments; who, or what he was, had never been conjectured, and what became of him nobody knew. . . . It was said, that strange appearances had been observed at the abbey, and uncommon noises heard; and though this report had been ridiculed by sensible persons as the idle superstition of ignorance, it has fastened so strongly upon

the minds of the common people, that for the last seventeen years none of the peasantry had ventured to approach the spot.[19]

The LaMottes' plan to hide out in the abbey depends upon a general indifference to penetrating and dissolving the abbey's mystery. That is, the peasants who understand the abbey as harboring a sinister, and even supernatural, presence combine that understanding with a refusal to investigate further—or even to "conjecture" as to the details of the story they accept on faith and fear. Knowledge in the novel is distributed according to strange and irregular patterns, through a process resembling contagion rather than education.[20] The passive voice with which the narrator conveys the peasants' reports ("strange appearances . . . had been observed," "uncommon noises heard") separates those sensory experiences from individuals and instead holds them in common—a kind of supernatural gossip. This collective registration of the abbey's mystery means both that the reports are unverifiable (just who would be questioned?) and also that verification is beside the point.

The novel features not one but two central mysteries: What *actually* happened in the abbey? And what is Adeline's origin? Both of these questions, we learn at the novel's end, turn out to have a single solution: her noble father was imprisoned (and later killed) in the abbey by her uncle, the Marquis de Montalt, who, over the course of the plot, attempts to have Adeline murdered in turn. When Adeline approaches this solution, discovering a manuscript written by her father and hidden in the abbey, she does not understand the full import of the message, in part because much of the manuscript has been obliterated over time, leaving a series of telegraphic exclamations. Instead, she understands the document as a validation of the popular superstition surrounding the abbey: "Some horrid deed has been done here. The reports of the peasants were true" (*RF*, 140). In a move typical of Radcliffe's novels, Adeline's validation of the rumors about the abbey elides the distinction between the reports of "a horrid deed" and the reports of a continued supernatural presence. In other words, what we might want to separate as true story on the one hand and superstitious gossip on the other are, for Adeline, inseparable. Significantly, it is not the contents of the letter that reveal the rumors to be true but instead the feeling that the letter prompts: "An unaccountable dread came over her" (*RF*, 140). As readers, we have the leisure to apply a more rational logic to this evidence: the letter writer cannot possibly have narrated his own demise, and so the letter is simply unable to provide proof of murder, let alone of a lingering specter. The inadequacy or irrationality of the evidence does not, however, pose a problem in this case. For Adeline, each piece of partial evidence—"the circumstances," "the reports," "the dreams," "the apparition"—*all* evidence, no matter its empirical verifiability, is connected metonymically and is mutually ratifying (*RF*, 141). Moreover, she understands the concatenation of these clues not as building to a deeper understanding but as indicating the more diffuse operations of an occult hand: "Such a combination of circumstances she believed could only be produced by some supernatural power" (*RF*, 141). Supernatural belief, however hastily verified, is understood retrospectively as a kind of legitimate knowledge. And, again, this is true not only of Adeline's response but for Radcliffe's valuation of that response: Adeline may overemphasize the supernatural content of the mystery, but, ultimately, we are led to believe that she is more or less correct in her suppositions.

When, at the novel's end, Adeline learns that the manuscript's author was her father—and that he was, indeed, murdered within the abbey's walls—she feels no shame in remembering her superstition but responds in precisely the same way she did when she first encountered the document: "When she remembered the manuscript so singularly found, and considered that when she wept to the sufferings it described, her tears had flowed for those of her father, her emotion cannot easily be imagined. . . . The narrative had formerly so much affected her heart, and interested her imagination, that her memory now faithfully reflected each particular circumstance there disclosed. . . . The anguish and horror of her mind defied all control" (*RF*, 347). Note again the conjunction of horror and remembrance, which we saw previously in the narration of Emily's encounter with the object behind the veil. "Horror" suggests the elimination of plot (a bracketing of "all sense of past, and dread of future misfortune," *MU* 249), while retaining the consistency of intense response over time that constitutes character. However much the manuscript's newfound content (that is, the identity of the victim and the truth of his fate) would seem to prompt an adjustment or improvement of response, Adeline seems nevertheless to relive, to reexperience, her previous response rather than revising or deepening it. In fact, shortly after this passage, we are told that she wishes she could eliminate this new information entirely: "There were times when she wished the secret of her birth had never been revealed." The narrator goes on to explicitly propose that Adeline's desire for erasure is indicative of her moral character: "If this sensibility was, in her peculiar circumstances, a weakness, it was at least an amiable one, and as such deserves to be reverenced" (*RF*, 347). More evidence, more facts, do not lead to a more rational understanding, nor should they.

While the banditti and fortune tellers, the kidnappings and imprisonments of Radcliffe's novels may give the impression of romance adventure plotting, the suspenseful narratives more often linger in moments of just that: suspense. Narrative time is held in the suspension of ekphrastic landscape description, the trancelike analysis of portraits and miniatures, and conversations with loquacious servants who seem never to get to the point. Such an emphasis on narrative pause and digression accords with my suggestion that Radcliffe is experimenting with duration, pacing, and, in particular, the aesthetic effects of prolonged inexperience. With Adeline, the defamiliarizing potential of the novice is particularly clear. The circumstances of Adeline's upbringing (we get the impression that she has seldom been permitted outside the walls of her cloister) mean that the natural world in which she suddenly finds herself is particularly new—even more so than for a heroine like Emily who is raised in a pastoral retreat. "With Adeline the charms of external nature were heightened by those of novelty: she had seldom seen the grandeur of an extensive prospect, or the magnificence of a wide horizon" (9). The extremity of Adeline's inexperience (that is, her inexperience of the natural as well as the social world) makes her an ideal perceiver of natural wonders.[21] Furthermore, Radcliffe takes care to note that Adeline's captivity has not damaged her perception nor her ability to find solace in natural wonder: "Her mind had not lost by long oppression that elastic energy which resists calamity; else, however susceptible might have been her original taste, the beauties of nature would no longer have charmed her thus easily even to temporary repose" (9). This sentence is a thorny one—not an uncommon quality of Radcliffe's digressions on aesthetic contemplation. Stressed here are the heroine's natural faculties ("her original taste") but, more so, the durability of her aesthetic response in the face of hardship ("that elastic energy"). It is this second quality that interests me and that I see reflected in the novel's working through of both aesthetic and ethical values. "Elastic" invokes a contemporary scientific neologism to suggest *not* Adeline's malleability or capacity for formation (this might be better rendered as "plasticity") but rather her tendency to snap back into her original shape after distortion.[22] Inasmuch as Adeline is praiseworthy, it is not for her original or natural capacities but for the concerted maintenance of those capacities, a task the novel shows to be demanding and often thankless even when worthy of praise.

I will first explain what I mean by the maintenance of aesthetic response before turning to the perhaps less familiar territory of the novel's ethical values. Radcliffe was, as critics have long noted, influenced by *A Philosophical Enquiry into the Origins of Our Ideas of the Sublime and the Beautiful* (1759), in which Edmund Burke identifies obscurity as a key component of the sublime.[23] We have seen this already in her theorization of terror and horror, the former essentially a rearticulation of the Burkean sublime. I have already shown how the distinction between terror and horror can get productively muddled in the novels (indeed, Radcliffe can appear to use the terms interchangeably as a novelist). As I turn to Radcliffe's engagement with Burke in *The Romance of the Forest*, I further contend that she significantly departs from Burke's empiricist aesthetics, sketching out, via the perception of the novice, a nonempiricist sublime.

Most work on Burke and Radcliffe is drawn, understandably enough, to the latter's descriptions of sublime scenes rather than to her exploration of the characters that inhabit those scenes. Radcliffe's extended ekphrastic passages, steeped in contemporary aesthetic theory, attract our attention for the way that they disrupt the forward movement of narrative. Indeed, narrative theory has long considered description to be essentially nonnarrative, as it views objects "in their spatial rather than temporal existence, their topological rather than chronological functioning, their simultaneity rather than succession."[24] This understanding of description seems particularly useful in considering the ways that Radcliffe's heroines encounter objects—not as changing over time, and so requiring repeated examination, but instead as arrested in a reliable state of permanence that seems to elicit a corresponding permanence in their perceivers. Indeed, the familiar complaint that description is associated with death (and narration, correspondingly, with lived experience) would seem to suggest that extended description is particularly suited to the Gothic mode.[25]

In drawing on this narratological understanding of description, I am suggesting that description in Radcliffe is attached to a viewer, usually the heroine, who *sees* nonnarratively, without progression. This way of seeing is as central to theories of the sublime as were the vistas being seen. For Burke, the sublime is, in Frances Ferguson's words "the *ne plus ultra* of experience," but exactly what kind of experience is this?[26] "It is our ignorance of things that causes all our admiration," Burke famously writes, "and chiefly excites our passions. Knowledge and acquaintance make the most striking causes affect but little."[27] "Striking causes," dramatic scenes, cannot alone produce sublimity but require a particular orientation on the part of the viewer. Indeed, Radcliffe's heroines, it would seem, embody personally the inexperience that Burke had associated with a more general phenomenology.[28] Thus Radcliffe suggests provocatively that a component of aesthetic experience might instead be a component of character identity, of a disposition toward inexperience that is not corrected away through experience and a disposition toward sublimity that is not eroded by exposure. Ferguson points out the problem that arises when Burke equates mental images of objects and objects themselves: "If objects can be known, in Burke's aesthetics, only through experience, the persistence of mental images, the accumulation of previous responses to objects (which he refers to under the general rubric of 'habit') of prior experience continually threatens to make present experience virtually illegible."[29] The novice short-circuits this problem by offering the possibility of an ideal sublime perceiver. Something closest to the pure present (what Radcliffe associates with the immediacy of horror rather than the anticipation of sublime terror) is achieved when the novice perceiver confronts the sublime. In this way, inexperience provides the surest registration of true experience, unmediated by past experiences. And yet, this true experience, poised outside of the accumulative erosion built into Burke's aesthetics, comes to look like an experience undreamed of by empiricism. We can see this virtually unmediated sublimity most clearly in the way *The Romance of the Forest* uses sublime scenes as domestic spaces without thereby domesticating them, rendering them habitable without removing their awful power. This is true both of the forbidden forest itself, with its ruined abbey turned safe haven, as well as for the sublimity topos of Savoy, the alpine wonders of which Adeline seeks for her eventual home by the novel's end.

That the kind of jaded, weary knowledge that Burke warns of should *not* come with repeated trial is signaled by Adeline's repeated reflection on her vulnerability to deception and her willingness to preserve this vulnerability. Radcliffe's narrator draws a connection between the aesthetic sublime and what I have come to think of as the ethical sublime. Even quite early in *The Romance of the Forest*, the narrator makes such a link explicit: "When from these objects [the romantic glades that opened into the forest] she turned her regard upon Monsieur and Madame La Motte, to whose tender attentions she owed her life, and in whose looks she now read esteem and kindness, her bosom glowed with sweet affections, and she experienced a force of gratitude which might be called sublime" (*RF*, 13). Radcliffe may flag the approximation here ("might be called"), but it is nevertheless true that her characterization of Adeline suggests that aesthetic appreciation and gratitude are analogous responses to overwhelming stimuli. For someone of Adeline's dark past—even by comparison with Radcliffe's other heroines, Adeline has led a life of extreme constraint and privation—human goodness is great and mysterious, inspiring its own kind of awe. Sent to a convent at seven upon the death of her mother, the adolescent Adeline refuses her father's demands to take the veil, becoming instead a novice of a different sort.

In a brief first-person interlude, she explains her background to Madame La Motte, revealing that the window between her time "immured in the walls of a cloister" and her abduction by the bandits who foisted her onto the La Motte family has been remarkably brief, consisting solely of a carriage ride with her father through Paris and into the countryside, where he keeps her locked in a cottage while deciding what to do with her. Adeline's relation of her travels through the city is remarkable for the way that her expectation accords with the reality of her fleeting glimpse:

> What days of blissful expectation were those that preceded my departure! The world, from which I had been hitherto secluded—the world, in which my fancy had been so often delighted to roam—whose paths were strewn with fadeless roses—whose every scene smiled in beauty and invited to delight—where all the people were good, and all the good happy—Ah! *then* that world was bursting upon my view. Let me catch the rapturous remembrance before it vanish! . . .
>
> What a novel scene! . . . Every countenance here was animated, either by business or pleasure; every step was airy, and every smile was gay. All the people appeared like friends; they looked and smiled at me; I smiled again, and wished to have told them how pleased I was. How delightful, said I, to live surrounded by friends! (*RF*, 38–39)

Adeline never spends enough time in Paris for her illusions about its general felicity to dissolve. Then again, the novel suggests that they may not have anyway, even with considerable exposure; these "fadeless roses" are made of silk. The stability of Adeline's sunny disposition is a cornerstone of her character—a topic of conversation from the novel's earliest pages when the La Mottes, before learning of the darkness of her background, assume that her sanguinity stems from a life of ease. "You speak, my dear," Madame La Motte says, "like one whose spirits have not been often depressed by misfortune, (Adeline sighed)" (*RF*, 29–30). Monsieur La Motte, too, assumes that contentment and hope are fragile, eroded by experience: "I once, like you, Adeline, could extract comfort from most situations. . . . The illusion is gone—I can no longer deceive myself" (*RF*,

30). Radcliffe is clear that it is possible, even normal, to lose the elasticity of youth, but Adeline's lack of prior experience with basic kindness leads her to greet "tender attentions" as if they are infinite; La Motte's ominous reference to illusion suggests that she should show more precaution in interpersonal encounters.

As La Motte sees it, Adeline's openness to deception is itself a form of *self-deception*, a favorite theme in Radcliffe. (Indeed, the *OED* traces the first non-biblical use of "deceive" in the reflexive—the act of deceiving oneself—to Radcliffe.)[30] In Adeline, as with other Gothic novices, perceptual deception (illusion) is conflated with moral deception (betrayal); the ability to trust the validity of supernatural phenomena translates into a tendency to extend credit (to the point of credulousness) to other people. Radcliffe's novels allow characters' testimony about the external world to be continually mistaken without any damage to their truthfulness to themselves. The prospect of love, especially after an early life devoid of intimacy, proves more challenging to Adeline's self-understanding. Thrust into a new family, she chooses to trust the La Mottes almost immediately. This trust is soon proven misplaced when Adeline is suspected by Madame LaMotte of having seduced her husband. As this is not in fact the case, Adeline cannot understand why her mother figure is increasingly distant. "With the warmth and candour of youth," she asks plainly why Madame LaMotte has changed her behavior but receives in turn no response other than additional "hints" that Adeline is not savvy enough to pick up on. Adeline's next step is true to form: rather than seeking an answer, she acknowledges her loss, affirms her own correct action, and vows to continue in her own feelings: "I have lost that affection . . . which was my all. It was my only comfort—yet I have lost it— and this without even knowing my offence. But I am thankful I have not merited unkindness, and, though *she* has abandoned *me*, I shall always love *her*" (*RF*, 74).[31] Again, as with Emily and the veil, we are told that Adeline conducts only the most cursory investigation, asking Madame LaMotte what troubles her, then never returning to the line of inquiry. We are told that Adeline's suffering lingers ("she would frequently leave the parlour, and, retiring to her chamber, would yield to . . . despondency") and her adolescent sulking only makes more poignant her insistence on her unrequited affection.

True, Madame LaMotte's coldness seems trivial in comparison to the further distresses Adeline is soon faced with. Her lover departs with his regiment just when her situation is beginning to look most dire; the Marquis wants to make her his mistress, with her dear Monsieur LaMotte acting as pander; even the trusty servant Peter (mistakenly) appears to carry her to the Marquis rather than helping her to escape. "Am I destined still to trust and be deceived?" Adeline asks (*RF*, 166). Adeline's question contains within it an implicit affirmative answer, not only because her capacity for trust is inextricable from her character identity but also, at the same time, because the conventions of the Gothic require that she, as heroine, be repeatedly victimized. But she also clearly considers her vulnerability to be the consequence of a *cultivated* inexperience, one that she chooses willfully to maintain: "Must I then believe that every body is cruel and deceitful? No—let me still be deceived, and still suffer, rather than be condemned to a state of such wretched suspicion" (*RF*, 150).

Adeline resists the development that would come with learning from her experiences because she associates that development with the hardening of skepticism and the loss of belief. In insisting that Adeline's sustained inexperience constitutes a choice, even an ethical imperative, Radcliffe extends a dignity to what might otherwise appear to be the privation of her experience. As Michel Foucault puts it, these novels are characterized by "the heroine caught in the trap of her own innocence."[32] We can add that the heroine, once sprung from that trap, returns to it, ensnaring herself yet again. That Adeline's insistence upon *remaining* deceived—that is, her production of an *ethos* of self-deception—is understood in the novel to be both wise and virtuous is registered in the ambiguity of the novel's references to "ingenuity," where the resourcefulness of "ingenuity" and the practical limits of "*ingénue*-ity" collide. In the late eighteenth century, "ingenuous" and "ingenious" were frequently used interchangeably, if erroneously so. While "ingenuous" can be traced to the Latin *ingenuus*, and "ingenious" to the Latin *ingeniosus*, both ultimately derive from the Latin *ingigno*, meaning "inborn." "The confusion seems to have been widespread," Susie Tucker writes, pointing out that the noun forms of each adjective were likewise often jumbled.[33] Indeed, in her *British Synonymy* (1794), Hester Lynch Piozzi includes "ingenuity" under the category "Candour, Purity of Mind, Openness, Ingenuity, Sincerity," and Ingrid Tieken-Boon van Ostade concludes that "ingenuous" and "ingenious" are used interchangeably in Austen's letters.[34] Epitomizing this telling confusion, Radcliffe's heroines collapse the distinction between heart and mind, sensibility and epistemology

Adeline makes a resource of her inexperience and, in doing so, extends it even after encounters with the world threaten to rob her of its power. The very susceptibility that renders the novice an ideal sublime perceiver also seems to leave inexperience as a concept open for *dis*ingenuous appropriation in these novels: hence the urbane Marquis, who had "discovered great knowledge of the

world; or, what is often mistaken for it, an acquaintance with the higher cir-
cles," but who nevertheless employs a pseudo-Sadean primitivism to justify his
ruthlessness (99).[35] And yet, in the end, the superiority of genuine, virtuous
inexperience is demonstrated perhaps most vividly when a terrified Adeline is
abducted and carried to the Marquis's pleasure palace (replete with silk sofas
and liquor and ice cream [*RF*, 156]) . . . only to quickly and easily escape out a
window: "She perceived that the window, which descended to the floor, was so
near the ground, that she might jump from it with ease: almost in the moment
she perceived this, she sprang forward and alighted safely in an extensive garden" (*RF*, 164). Likewise, Emily St. Aubert spends hundreds of pages trapped
within Udolpho, only to walk out, casually and unscathed. The plot points that
these narratives might appear to build toward are revealed to be arbitrary rather
than climactic. In this sense, it might be better to locate the bathos of Radcliffe's
plots less in the explained supernatural itself—which, as I argue, does little to
disabuse her heroines of their illusory understandings of their worlds—than in
the very success of those false understandings: their capacity to shield Adeline
and Emily from the ends they fear. This quality makes the heroines appear as
if enchanted: not just unworldly but *other*worldly, not just isolated from the
world but insulated from its effects. We see in the frictionlessness of these escape routes less "virtue in distress" than virtue mildly inconvenienced.[36] Radcliffe's protection of her heroines endorses their ingenuousness while granting
it an almost supernatural fortitude.

As if run through Pitt's "machinery," the threat of a "midnight murder" is
swapped out for a "marriage." Likewise registering the anticlimax of Radcliffe's
climaxes, Terry Castle has observed that the explained supernatural in Radcliffe is "not so much explained . . . as it is displaced."[37] Otherworldliness is not
evacuated from the action of the novel but instead rerouted onto characters
that we would expect to remain resolutely mundane. This is most true, as Castle notes, of the heroine's lover, who can be found "haunting" the places significant to their union and who likewise "haunts" the heroine's thoughts when he
is absent.[38] But Castle has less to say about what this displaced supernatural
says about the heroine *herself*, who is visited not only by the ghosts that turn
out not to be but also by the ghosts who steadfastly remain, albeit in human
forms. We might venture to think of these heroines as possessing a special *capacity* for that haunting, for being *mediums* for supernatural phenomena. Such
an analogy is, admittedly, an anachronistic invocation of what we tend to think
of as a Victorian preoccupation, but it emphasizes the sense that these heroines

have little significant or lasting experience of their own and instead act as *conduits* of sorts for the experiences of others.[39] They are thus, on the one hand, unchanging and, on the other, able to create possibilities for others through means that go beyond the proffering of moral exempla.

The (In)experienced Gothic Reader

An early anonymous reviewer of Radcliffe remarked that "her ignorance was nearly equal to her imagination, and that is saying a great deal."[40] The review is referring most explicitly to the frequent misquotations and historical inaccuracies that pepper Radcliffe's novels, but at this point we might pause at the felicity of the reviewer's conjunction of ignorance and imagination.[41] In this final section, I draw a connection from the cultivated ingenuousness of Radcliffe's heroines to a recursive, and voracious, reading practice that likewise relies on the novice's capacity to sustain openness. By limning the power of inexperienced vision, Radcliffe's attention is drawn not to the romance heroine (as Duncan would have it) but to the romance reader—a character with an equally venerable legacy, from Don Quixote to Charlotte Lennox's Arabella, from Harriet Smith to Madame Bovary to Lord Jim.

Indeed, the confusion between ingenuity and ingenuousness is perhaps best captured in the struggle to understand that quintessential figure of inexperienced self-deception, to translate properly into English the full title of Cervantes's novel: *El Ingenioso Hidalgo Don Quixote.* (Tobias Smollett was not alone in addressing the conundrum by dismissing it entirely; his influential 1755 edition of Cervantes bore the straightforward title, *The History and Adventures of the Renowned Don Quixote.*)[42] Several eighteenth-century abridgements stressed the amiable adventures of the first part of the novel, underplaying the corrective force one might well read into the hero's eventual conversion and death. In one 1776 adaptation, targeted at children, Don Quixote does not even die, and in several he appears as a youth rather than as the gray-bearded nobleman nearing (I'm sorry to break this to you) the ripe old age of fifty.[43] For all his follies, the admirable vision of Quixote is emphasized even by some of his most moralizing readers. Samuel Johnson, for example, stresses the universality of Quixote in *Rambler* 2: "Very few readers, amidst their mirth or pity, can deny that they have admitted visions of the same kind; though they have not, perhaps, expected events equally strange, or by means equally inadequate. When we pity him, we reflect on our own disappointments; and when we laugh, our hearts inform us that he is not more ridiculous than ourselves, except that he tells what we have only thought."[44] But it is in Lennox's *Female Quixote* (1752) that we can most clearly discern the self-deceiving visions of young, inexperienced women. Henry Fielding's review of the novel in *The Covent Garden Journal* notes Lennox's ability to inspire affection for her heroine by maintaining what he refers to as her "integrity": "Both Characters [Quixote and Lennox's Arabella] are accordingly presented as Persons of good Sense, and of great natural Parts, and in all Cases except one, of a very sound Judgement, and what is much more endearing, as Persons of great Innocence, Integrity, and Honour, and of the highest Benevolence."[45] While what Fielding breezily refers to as the single exceptional case—namely, a madness inspired by an overactive imagination—is hard to ignore, commentators repeatedly stress the power of the visionary novice to shape her world and to provide readers with a bold model of lived virtue.

In recognizing this type, Catherine Gallagher places inexperience at the heart of what she calls, in her widely influential 2006 essay, "The Rise of Fictionality."[46] Gallagher offers a compelling literary historical argument about the emergence of fictionality as a concept in mid-eighteenth-century Britain, but, in focusing on the decoupling of fiction from the incredible (in the novel's move away from romance), she overstates the degree to which inexperienced characters were understood to be negative examples: "The early novel's thematic emphases on gullibility, innocence deceived, rash promises extracted, and impetuous emotional and financial investments of all kinds point to the habit of mind it discourages: faith. The reckless wholeheartedness of its heroes and heroines, their guileless vulnerability, solicits our affectionate concern and thereby activates our skepticism on their behalf. Hence, while sympathizing with innocent credulity, the reader is trained in an attitude of disbelief, which is flattered as superior discernment."[47] The reader, so this argument goes, is prompted to think *for* the novice, to anticipate the plot's twists and turns, and so to practice such a prudential perspective for subsequent applications to real life. However, narratives of inexperience in fact trouble the reader's inclination to anticipate and even indicate that such anticipation would be morally suspect. Instead, early novels force readers to pare away the accretions of modern life that would prevent them from acting without forethought. This is precisely the novel's ethical challenge: inexperienced characters dare readers to embrace a credulous openness to the world even after reading of the hazards incurred by that very ethos.

With his head in the clouds and his feet on the ground, the romance reader cannily figures the novel's cooptation of romance possibility within early realism's more bounded fictionality. When Gallagher points out that "early novels gave us numerous Quixotic characters to laugh at for confusing textual with actual people," she is certainly right that readers were not expected to be confused about the ontological status of the characters and scenes they read about.[48] At the same time, however, it is important to keep in mind that more than ontological credibility is at stake in these narratives. Namely, to maintain a moral capacity for trust, readers were required to value the novice's amnesiatic denial of the prior encounters that might inform present action, an amnesia captured by David Simple, for whom, with each new encounter, "the World was to begin again with him."[49] Sarah Fielding's novel—about a good-hearted man, disinherited by his more duplicitous brother and repeatedly confronting deception with durable optimism—marks just the first of Sarah Fielding's numerous sustained explorations of inexperience in both her fiction and criticism. In an authorial intrusion to her experimental novel *The Cry: A New Dramatic Fable* (1754, cowritten with Jane Collier), she likewise defends both Don Quixote and her brother's "English Quixote," Parson Adams, maintaining that readers who "laugh at" such characters are missing the point:

> That strong and beautiful representation of human nature, exhibited in Don Quixote's madness in one point, and extraordinary good sense in every other, is indeed very much thrown away on such readers as consider him only as the object of their mirth.
>
> Nor less understood is the character of parson *Adams* in *Joseph Andrews* by those persons, who, fixing their thoughts on the hounds trailing the bacon in his pocket (with some oddnesses in his behaviour, and peculiarities of his dress) think proper to overlook the noble simplicity of his mind, with the other innumerable beauties in his character; which, to those who can understand *the word to the wise*, are placed in the most conspicuous view.[50]

This is not the place to determine whether Sarah Fielding's reading of Parson Adams is justified by the text—though it is important to note that she insists on the soundness of her reading: "That the ridiculers of Parson *Adams* are designed to be the proper objects of ridicule (and not that innocent man himself) is a truth which the author hath in many places set in the most glaring light."[51] Nevertheless, Sarah Fielding's full-throated defense raises significant implications for how we read inexperienced characters.[52] Her assessments of Don Quixote and Parson Adams quite clearly resist the urge to deride these characters or even, as Gallagher argues, to protect them; instead, Sarah Fielding suggests that at least some readers (and critics) were longing to respond to texts with concerted sincerity, wishing to believe not less but *more*.

It is no coincidence that the naïve figures on which I have focused in this chapter—servants and young women—are also the figures considered at the time to be the most voracious readers of Gothic fiction. Radcliffe identifies Adeline as being particularly well read: "From books indeed, she had constantly derived her chief information and amusement: those belonging to LaMotte were few, but well chosen, and Adeline could find pleasure in reading them more than once" (*RF*, 82).[53] It is significant that reading in this scene is less formative than therapeutic: "When her mind was discomposed . . . a book was the opiate that lulled it to repose" (*RF*, 82). Experience is figured here as a means of corruption, of *dis*organization, that must be undone by the suspension that reading provides. Elsewhere in the novel, we see a similar scene of reading as not only a kind of positively valued self-deception but also as self-medication: "Books were [Adeline's] chief consolation. With one of these she would frequently ramble into the forest, where the river, winding through a glade, diffused coolness, and with its murmuring accents, invited repose: there she would seat herself, and, resigned to the illusions of the page, pass many hours in oblivion of sorrow" (*RF*, 34–35). Reading in *The Romance of the Forest* does not help Adeline in thinking through her decisions so much as it allows her to think *less*, to *simplify* her thinking. The insistence that these novels place on essential moral competence reveals that novels are not equipped to teach that competence—or, to put it differently, that that competence cannot be taught. Instead, it can only be reinforced, its significance emphasized, and its benefits highlighted. In a pointed reference to Richardson's *Pamela*, and thus a final explicit endorsement of inexperience, Adeline concludes her narrative with "[her] virtues greatly rewarded" (*RF*, 363).

We might contrast Adeline's repetitive reading practice to the critical commonplace found in reviews of Radcliffe that the explained supernatural rendered her novels unrereadable. This line of reasoning held that the twist endings removed any suspense, and thus any satisfaction, that a reader might find in a second reading. (In other words, these critics saw Radcliffe as the M. Night Shyamalan of her cultural moment.) Against just that sort of claim, Deidre Lynch has recently argued that the Gothic created a body of "knowing" readers who could predict with increasing facility the genre's conventions *without* compromising the possibility of rereading.[54] On the contrary, familiarity with Gothic convention seemed instead to *encourage* rereading: to produce a knowledge system decoupled from a developmental teleology. This kind of voracious reading resembles the recursive path of the novice not only in that the immersion of private reading can resemble the novice's isolation from the wider world but also because these readers, like Radcliffe's heroines, exhibit a willingness, even an eagerness, to start over again at the beginning, to withhold even from themselves their awareness of what is to come.[55]

Radcliffe's readers, I want to suggest, were not so much encouraged to nurture their own inexperience (to develop their own characters along the lines of Radcliffe's heroines) so much as to engage in a recurrent uninquisitiveness: a suspended (rather than a penetrative) mode that promised to reveal and recenter an essential goodness that was always already there. This sense of centeredness, of self-sameness validated through a recursive reading practice, comes to resemble a love of books and reading even as it replicates the oscillation between knowing and ignorance mobilized and thematized by Radcliffe's Gothic. But, rather than see this mode as one of momentary suspension only, I want to emphasize the duration of such a pose. Readers of Radcliffe were inclined to say, along with Catherine Morland, "I should like to spend my whole life in reading [this book]."[56] A novel like *The Romance of the Forest* acknowledges a valid knowledge system that is activated by the act of reading itself.[57] Catherine, like Quixote before her, allows us to understand this kind of reading not as a foolish escape from life but as a reinvigoration of the moral faculties.

CHAPTER 4

Starting from Scratch

Frances Burney and the Appeals of Inexperience

Man develops but littlè, though he experiences much.

—MR. TYROLD IN FRANCES BURNEY, *Camilla*

Not unlike Radcliffe's Adeline, the eponymous protagonist of *The Unbreakable Kimmy Schmidt* (2015–19) owes her pluckiness to a missing childhood that renders her young adulthood a continuation of her prepubescence. Abducted and imprisoned underground by a cult leader for fifteen years, Kimmy (Ellie Kemper) exemplifies the survivorship implied by the show's title. "Yes, there was 'weird sex stuff' in the bunker," she huffs in the pilot—less a revelation than an affirmation of the obvious.[1] She has withstood unspecified sexual assault and, subsequently, the secondary violation of the talk show circuit that holds her up for public inspection. (We may be reminded of the ways that both Clarissa's imprisonment and her disregard for social life make her particularly desirable as an object of public regard.) Kimmy's irritation signals her recognition that the salaciousness of probing questions only compounds the indignity she has already suffered. That is to say, *Kimmy Schmidt* is a comedy, but its satire is trained less on Kimmy's inexperience than on the sordid prying of the outside world into which she has been thrust. The show's innovation is to take up a perennial topic for television entertainment (sexual violence against women) as a precondition for plot rather than as its central organizing principle—less

What happens when a woman is raped? than *What kinds of lives might be led by women who have been raped?* The show is canny about the limits of the cultural cathexis on the "Strong Female Lead": "Females are strong as hell," the theme song assures us, but what choice do they have in the matter? Kimmy does not break, but nor does she bend, even as she pursues a series of personal milestones that should ostensibly signal maturity (renting her first apartment, getting her GED, having a boyfriend, etc.). This arrested development is explained in part by fresh trauma: as her roommate exclaims while urging her to see a therapist, "You yell in your sleep. You bite *my* nails. And we still don't know why you're afraid of Velcro!" Kimmy's stasis also drives the episodic comedy that mines the heightened potential, and likelihood of false starts, inherent to a young woman's life. As the show's creator, Tina Fey, puts it, *Kimmy Schmidt* "is like a very heightened version of [the HBO dramedy] *Girls*. Like, 'I'm here, and I'm new, and I don't know what I'm going to do with my life.' A woman who's an extreme case of that, because she's lost a chunk of her life. She doesn't know anything."[2] Kimmy's attempt to make up for lost time does little to advance her psychological growth. Her trauma is accompanied by a serious case of what one psychologist has called *pronoia*: the delusion that the world is conspiring to help you.[3] That essential trust and goodwill, maintained in defiance of her experience of the bunker, lead her into hijinks from which she will emerge more or less unscathed. Kimmy is a novice not only because her knowledge of the world was paused in the eighth grade but also because she continues to bring to each encounter the guilelessness of an adolescent with infinite possibilities before her.

Kimmy has a Gothic past, but her cartoonish imperviousness to accumulated experience places her firmly in a line of sentimental protagonists who, in assuming the goodness of others, merely project their own minds onto those they encounter. We have met several of these sentimental novices already. Parson Adams, we are told, is "entirely ignorant of the Ways of this World, as an Infant just entered into it could possibly be. As he had never any Intention to deceive, so he never suspected such a Design in others."[4] Or, clearly influenced by Adams, Sarah Fielding's David Simple, "as he was too young to have had much Experience, and never had any ill Designs on others, never thought of them having any upon him."[5] As we will see in this chapter, Frances Burney's interest in this type is evidenced not only in her novels but also in the sketches that exist only in manuscript form. Take this example, from the scraps of writing—mostly plans, lists, and snatches of dialogue—that would eventually turn into her third novel, *Camilla* (1796):

Mr. Medito has spent his life in the rural scenery and studious contemplation; practicing every virtue without knowledge of any vice, and investigating the works of Nature with almost holy wonder.

Brought by circumstance to the metropolis, he is the dupe to every profes-sion [?], for duplicity is not in his conception. Amazed at every deviation from right, he [expresses?] himself with the horror or the pity belonging to criminals upon the frailties and even foibles of daily occurrence. Accustomed only to the pleasantry that flows from domestic concord, the ridicule he finds spread around upon all things shocks or [?] him.[6]

For the protagonists of these stories, inexperience often looks like skepticism's opposite: the comfortable assumption of knowledge of other minds, inasmuch as those minds are mere replications or extensions of one's own. This is a fan-tasy of expansive interiority, but one with significant consequences. This is not a desire to know the mind of the other but the inexperienced assumption that that mind is already known. The benevolent innocent poses not only a prob-lem for identification (for our registration of the figure as a model seems al-ready to presuppose our knowingness) but also for ethics, since this variety of benevolence would seem to obviate the very idea of alterity upon which the ethical is typically grounded.

In considering the novice's curious externalization of her own interiority, this chapter works through a problem posed by Burney's notoriously puzzling preface to *Camilla*, in which the novelist sets herself the challenge of "investi-gat[ing] the human heart."[7] She judges this task to be nearly impossible, though worthy of attempt: "[The heart's] qualities are indefinable, its resources unfath-omable, its weaknesses indefensible. In our neighbours we cannot judge, in ourselves we dare not trust it. We lose ere we learn to appreciate, and ere we can comprehend it we must be born again" (7).[8] Indeed, as you may already be thinking, "notoriously puzzling" is generous. The preface was also ruthlessly par-odied, as in the preface to the satirical novel *Azemia*, published pseudonymously by William Beckford in 1797 under the name Jacquetta Agneta Mariana Jenks. A harsh critic of the "explained supernatural," Beckford largely lampoons Rad-cliffe in the narrative itself, but the stylistic effect of the parody's preface is that of Burney liberally translated via thesaurus:

The narrator of the adventures of juvenile humanity finds less of labrynthine involutions in the eccentricities of accumulated improbabilities, less of inde-scribability in the multifarious camelionity of terraqueous variety, or in the revolutionary scenery of planetary evolution, than dismaying-incomprehensibility in the enfoldings and vicissitudes of the involucrums of the pericardic region. . . .

It forbears to palpitate, and we lose ere we can analyse it. The vacuity is inscrutable unilluminated profundity, and conjectural sensibility waves over it her many-scintillating banner in vain!⁹

While Beckford's response is no doubt extreme, I see it as evidence that contemporary readers both noticed Burney's philosophical turn in *Camilla* and considered it worthy of ridicule. (She would go on to remove this preface from the heavily edited second edition of the novel.) As critics have long pointed out, Burney is defining her project as partaking in a Richardsonian mode, and we have traditionally taken this task of cardiography (of mapping the heart), to be the project of what we now call the psychological novel. But it is worth pausing to consider the specifics of the preface's description of the novel's aims. Here, the idea of being "born again" most obviously invokes the New Testament ("Except a man be born again, he cannot see the kingdom of God").¹⁰ However, in domesticating the biblical injunction, Burney also suggests that knowledge of the other presupposes inexperience with the world. This may strike us as odd; as Margaret Anne Doody puts it, "A stance taken on philosophical ignorance is not that of conduct books or educational tracts."¹¹ And yet, I argue that the preface to *Camilla* marks Burney's most explicit statement of a preoccupation with the erasure of experience that follows her throughout her career and reaches a height in that novel. While I ultimately contend that Burney is ambivalent about the ethical potential of such erasures, her repeated return to this topos suggests a sustained project worthy of further attention.

Miss in Her Teens

Just as she reached adolescence, Frances Burney decided to start over. On her fifteenth birthday, against the protestations of her sister, Burney cremated her juvenilia in a bonfire behind her house. Years of writing, including a full novel manuscript, were committed to the flames. Burney relates the story nearly fifty years later in the preface to her final novel, *The Wanderer* (1814):

> So early was I impressed myself with ideas that fastened degradation to this class of composition [that is, novel writing], that at the age of adolescence, I struggled against the propensity which, even in childhood, even from the moment I could hold a pen, had impelled me into its toils; and on my fifteenth birth-day, I made

so resolute a conquest over an inclination at which I blushed, and that I had always kept secret, that I committed to the flames whatever, up to that moment, I had committed to paper. And so enormous was the pile, that I though it prudent to consume it in the garden.[12]

Burney's embarrassment about fiction writing (a "degrad[ing]" pastime that makes her "blush") is associated with the onset of adolescence—as Burney suggests, fifteen was, in the late eighteenth century, the age at which adolescence was conventionally understood to begin—and, not coincidentally, with those prurient desires that novel *reading* was suspected of stoking. The backyard conflagration is intended to be a triumph of self-fashioning, a repudiation of a disagreeable "inclination" in favor of a more cultivated self-control. This is maturity: the putting away of childish things in order to take on the challenges and promises that come with entering into adult life.

But for Burney, writing decades later, this moment of concerted teenage repression also serves as an occasion to consider the childhood being erased. Recounting this scene from a position of security and success, Burney carefully indicates that her passion for writing begins much earlier than adolescence, is even preternatural: "So early," "even in childhood," "even from the moment I could hold a pen." Of course, Burney has to accentuate her precocity because she has, in that rash moment, eliminated any evidence of it.[13] And, in fact, it is likely that she is *over*emphasizing that early talent here; we know that, far from being prodigious, she was slow to learn to write.[14] Just how precocious Frances Burney was, just how much she could be considered a remarkably *young* woman first and a writer second, has been central to both her contemporary and her modern reception.

To pause briefly on the former, I will draw your attention to her friend Samuel Johnson's sense that Burney's particular gift was to conjure an illusion of experience from its absence: "Poetical abilities require not age to mature them; but 'Evelina' seems a work that should result from long experience, and deep and intimate knowledge of the world; yet it has been written without either."[15] Indeed, however contradictorily, Burney's own youth is repeatedly understood by her supporters and fans as offering precisely that insight into human nature that characterizes her genius. In other words, Burney was herself, like the novices we have encountered so far, thought to possess special insight because of her inexperience. In perhaps the most alarming example of Burney's genius being conflated with her youthfulness, she relates the story of an evening with

Johnson also attended by Edmund Burke. The recent publication of *Cecilia* cementing Burney's reputation, Johnson relates Burke's plea, "Miss Burney, die to-night!" rather than continue to age and so leave behind her famous (and lucrative) inexperience.[16] Here, the inexorability of experience becomes a miniature Gothic tale. Burney would, in aging, cease to be herself—so much so that death would be preferable, capturing her youth as if in amber and cementing her legacy as a perpetual adolescent. Burke is no doubt joking here (please let him be joking), but his exclamation nevertheless captures a common sentiment aligning the power and fragility of Burney's personal inexperience, a sentiment she would exploit through, among other measures, repeating and publishing anecdotes such as this one.

To detractors, Burney's exploitation of the idea of youth was misleading and even illegitimating. In a series of reviews that resemble nothing less than twenty-first-century tabloid journalism, the critic John Wilson Croker accused Burney of manipulating readers by lying about her age and capitalizing on the idea of her precocity.[17] He zeroes in on Johnson's appraisal in particular, suggesting that Burney's gift (of appearing, in her writing, to have deep experience of the world when she had none) would be rendered effectively absent were her friends and readers to know that she had actually been several years older when *Evelina* was written. An extended quotation from Croker's review demonstrates the extent to which he particularizes his understanding of youth alongside his argument that Burney was *not* authentically youthful. He begins, as does Johnson, with incredulity at Burney's ability to have written *Evelina*, but where Johnson's disbelief turns into awed admiration, Croker's skepticism only deepens into dismissal:

> We are utterly at a loss to comprehend how a girl of *seventeen*, slow, shy, secluded—almost neglected—never having been, as it would seem, from under the parental roof, and having seen little or nothing of life (but her own little play-room), could have written such a work as "Evelina." We are not blind to its faults—the plot is puerile enough—the denouement incredible—the latter part very tedious—there is much exaggeration in some of the minor characters, while that of the heroine herself is left almost a blank—but the elegance and grace of the style, the vivacity of many of the descriptions, the natural though rather too broad humour, the combination of the minor circumstances, the artist-like contrast of the several characters, and, above all, the accurate and distinctive knowledge of life and manners of different classes of society—from what sources did

this *child, writing by stealth, in the play-room*, derive them? If she had lived a few years in the world there would have been not much to marvel at—at *five and twenty*, "Evelina," though a clever work even for a writer of that age, would not have been such a wonder as the world has been accustomed to consider it; nor would it, we are persuaded, have excited anything like the public enthusiasm which, when the author's age and situation became known, "Evelina" produced.

Not content to merely speculate on Burney's age, Croker launches an investigative report into the facts of Burney's birth, going as far as to travel to her home parish in order to sniff out relevant documentation. What he discovers there (that Burney did, indeed, shave years off her age in the years following the publication of her first novel) convinces him that she is a fraud. His disgust finds its outlet in epithet: "Even up to 1787, the last date to which these volumes [under review] carry us, when she had attained the mature age of 35, we find her still playing off all the little airs and manners of '*Miss in her Teens*.'"[18] For Croker, Burney's assumption of youth is not just a matter of factual manipulation but rather of extending and embodying an entire character (a set of mannerisms and associations) to which she no longer holds a right.[19] I want to draw out an important point from Croker's antagonistic attack. He understands adolescence to be a meaningful category of identity; he is thoroughly convinced of the unmistakable difference between seventeen and five-and-twenty. And I would suggest that he believes this to be the case in no small part because of his reading of Burney's own fiction.

That Burney could purport to be an adolescent while in fact being, as Croker puts it, "mature" destabilizes her identity, rendering her, like Evelina "almost a blank." Indeed, this idea that Burney's heroines (and even Burney herself) offer a troublingly vacant model of identity has only solidified in responses from modern critics. So strong was the aura of the teenage Burney that when Burney's status as an early novelist was recovered by feminist literary critics in the 1980s, one of the first points of business was to convince scholars to stop referring to her affectionately, but condescendingly, with the diminutive "Fanny."[20] Unlike Croker, we are keen to have a mature Burney, to take the elimination of her juvenilia to be a gesture of maturation, and to see in the manipulation of her age a quite understandable, even admirable, attempt to take advantage of the market's willingness to see her as personally underwriting the content of her novels.

I have lingered a bit longer than might be expected on Burney's biography not only because it underscores a rather obvious point about her choice of subject matter, but also because her incessant revisiting of her own youth and the subject of youth performs the very vertiginous recapitulation that her novels formally reinforce. For youth, in Burney's rendering, is not stadial as much as it is recursive. Burney's account of this fire is as much a reflection back on her career as a writer as it is a reflection on its second beginning: her birth from the flames. Adolescence, for Burney, marked a beginning—not, as she had hoped at fifteen, of a mature life that would leave the embarrassments of the novel behind her but one precisely of novel writing. Adolescent beginnings became, for Burney, a central thematic concern. Most famously, Burney considers the second birth of adolescence in her first novel, *Evelina: or the History of a Young Lady's Entrance into the World* (1778), published when she was twenty-six (though, as Croker reminds us, she claimed to be seventeen). Feminists critics have noted that, for Burney, the cusp of adulthood was a time not primarily of social education but, more disconcertingly, of uncertain identity. Margaret Doody writes, "In her novel [*Evelina*], Burney explores the universal adolescent experience of making an entrance into the world as 'nobody,' without an established or fixed social self."[21] Catherine Gallagher writes of Evelina's "constant teetering on the brink of social nonbeing."[22] Susan Fraiman notes, "What Burney's subtitle calls 'a young lady's entrance into the world' might be more accurately described as a young lady's floundering on the world's doorstep."[23] As we turn now back to *Camilla*, we see that this conceit of the instability of the novice's identity is only heightened later in Burney's career. In fact, the plot of *Camilla* suggests not only that inexperience of the world affords better access to the human heart but also that adolescence in particular—a period of distilled inexperience and unstable personhood—offers the fittest subject for the novel's form.

Bad Education

Sorting through the scraps of drafts of *Camilla*, it is possible to see Burney paring away the novel's *Bildung*. In one draft, the heroine finds herself caught up in a disastrous marriage, a defining event only threatened by the time we reach the published version. The drafts dwell on the heroine's self-recrimination: "In all ways, she cried, then, I am culpable As well as unhappy! in every plan, every effort & even in every sacrifice. I am culpable!"[24] I will return later in this chapter to the published *Camilla*'s sorting of its protagonist's debts and crimes— which she can be held responsible for and why—and we will see a stark contrast to the moral accounting of these early attempts. Tracing the novel's composition history, Doody offers a persuasive reading of *Camilla* as an anti-*Bildung* revelation for Burney.[25] The earliest drafts of the novel—which Doody treats as an entirely separate novel she calls "Clarinda" after the earlier version of the protagonist's name—*do*, in fact, come together as a recognizable novel of education, but Burney finds herself uncomfortable with this form and starts over. The result is a far less didactic, but far stranger and more philosophical, novel: *Camilla*.

But if the minimal plot of *Camilla* is not that of the *bildungsroman*, or plot of development, but instead what I call the plot of inexperience, then it would be fair to ask just what that plot consists of. In this case, chiefly the maddeningly deferred courtship of Camilla and her childhood companion Edgar Mandlebert, who become engaged around the novel's halfway point and then require another 450 pages to cement their union. The dilation of their courtship is due to a series of what Julia Epstein calls "delaying actions"—that is, the kinds of obstacles that must always thwart narrative closure, lest closure come far too soon.[26] But we can attribute that delay specifically to the bad advice Edgar receives about the *kind* of experience on which love and marriage must be grounded. When, early in the novel, Edgar discloses his love for Camilla to his tutor and confidant, the learned Dr. Marchmont, he is warned not to enter too hastily into an engagement. Marchmont pointedly dismisses the couple's long period of acquaintance—they have been close "almost since infancy," when the orphaned Edgar was entrusted to Mr. Tyrold's care—and he instead enjoins Edgar to observe Camilla as if encountering her for the first time. In doing so, Marchmont raises a curious epistemological puzzle that the entire novel will struggle to unravel: Camilla is deemed of dubious suitability because of her newness, and yet Edgar is urged, in turn, to cultivate newness (a kind of affective objectivity) in order to judge her properly. Her inexperience obviates his experience of her.

Adolescent women, for the purposes of Marchmont's experiment, are merely theoretical persons. His warning to Edgar takes Camilla's youth as a hypothesis, one that has yet to be subjected to empirical trial: you must wait, he cautions, "till you have positively ascertained her actual possession of those virtues with which she appears to be endowed"; "do not mistake promise for performance" (159). Here, theory is judged inadequate in comparison to a praxis that is assumed inevitable. In other words, Camilla's youth is understood to be both preliminary and temporary, a stage before real experience begins. Marchmont's suspicion, of course, raises the problem of how virtue might be proven, a question of central importance to early realism more generally, which sees natural virtue as both endangered by the world and, at the same time, tempered by constant trial.[27] This is precisely the novice's double bind. Camilla's goodness and her youth (qualities that, in this novel, are virtually synonymous) testify to her innocence, her insulation from any worldly activity, and yet that very inexperience is precisely what renders her suspect because it is deemed too abstract to count as admissible evidence.

Indeed, by insisting on positive proof of a figure essentially defined through negation or apophasis (Camilla is *not* experienced, *not* worldly, *not* knowing, *not* guilty), Marchmont sets Edgar up to fail. His test appears, at best, overliteral: never having been a wife, Camilla cannot adequately prove her fitness as a wife. The concept of proof is central to the ensuing debate between Edgar and Marchmont.[28] Edgar cites as evidence of Camilla's goodness his long knowledge of her: " 'Let me, then, be her guarantee!' cried Edgar, with firmness; 'for I know her well! I have known her from her childhood, and cannot be deceived. . . . I can trace to a certainty, even from my boyish remarks, her fair, open, artless, and disinterested character.' He then gave a recital of the nobleness of her sentiments and conduct when only nine years old" (158). In other words, love is, by Edgar's account, a longitudinal study. The sheer duration of his knowledge of Camilla would seem to certify the validity of his knowledge. Edgar might be understood to be invoking a "truth-will-out" model of courtship popularized during the anti-*Pamela* debates of the mid-eighteenth century that I discussed in chapter 2. Recall that readers of Richardson's novel were warned against hasty marriages, especially to social inferiors, in favor of long engagements during which faults (or schemes) would be inexorably revealed.[29] According to such a model, Edgar certainly has enough evidence to commit to a marriage with Camilla. Of course, this is only true if all parties are able to agree upon a suitable duration for determining fitness. Here is where Edgar deviates from the skeptical model. Trusting Camilla, Edgar thinks her probationary time is already up. But the suggestion of the long engagement implicitly supposes a revelation of inadequacy. It is founded on the assumption that inexperience will resolve itself into experience, that stability is a moral and characterological impossibility.

Marchmont's idea of praxis, and of valid proof, only further complicate his plan for Edgar. His idea of trial requires a purportedly neutral observer: "you must study her, from this moment, with new eyes, new ears, and new thoughts" (159).[30] Edgar's familiarity with Camilla is, by this competing account, evidence not of expertise but of bias: it is the very thing that will prevent him from judging her suitability for marriage, even though, as he himself insists, it is that very familiarity that has grown into affection and then love. If Edgar's argument resembles eighteenth-century warnings for young men to beware short acquaintances, Marchmont's advice would seem just as strenuously to warn against long ones. This is because it draws on another discursive commonplace: eighteenth-century experiential aesthetics that grounds itself on infancy as the time of wholly new sensory experience.[31] According to this line of thought, empiricism is the origin of and basis for aesthetic value. As Samuel Johnson writes in *Idler* 45: "We are naturally delighted with novelty, and there is a time when all that we see is new. When first we enter into the world, whithersoever we turn our eyes, they meet knowledge with pleasure at her side; every diversity of nature pours ideas in upon the soul; neither search nor labour are necessary; we have nothing more to do than to open our eyes, and curiosity is gratified."[32] The value of novelty as an aesthetic category rests in its primariness, its status as our first introduction to the aesthetic as such. Marchmont's innovation is to attach this way of thinking to a strategic approach to marriage. It is sight, especially— that most passive of senses ("we have nothing more to do than to open our eyes")—that is perverted, for Edgar, into a method of surveillance. Under Marchmont's tutelage, Edgar observes Camilla both in private and, especially, in public, refusing to compare or to replace her appearance with his previous knowledge of her heart. The "pleasure" of empirical knowledge is corrupted, and Edgar's vigilance obscures his vision: "A general mist clouded his prospects, and a suspensive discomfort inquieted his mind" (162).

It is tempting to side with intimate familiarity here and to reject this cooptation of the aesthetic of novelty for this conjugal scouting mission. Marchmont's injunction, which Edgar is himself slow to accede to, threatens to empty out the experiences that Camilla and Edgar have shared. Nevertheless, we should pause before dismissing Marchmont entirely, even if he is the cause of hundreds of pages of heartache as Edgar repeatedly mistakes Camilla's inexperience for coquetry. This is because Marchmont's command to see one's lover anew also brings the reader back to Burney's preface, where she proposes that being "born again" is the only way to fathom the human heart. By this light, what Marchmont gets wrong is not the *idea* of starting over but the reasons for doing so. He twists a principle of equity into a practice of misogyny, and he mistakes a difficult ethical practice for a means of self-preservation. In fact, Marchmont is quite frank in his entreaty for Edgar to act out of self-interest: "Nothing must escape you; you must view as if you have never seen her before; the interroga-tory, *Were she mine?* must be present at every look, every word, every motion; you must forget her wholly as Camilla Tyrold, you must think of her only as Camilla Mandlebert; even justice is insufficient during this period of proba-tion, and instead of inquiring, 'Is this right in her?' you must simply ask, 'Would it be pleasing to me?'" (160). This proleptic, counterfactual marriage threatens to overwhelm their actual, incipient marriage, swallowing it in a subjunctive. Marchmont's impatience with "even justice" demonstrates that the newness he proposes only superficially resembles the one that Camilla herself represents in the novel. What is "right" becomes what is "pleasing," but the very idea of plea-sure is so vacant that it is unclear what Edgar is supposed to desire.

It is Marchmont's bald self-interest that Burney is exposing for criticism here, and it is a quality that Edgar, to his credit, never quite masters, though his studied suspicion of Camilla throws up substantial obstacles to their hap-piness. Marchmont's advice is logically incoherent (How can one observe with "new thoughts" when those thoughts are simultaneously to be trained on one's own self-interest? Is this understanding of self-interest so basic as to *precede* all thought and experience?), and, moreover, he is also revealed to have been load-ing this advice with the baggage of his own disastrous experiences with women.[33] Marchmont, in advising Edgar, does not start from scratch. We learn, by the novel's end, that Marchmont has had two unsuccessful marriages, which leave him unable to entertain the kind of ethical knowledge of the other that Burney endorses. Unable, that is, until he finally sees Camilla as Edgar has always seen her: "And Dr. Marchmont, as he saw the pure innocence, open frankness, and spotless honour of [Camilla's] heart, found her virtues, her errours, her facility, or her desperation, but A PICTURE OF YOUTH; and regretting the false light formed from individual experience, acknowledged its injustice, its narrowness, and its arrogance. What, at last, so diversified as man? what so little to be judged by his fellow?" (913). These are the novel's closing lines. The plaintive final ques-tions suggest—bookending the preface—that true knowledge of another is merely aspirational. By the end of *Camilla*, the character who is chastened, who must recognize, with some degree of shame, that life is not as it had been as-sumed, is not the heroine but instead the older, male teacher figure. The novel's true lesson is learned not by its protagonist but by its narrative engine, March-mont, who comes to understand that his life has *not* furnished him with the authority to instruct his pupil. To point this out is not simply to relish a sense of feminist triumph, though there is certainly nothing wrong with that. Marchmont comes to understand that experience is a poor basis for authority. Thus, ironically, the one character who undergoes a developmental arc in Burney's novel does so only by learning that his lifetime of lessons have done him no good and that his "individual experience[s]" only perpetuate harm. In other words, the novel insists that particularized experience (the kind that makes an individual an individual, that makes humanity "so diversified") is not only harmful for individuals; individual experience harms others as well. No wonder the novel reserves for its heroine a life unmolested by experience, a plot that is not really much of a plot at all.

Teenage Dream

One way to render *Camilla*'s moral might be: experiences, unlike loans, are nontransferrable. Camilla's theoretical personhood, the novel's tendency to understand her as an abstraction, finds expression not only in its marriage plot, where Edgar tries, and fails, to assess her objectively, but also in the almost picaresque series of scrapes Camilla finds herself caught up in over the course of the novel's second half. As this secondary plot becomes primary—in part due to Edgar's exasperated departure from the scene—Burney considers the ways that legal formalism (the slotting of persons into categories of responsibility without regard to mental states) likewise calls Camilla's experiences into question, absolving her of responsibility even as she sinks into self-recrimination. Here, again, we see Burney experimenting with the removal of embarrassing youthful experience epitomized by burning her juvenilia.

Camilla repeatedly uses the counterfactual present to wrest its heroine's perspective from the reader's judgment of her encounters, especially in showing her extreme response—we might say her adolescent taste for melodrama—to be unwarranted when compared to the facts of her case. Though early readers often attempted to understand Burney's novel in the tradition of the conduct book, as a means of educating young women about proper behavior, they also —however contradictorily—faulted the novel for containing incidents that were too inconsequential, too *minor*, to produce the effects that ensued. The plot's thinness therefore threatened to unravel its didacticism. William Hazlitt, highlighting the subtitle to Burney's final novel, *The Wanderer*, sees triviality of narrative incident as characteristic of Burney's fiction: "The difficulties in which [Burney] involves her heroines are indeed 'Female Difficulties'; they are difficulties created out of nothing."[34] As a writer for the *British Critic* puts it,

"Camilla . . . falls into these inadvertencies rather too frequently, and the consequences of some of them are disproportionately serious."[35] These "inadvertencies" largely consist in cringe-inducing lapses in propriety, as when she pays too much attention to an elderly gentleman, not realizing that he is then taken to be her suitor. For yet another critic, these narrative problems, the bathos of Burney's novels, are attributable to a personal defect of the author: "Her innate propensity was to *make mountains of mole-hills*."[36] What contemporary critics understand to be Burney's disproportionate punishment of her heroines, I take to be a ratcheting up of the stakes of the novice's misfit with the world at large.

Camilla's errors are increasingly errors of literal miscalculation; like Edgar the recipient of poor counsel, she repeatedly allows articles to be purchased in her stead that far exceed her carefully estimated budget. If *Camilla* is a novel about the psychological effects of racking up debt (as Deidre Lynch and others have argued), then it has to be acknowledged that those debts are relatively minor.[37] (Doody does the math: if we exclude the debts Camilla contracts via others who borrow in her name, her balance comes to a mere eighteen pounds—an amount easily raised by her sisters once she finally asks them for assistance.[38]) But these debts are not just themselves minor, inconsequential, they are also the debts *of a minor*: of one who could not be expected to avoid them when left unsupervised. The *Critical Review* faulted Burney for seeming to call for the correction of errors that simply did not count precisely because they are incurred by a young girl: "[Burney's] female characters are too *young* to act the part she assigns them. The errors of Camilla are not errors in one who is almost a child."[39] This critic, though clearly speaking out of frustration, is nevertheless onto something: Camilla's errors are not significant enough to contribute to our understanding of her character, even if—*especially* if— she understands them herself to be grave errors in judgment. And, as we shall soon see, this truth about the novel is only highlighted if we consider the fact that it was written at a time when eighteenth-century law was beginning to question whether minors, like Camilla, could be held responsible for anything at all.

Spiraling her briskly into disaster, Camilla's financial troubles are the result of two problems of credit: first, she is extended credit repeatedly even though she is a minor without the legal standing to enter into such a contract. Second, her *word* is not credited: her repeated insistence that she is *not* Sir Hugh's (her uncle's) heir (and thus not capable of taking on large debts) is taken to be a polite demurral. This double negation is consistent with the ultimate anticlimax to which these debts lead. After all, if, by the novel's end, Camilla *does* learn anything about debt, those lessons in household economy are of little use to her now. Edgar, whom she does finally marry, is, unlike Camilla, quite wealthy, and he demonstrates this by offering to pay off, with ease, all debts incurred by others. Fittingly, then, when these minor debts lead Camilla to curse her fate and threaten to take her own life, these threats are shown by the novel's final expediency, as its early readers pointed out, to be rather out of proportion. And, even before this, Camilla's desire for death, while seemingly heartfelt, is treated by its witnesses (and by the novel itself) as a fit of adolescent sensibility. Her anguished cries are met with only eye-rolling by the innkeeper and his wife who take her in (the latter is "sure, after a little sleep, [all] would be forgotten" [876]). Even Burney's immolation of her juvenilia seems to be invoked and, to a significant degree minimized, in the accidental burning of Camilla's most plaintive letter to her parents in the novel's final volume. It is in this letter that she commits to paper her wish for death—and that wish's apparent fulfillment. (That is, she warns her parents that she may be dead before they receive the letter.) The letter goes up in smoke, leading to Camilla's darkest moments of apparent abandonment. But the fact that the letter is destroyed in such a silly way (the man entrusted with it accidentally sets it alight while lighting his pipe, then, worried he will lose his fee, lies to Camilla that the letter received no response), suggests a providential pardoning of Camilla, shielding her from the embarrassment of the letter's ever being read. (If only we could all have such divine management of our juvenile embarrassments.)

Finally, in the depths of a fitful, Gothic nightmare, Camilla is enjoined to commit her crimes to the "Records of Eternity," but when she finally brings herself to look over "the guilty characters" in which she records her crimes, she sees that "her pen made no mark! . . . the paper was blank!" (875–76). She awakes unable to distinguish her dream from reality, frozen in a "suspensive state" (876). No writing. Nothing. Not in the red. Not a blot. Not a black mark. Camilla's own blankness is, by the novel's end, tenaciously thematized—the reference to Locke's infamous sheet of white paper is conspicuous to the point of comedy. Rather than a problem of bathetic narrative, as Burney's early critics would have it, the evacuation of Camilla's experience—the suggestion that her errors are literally unremarkable, not noteworthy—has to be understood as a study in narrative abstraction. As I show, the law's formal treatment of minority (as innocent regardless of intention) upholds Camilla's essential moral integrity even as her increasing acquaintance with the world causes her to stumble or, to recall Fraiman's memorable phrase, to "flounde[r] on the world's doorstep."

The Presumption of Innocence

Camilla is not a "guilty character"—not because she has no experiences but because those experiences *just do not count.* She cannot be held liable. This is true both according to the novel's moral mathematics but also through its invocation of contemporary legal thought. Sandra Macpherson has advanced an ambitious, polemical argument about liability and the early novel, one that sees the novel as severing the connection between intention and effect, instead offering a radically material understanding of personal responsibility.[40] Whether or not we intend to, Macpherson tells us, we cause harm—harm for which, according to changes in law that pick up speed during the eighteenth century (broadly categorized as "strict liability"), we must take responsibility. Macpherson's argument forces us to question traditional understandings of the novel form's relationship to character psychology. But Burney's novel, in turn, forces us to consider a fact of eighteenth-century law that falls beneath Macpherson's notice: legal liability for minors, once identical to liability in adults, is eroded over the course of the century and virtually disappears by the Romantic period. Consider Samuel Comyn's *Treatise of the Law relative to Contracts and Agreements* (1807): "All contracts with infants [those under twenty-one], except for necessaries, are either void or voidable: the reason of which is, the indulgence the law has thought fit to give infants, who are supposed to want judgment and discretion in their contracts and transactions with others, and the care it takes of them in preventing them from being imposed upon or overreached by persons of more years and experience."[41] As legal historian Holly Brewer points out, Comyn adds "void" here, further strengthening what was already a robust defense of minors. Moreover, by this time, a decade after the publication of Burney's novel, the phrase "except for necessaries" had become effectively null, as courts drastically shortened the list of those goods that qualified as basic needs.

In other words, while in the early eighteenth century minor responsibility was linked to intentionality, that link was removed decades later—and *not* in the way Macpherson sees happening in the law elsewhere. This is key: as strict liability started to hold individuals responsible for their actions regardless of intention, the same legal culture established that minors *even with avowed intention* could not be held responsible for their harms. (We might recall that "innocent" derives from "not harmful" or that Milton said of the guileless serpent, before being inhabited by Satan, that he was "not . . . nocent yet.") Here is Brewer: "It was generally agreed during the early eighteenth century that infants should be liable in cases where they intentionally caused damage or acted deceitfully, such that they, for example, sought to sell goods not their own or pretended that they were of age. By the early nineteenth century, children had largely lost this liability."[42] My aim here is not to lodge a quibbling historical objection to Macpherson's argument. Rather, I hope to illuminate two primary implications of this change in the legal status of minors. First, it is important to note the extent to which the law, even with such dramatically divergent results, nevertheless *maintains* the divestment of liability from intention that Macpherson sees in strict liability. That is, that effects can be separated from mental states is central to the law *even when* responsibility is deemed irrelevant or impossible. Second, this change shows just how central (and vexed) the consideration of minority is in this period. The mental states of minors are posited (they are presumed here to consist universally of inexperience, or "want of judgment and discretion") at the same time that they are legally evacuated. Minority places significant pressure on the law's understanding of personhood. This is more true of adolescence, the stage at which Camilla finds herself. While adolescence is not a legal category, it is a significant social one in precisely the ways Burney's novel illustrates. Indeed, adolescence is the period of *uncertain* personhood, when we might ask of a woman, *Is she an adult, or is she a child?* just as Mary Crawford asks of Fanny Price, "Is she out, or is she not?"[43] This uncertainty raises the possibility that one might encounter—or contract with—a seeming person who is not one, a grown-up woman who is actually an infant.

As Frances Ferguson has argued of rape law, the legal formalism that considers children under a certain age unable to consent raises uncomfortable questions about psychological states; that is, if a child may *indicate* a consent that is legally impossible, the result is that legal consent and personal intention become untethered:

> The statutory definitions establish the possibility—and indeed the inevitability —that consent and intention will be self-contradictory, or impossible, notions. They thus create the categories of consent that is not consent (for some hypothetically consenting female who has not reached the age of consent) and intention that is not intention. . . . And these categories . . . solve a certain conundrum that appears in the interpretation of testimony about rape . . . by insisting upon it, by saying that even where there might appear to be consent, even where there might appear to be intention, there can be none.[44]

Legal formalism designates categories of persons for whom consent is impossible, thereby eliminating intention from the calculation of responsibility. The same might be said in Burney's novel of intention and responsibility. Camilla's decisions, even when rash, are eliminated by the denouement's strictly legal accounting, wherein any transaction she could not legally enter into seems never to have existed. Legal minority is a status that, as we have seen with eighteenth-century culture more broadly, does not differentiate between the young woman of seventeen and the infant. This means what is perhaps Camilla's least excusable offense, her arrangement with a usurer, never happened. As the novel concludes, it is repeatedly emphasized that her contract with the usurer is invalid. In fact, it is invalid twice over: first, because usury is itself illegal, and, second, because Camilla, as a minor, cannot enter into a contract.[45] Only the second reason is repeatedly, emphatically, emphasized.

My point here is not that minors in this period could not be held responsible for harms that they caused. Rather, what I want to stress is the way that the law, like the sentimental novel, *requires* inexperience of its protagonists. What is more, the law, like Camilla, assumes that those it encounters are good at heart (if they have done wrong, they did not know better; if they had known better, they would not have done it). The changes in law for minors fashion the sentimental subject position as a formal category, while, at the same time, ensuring that, as a shared category (minority) it can only ever conjure the *illusion* of subjectivity. Moreover, what the law thinks of minors, the protagonist thinks of *everyone*. The assumption of continuity between the novice's mind and other minds is a replication and exaggeration of this formal stipulation of goodness.

Macpherson contends that liability, the status of being responsible for one's effects (even when, as with strict liability, one intends no harm) is central to the novel form, but Camilla's insulation from liability (and her attendant insulation from plot) reveals the novel form's uneasy relationship with abstraction. Camilla's actions, the novel tells us, occur independently of *both* their intentions *and* their effects, subordinating her experiences and elevating her merely hypothetical personhood. If the literary payoff of Macpherson's argument about strict liability is the theorization of what she calls, following Paul Ricoeur, "emplotment" ("a formalist account of action indifferent to questions of motive and practices of interiority"), then *Camilla* raises the possibility of an even stranger account of character's intersection with plot.[46] Call it "deplotment": the prying apart of character and plot; an ultimate standoff between the novel's constituent parts; a narrative that unravels itself, leaving only a picture behind. A picture of youth.

Emma's Dystopia

It is with some trepidation that I reach the end of a book that is throughout ambivalent about endings. By attending to suspended or eliminated character formation, I have illuminated the ways that the early realist novel holds endings in abeyance and questions their explanatory value. In the novels on which I have focused, endings can feel particularly rushed (as when Sophia Western hastily withdraws the terms of engagement she has just set) and can even seem to undermine the preceding narrative (as when Camilla Tyrold's mounting debts—so consequential to her fate—are instantly evaporated upon her marriage to Edgar). We have also seen how an unsatisfying ending—like Clarissa Harlowe's protracted death—prompts observers to compensate by generating formation where it is otherwise absent, an attempt to craft an ending that feels adequate to the task of enclosing an exemplary life. In noting how such endings unsettle and undo, I have been drawn to the literary theoretical models with which we attempt to understand this kind of pacing: chiefly bathos and its narrative mode, anticlimax. Both are models of suddenness, of being thrown off-kilter; both offer a kind of consolation for the otherwise unsatisfying sense that these novels conclude simply because they must.[1] These terms also begin to capture the sometimes cruel comedy that can inhere in these narratives, the sense that the characters are being moved about like dolls that must soon be placed back in the toy box. Recall the way that Adeline's imprisonment by the Marquis de Montalt is cut mercifully short when she slips safely out of a window, sparing her a seemingly inevitable rape (and likely murder) while also feeling deflationary and overly convenient. Defenestration ex machina. In shaping an argument that privileges beginnings, about texts that make origins thematically and conceptually central, I have come to treat endings rather lightly, to see the ways that narrative convention can require a closure that is minimally loaded in comparison to the stasis, duration, and repetition otherwise highlighted by these narratives of inexperience. My aim in this book has been to develop a conceptual vocabulary that will both train readers' attention onto inexperienced characters and, what can be considerably more difficult, help keep them in focus even as the incidents of narrative time may appear to warp and transfigure them.

This is not to suggest that such superficially developmental endings (marriage, centrally, but also often varieties of salvation that may or may not coincide with marriage) necessarily undo inexperience or resolve it into experience. I mentioned in the introduction that the widespread depiction of inexperienced older men in eighteenth-century texts reveals a belief that inexperience might extend indefinitely past the parameters of biological youth. When Parson Adams, the quintessential figure of advanced inexperience from Fielding's *Joseph Andrews*, returns at the end of *Tom Jones* to become the tutor to Tom and Sophia's children, how else are we to read this cameo than as the assertion of naïveté's continued and valued presence in the Jones household? Perhaps Tom has been "fixed," solidified by his marriage to Sophia, but her reckless concession in accepting him only sets a new precedent for the priority of willful ignorance over prudence. Still, where novels center on youth, this extension of inexperience is often less certain, perhaps even unknowable. Will the novices on whom I focus remain inexperienced beyond the confines of their narratives? To answer this question is to bring to bear a conception of character as exceedingly referential, as alive off the page—a conception that I cannot quite embrace, whatever the pleasures it may otherwise afford.

We can see this extrapolation of character beyond diegetic time in Edmund Wilson's well-known conjecture on Emma Woodhouse's married life, in which he imagines her beginning her narrative all over again, "discovering a new young lady as appealing as Harriet Smith, dominating her personality, and situating her in a dream-world of Emma's own in which Emma would be able to confer on her all kinds of imaginary benefits, but which would have no connection whatever with her condition or her real possibilities."[2] Wilson is condemning Emma here, and his censure inspired a series of heated responses that, in coming to Emma's defense, assured readers that her development was secure, that she was—to paraphrase a skeptical Eve Sedgwick—a girl who had been taught her lesson.[3] Among these defenders is Wayne Booth, who rhapsodizes about the novel's "perfect" ending in *The Rhetoric of Fiction*:

> All of the cheap marriage plots in the world should not lead us to be embarrassed about our pleasure in Emma and Knightley's marriage. It is more than just the marriage: it is the *rightness* of *this* marriage, as a conclusion to all of the comic wrongness that has gone before. The good for Emma includes both her necessary reform and the resulting marriage. Marriage to an intelligent, amiable, good, and attractive man is the best thing that can happen to this heroine, and the readers who do not experience it as such are, I am convinced, far from knowing what Jane Austen is about.[4]

"What Jane Austen is about," for Booth, is the prospect of a formative marriage, one that not only coincides with "reform" but indeed generates it. To be "*re-formed*," for someone of Emma's overlong adolescent "wrongness" is effectively to be formed for the first time—to achieve, however belatedly, a mature and fully developed "rightness." In reading closure lightly, I have come to question some of the formalist criticism that has otherwise shaped my own engagement with the novel form. Surveying the midcentury criticism on the novel, Claudia Johnson has diagnosed in Booth's example the tendency of "a generation of Aristotelian-oriented formalists" to read "the novel's comic structure and moral lesson [as] one and the same."[5] But this tidy way of reading is not limited to the Chicago school critics to whom Johnson explicitly refers; we could, for example, as readily fault the New Critics for offering lyric as the prime example of artistic wholeness (and so inspiring generations of readers who have attempted to stuff novels into urns). The theorization of closure has been perhaps one of the most influential contributions of formalist literary criticism of the past few decades. Johnson sees the solution for this problem in a more robust historicism, but it may also be that another formalism is in order, one that distributes attention otherwise.[6] Such a formalism is anticipated by eighteenth-century readers' own disregard for final endings, from the enthusiastic rewritings that greeted the final volume of *Clarissa* to the popular fascination with Don Quixote that paid little mind to the character's deathbed conversion.[7] Attuned to the counterfactual logics set in motion by inexperience, this formalism would recognize the embedded, implicit seriality of fiction well before the height of serialized fiction in the British nineteenth century.

Emma Woodhouse does not face these problems herself because she does not read endings. It is a defect of her character, or so Knightley suggests, that she is always drawing up lists of books to read without actually finishing them, that she embarks on schemes of self-improvement without following them to fruition. Emma is drawn to new beginnings. We can see this compulsion not just in her own aborted attempts at self-cultivation but also in her intense fascination with Harriet Smith, novice par excellence. If Emma's development is minimal (and I believe that it is), then she may take something of a cue from Harriet, who, despite Emma's feverish interventions, ends the novel just as she began, married to the man on whom she had already set her eye. Hers is not a story of social or class mobility. A foundling, Harriet Smith never quite takes her place in the long line of illegitimate heroes of British fiction. Her placeholder name recalls that of Tom Jones, her mysterious parentage that of Evelina.[8] While these characters are protagonists because their unclear origins leave them more socially mobile, more observant as outsiders, Harriet is decidedly second string, a minor character if ever there was one.

Emma may seem an unlikely text for this study to end on. You may have come to expect a conclusion that lingers a bit longer with Catherine Moreland's childishness, perhaps Fanny Price's stunted adolescence, even the lost-and-found youth of Anne Elliot, whose faded bloom returns, injecting youthfulness back into her life.[9] Emma is not much of a novice. First, the novel's protagonist is a wizened twenty-one at the start of her narrative—only dubiously a "young person" by most contemporary measures (including legal ones) that would consider her age to be the onset of adulthood. Were she a man, Emma would have reached "man's estate." Nor is Emma entering the world. She is firmly established in her world, whether we understand "world" to name the physical locus of Highbury or the minimal high society it maintains. As the brief survey above indicates, *Emma* is notorious for its focus on its heroine's development, making it a quintessential bildungsroman, the critical reception of which has long been focused on just how Emma matures, grows, progresses—or, in a related line of thought, is chastised, humiliated, forced to submit. Still, Emma believes herself to be in a plot of inexperience. She is certainly sheltered (she seldom leaves the village), and she believes herself capable of transforming her world with her vision of a better life. That Emma does not get to stay in her plot of inexperience has long been of interest to Austen critics, though not in precisely these terms. Indeed, *Emma* rankles inasmuch as it wrests Emma out of her inexperience—which would in part consist in her ability to continue, as she desires, unmarried—and into *Bildung*.

I do not see Emma as the next in the series of novices that this book tracks so much as I see in the novel Austen's awareness of and affection for the kinds of novels I have focused on thus far. Emma is not herself a novice, but she sure knows one when she sees one. *Emma* stands in relation to these novels in much the same way that *Northanger Abbey* does to the Gothic fiction of Radcliffe and her ilk: as an affectionate slant imitation that exposes the mechanisms by which the genre operates. Consequently, Harriet finds herself shunted to the side in Austen's novel, not the protagonist she would be in an earlier narrative but the hapless friend—the object, not the subject, of the novel's plot. And Emma, no longer an adolescent, is attracted to the charms of inexperience even though (or perhaps because) she herself has all the experience she is ever going to need. As William Galperin has observed in a spectacular reading of Amy Heckerling's *Clueless* (1995), even as the film pulls Emma back from twenty-one to sixteen, it nevertheless produces a faithful adaptation of Emma insofar as it reveals how limp Emma's *Bildung* ultimately turns out to be. Austen, Galperin contends, "leaves the story of Emma's development intact, but as an object of interpretation from which the novel overall is increasingly dislocated. And so it goes in *Clueless*, where the developmental narrative is, for all intents and purposes, nonexistent or, when existent, doggedly plot-driven and even a little pathetic. . . . Cher has learned everything that she needs or, better still *should have learned* by the time we first encounter her in late 20th-century Los Angeles."[10] Cher may be a "virgin who can't drive"—and so she has yet to clear the rites of passage into late twentieth-century adulthood—but her inexperience poses no significant obstacle. Emma may develop by the novel's end, then, but what *Clueless* suggests by bringing Cher's minimal experience to the surface is that Emma's development is the least interesting part of Austen's novel. Here, again, an anticlimax. And so the film can end with a wedding that is not Cher's own ("I am only sixteen, and this is California, not Kentucky"); the latent potential of her adolescence remains intact.[11]

I began this book by suggesting that eighteenth-century narratives of inexperience highlight a realism that is always implicitly idealist in its selectivity. Because of this, early realist novels hold in tension the representation of the world as it is with the representation of protagonists who exceed the possibilities of that verisimilar ordinariness. And so with *Emma*. Dystopia, for Emma Woodhouse, is a world uncoupled, her matchmaking a world-building vision that promises to right the injustice of singleness.[12] The role she proposes for herself in this utopia may be a modest one—"a something between the do-nothing and the do-all"—but her vision is tantamount to revelation: an insightful and inspired understanding of the day to day operations of Highbury her neighbors continue to misconstrue.[13] I exaggerate, but part of what makes Emma appear more youthful than she is, is the forcefulness and clarity of her claims—what D. A. Miller refers to as the impersonality of her "style." As Miller observes, Austen's world operates according to a "depressing law of universal conjugality."[14] Emma senses that Highbury, with its scatterplot of persons, requires her governing hand to bring order, and she excludes herself from this universal law even as she works to uphold it. Explicitly, she insists on the viability of a single life for herself, noting the gratuitousness of marriage for a woman of her means. Implicitly, her series of overlapping infatuations (notably, Harriet, Frank Churchill, Knightley) charts constellations that are not organized in twos.

The singleness of others poses a dystopian prospect for Emma, but, more profoundly, the most insistent threat to her happiness is the finality of singular choice. What *Emma* may evince most strongly is the desire to be more than one person, to live out more than one possible path. For someone with such circumscribed parameters—that is, for someone who never leaves Highbury— Emma wants to live out as many possible lives as she can. Austen provides an unlikely and easily overlooked model for this abundance in Frank's mother, the first Mrs. Weston, whom, we are told, "did not cease to love her husband, but she wanted at once to be the wife of Captain Weston, and Miss Churchill of Enscombe" (13). Where Mrs. Weston fails, Emma may very well succeed. Emma's achievement is to carve out a conjugal life that deviates minimally from the life she presently enjoys. Edmund Wilson gets this right. To marry Knightley is to marry while also continuing to live as she has been living, to remain in Hartfield, to remain with her father. She effectively suspends her possible worlds, managing at once to be the wife of Mr. Knightley, and Miss Woodhouse of Hartfield.

But what happens if we follow out the logic of Emma's modest utopianism? Contemporary dystopian young adult fiction, with its impossibly good, impossibly brave teenagers, owes a great deal to the kind of plot that I have discussed in this book. It may be fair to say that, as the novel's realism has, over time, become less open to the jostling worlds and competing visions I have outlined, and as it has loosened its grip on idealism of the sort that inexperience magnifies, the novice has found a more welcome home in subgeneric than in literary fiction, so-called.[15] Young adult fiction is of course drawn to the possibilities inherent to adolescent life, but it is in dystopian YA in particular that I see the legacy of the novice carried on most forcefully. The idea of the adolescent heroine who, in just entering the world, seems uniquely capable of diagnosing and addressing the world's problems is fundamentally indebted to the novice figures of the early realist novel. These adolescent protagonists have become so popular as to spawn something of a parody industry. I include here just two comments, both in the form of tweets that ventriloquize the subjectivity of novices. First, from an account built around this kind of analysis, which calls itself "Dystopian YA Novel":

> This is a lot of responsibility, being 16 and being the only one who recognizes the problems with totalitarianism.

The second from a literary critic who insightfully compares dystopian YA to precisely the literary fiction it is so often compared to unfavorably:

> adult fiction: I am riddled w ennui shall I cheat on my wife perhaps
> YA fiction: overthrow govt and also kill its grasping maoist successor[16]

These winking send-ups of YA fiction capture both the implausibility of its generic conventions and the humorous ill fit between the weight of the world in crisis and the more mundane responsibilities that are usually thought to attend modern adolescence. (I'm the only one who can take out an authoritarian dictator, but first I have to study for this chemistry test!) These observers rightly identify as central to YA the figure of the powerful novice, who, though young and more or less defenseless, brings to a corrupt world both an unshakeable moral center and a persistence bordering on the pathological. Without mentioning the series by name, both tweets readily bring to mind Suzanne Collins's wildly popular YA series The Hunger Games (2008–10).

At first, The Hunger Games appears to be structured around coupling of a different sort than the one Austen holds up for our inspection. Collins's novels take place in Panem, a postapocalyptic North America, each district of which sends one boy and one girl ("tributes") to fight to the death until a single survivor remains. Broadcast to rapt viewers, the event (called "the Reaping") has been instituted as punishment for a failed uprising some years before, but it also serves as a kind of appeasement, providing entertainment for a populace trained to cathect onto the lives and fates of their representatives. A key insight of this authoritarian regime is its recognition that the inherent narrative structure of adolescence heightens the promise of possibility even where extreme constraint—postapocalyptic Panem, Regency girlhood—renders actual prospects severely limited. The premise of the Reaping, Collins has explained, is based on the myth of Theseus: Crete forces Athens to send seven boys and seven girls into the labyrinth to confront the Minotaur. Like an inverted marriage market, the object of the Reaping is to be the last person standing. But Collins's classical model quickly bends to novel logic; in the first book of the trilogy, the rules are changed. Where the games once served a logic of the individual (only the strongest survives), now a district's couple may be cowinners, rewarding not just might but also love. Or, that is, the appearance of love. Postapocalyptic Panem is a continually surveilled world where true intimacy has been all but eradicated; compulsory viewing of the Games foments an investment in the romantic lives of the tributes that puts the "tittle-tattle of Highbury" to shame. For Katniss Everdeen, romance quickly becomes a strategy for survival. One element of the proceedings is that sponsors can support favored participants by sending donations of supplies, and there is some suggestion that the orchestrators of the game's essential elements—like producers of a reality television show—are attentive to the pulse of the audience. Fabricating a convincing courtship plot becomes quite literally a matter of life and death.

As with *Emma*, the novel most insistently finds Katniss drawn to novices rather than resembling one, but the superficial resemblances to the novel of inexperience are nevertheless there. Katniss's provincial upbringing (her district was once Appalachia) means that the decadence of the Capitol is all the more disorienting. Katniss Everdeen is a heroine not merely because she is good with a bow and arrow but also for her exemplarity: she displays a moral courage that is, in her battered and broken, corrupt and exhausted postapocalyptic world, nearly unprecedented. ("What I did was the radical thing," she acknowledges.[17]) Katniss risks sacrificing herself for her sister (twelve-year-old Primrose is chosen to participate; Katniss volunteers to take her place) and is later drawn to another young girl, Rue. The innocence of Primrose and Rue is overdetermined; they are no more innocent than Katniss, whose only additional experience has been the care of her family, and yet they bear the loaded cultural weight of a more extreme privation. Like Emma, Katniss envisions a life for herself that defies the expectations of her society. And yet, Katniss's desire to remain single appears to foreclose the very counterfactuality that Emma embraces. Confiding in her inevitable love interest early in the series, she refuses to entertain the prospect of a life livable otherwise.

> "I never want to have kids," I say.
> "I might. If I didn't live here," says Gale.
> "But you do," I say, irritated.[18]

Katniss imagines a life without children both because her hard-won practicality knows the difficulty of another mouth to feed and also because the circumstances of her life have foreclosed all meaningful futurity. (*The Hunger Games* is narrated in the first-person present tense, refusing the projected futurity that would be implied by retrospective narration.) Gale's willingness to entertain counterfactual possibility marks him in this moment as an inappropriate partner, and it exposes Katniss's utter inability to imagine her life differently: "We can't leave, so why bother talking about it? And even if we did . . . even if we did . . . where did this stuff about having kids come from?"[19] But not long after this moment, the novel turns to the improbable: despite having entered the Reaping's lottery just once (compared with Katniss's twenty entries), Primrose is chosen. The series' famously eerie refrain ("May the odds be ever in your favor!") is ironized once by Prim's sheer bad luck and then again by the fact that surviving the games has little to do with probability.

Because the annual Games are compulsory viewing, Katniss has accumulated a lifetime of vicarious experience. She is familiar with the contours of the Games' narrative arc; she can predict with considerable accuracy what the audience will demand and what the Gamemakers will offer in return. She knows when her own interventions in the Games are unprecedented and therefore particularly risky.[20] Her clever final move—threatening a double suicide that would rob the Capitol of a winner—is seen, quite rightly, as an act of rebellion, and so her allies advise her to present herself as incapable of the strategy she has just enacted. Here, the cooptation of love as strategy becomes useful yet again, granting Katniss plausible deniability: she did not orchestrate a double suicide to thwart the propaganda machine of the Capitol; she was just in love— the kind of crazy, teenage love that causes you to do reckless things. This claim can only be made implicitly, and Katniss's loyal handlers go to work crafting an image of sweet guilelessness. For an adventure novel, *The Hunger Games* spends a lot of time carefully describing dresses, and Katniss's final gown is no exception: it is both modest and alluring, a sunny yellow with an empire waist. "I look, very simply, like a girl. A young one. Fourteen at the most. Innocent. Harmless. . . . This is a very calculated look" (355). To survive long enough to consider her next move, Katniss will "need to look as girlish and innocent as possible" (360). Katniss's masquerade as a novice saves her life, for now at least, obscuring the knowingness that makes her a formidable threat to the stability of the regime. If, as I argued, the remainder of Richardson's novel after Clarissa's death worked to fabricate a *Bildung* Clarissa herself defied, we see something of the opposite in the denouement that follows Katniss's climactic victory in the Games. Only a novice (whether genuine or counterfeit) can survive in a world that weaponizes the appeals of adolescence.

Even after winning the Games, Katniss continues to resist the prospect of marriage and children. "It's no good loving me because I'm never going to get married anyway. . . . I'll never be able to afford the kind of love that leads to a family, to children. And how can he? How can he after what we've just been through?" (372–73). Does it matter, then, that the final installment of the trilogy concludes with an epilogue that finds Katniss married with children? She makes her reluctance clear ("It took five, ten, fifteen years for me to agree"), but the reader is led to believe that the choice to have children is less a personal decision than the act of a representative.[21] The resistance needed a novice and, now that revolution has been achieved and a new world is in view, it needs *Bildung.* To have children is to legitimate the end of the Games, to lend solidity to the fragile peace that follows the war against the Capitol. Katniss has to grow up—and to present the tokens of maturity—to assure her people that the possibilities ahead are circumscribed in the right ways—that their future is not martial but domestic. Yet the bathos of this *Bildung,* the sense that Katniss has not exactly chosen this path, continues to attest to the series' more fundamental commitment to inexperience's logic.

Collins has resisted allegorical readings of her novels that threaten to temper their dystopian bleakness ("I don't write about adolescence. . . . I write about war. For adolescents").[22] And yet, The Hunger Games does make use of adolescence in much the way that *Emma* does, as a figure for possibility and a structure for the generation of conceivable lives. It has become something of a journalistic commonplace to note that young adult fiction like *The Hunger Games* is so popular that it has spawned marketing designations like "new adult" or "emerging adult" to name a wide readership drawn to the lives of adolescents. These designations draw attention to without solving the ambiguity of a designation like "young adult"; these categories are just the latest attempt to capture what eighteenth-century Britain thought of as the entrance into the world. As I have argued, the novel has, since its reflourishing in mid-eighteenth-century Britain, been attuned to the lives of young people and has seen them, moreover, as uniquely capable of testing the limits of the novel's form. Does the novice disappear once *Bildung* becomes central to the novel's conception of character? *As if*. This book has aimed to show that the affordances of adolescence for both character and narrative exceed *Bildung* and overspill the literary historical moment in which they are first theorized.

Notes

INTRODUCTION: Entering the World

1. Frances Burney, *Camilla*, ed. Edward A. Bloom and Lillian Bloom (Oxford: Oxford UP, 1972), 523.

2. We may also justly ask whether it is possible to imagine the novel without the subject. Indeed, this question motivates some of the most exciting work in novel theory of the past decade. See, for example, Jonathan Kramnick's emphasis on externality (rather than inwardness) in *Actions and Objects from Hobbes to Richardson* (Stanford: Stanford UP, 2010); and Sandra Macpherson's emphasis on harm (rather than responsibility) in *Harm's Way: Tragic Responsibility and the Novel Form* (Baltimore: Johns Hopkins UP, 2010). While this book will by no means take subjectivity as a given, I do understand the novels I read here to experiment with the coherence of a self unimpinged upon by the outside world.

3. While Philippe Ariés influentially solidified a long-held argument that adolescence did not exist in preindustrial Europe (*Centuries of Childhood: A Social History of Family Life*, trans. Robert Baldick [New York: Knopf, 1962]), I hold with a generation of scholars who have since pushed back against this claim. See, for example, Ilana Krausman Ben-Amos, *Adolescence and Youth in Early Modern England* (New Haven: Yale UP, 1994); and Helen Yallop, *Age and Identity in Eighteenth-Century England* (London: Pickering and Chatto, 2013). I would add quite simply that the claim that adolescence (most often referred to simply as "youth" in this period) does not constitute a distinct life stage evaporates once we turn our attention to these novels.

4. Eliza Haywood, *A Wife to be Lett: A Comedy* (London: 1723), act 5, scene 1.

5. An earlier instance occurs when Mr. Tyrold praises his youngest daughter, Eugenia. There, the phrase acts not as an accusation, as it does when uttered by Lionel, but a panegyric. The versions of inexperience exhibited by the Tyrold daughters (Camilla, the disfigured scholar Eugenia [whose name invokes and is frequently coupled with "ingenuous"], and the bland-to-the-point-of-invisibility Lavinia) suggest that Burney is experimenting (as she does throughout her oeuvre) with the sheer variety of representations of female adolescence.

6. Anna Laetitia Barbauld, "Life of Samuel Richardson, with Remarks on His Writings," in *The Correspondence of Samuel Richardson* (London: 1804), x. I follow Michael McKeon in understanding the origins of the novel and the registration of its newness as separate phenomena: "The emergence of the origins of the novel into public consciousness and controversy marks the point at which the genre is . . . identified as such, as a 'new species.'" *The Origins of the English Novel* (Baltimore: Johns Hopkins UP, 2002), 418. Without wishing to pinpoint an origin, my study attends to this moment when novelty becomes a matter of public debate, and it begins, then, where McKeon's leaves off.

7. Frances Burney, *Evelina, or A Young Lady's Entrance into the World*, ed. Edward A. Bloom (Oxford: Oxford UP, 1970).

8. On "coming out" as a regulated, even mechanical process that makes women into automatons, see Julie Park, *The Self and It: Novel Objects in Eighteenth-Century England* (Stanford: Stanford UP, 2010).

9. My thinking about this opposition is informed by the discussion of *Bild* and *Bildung* (form and formation) in Hans-Georg Gadamer's *Truth and Method*, trans. Joel Weinsheimer and Donald G. Marshall (London: Bloomsbury, 2013).

10. Recent scholarship has started to dislocate the centrality of progress narratives to novel theory by locating in novels pockets outside of the thrust of developmental time. Anne-Lise François counters the "normative bias in favor of the demonstrable, dramatic development and realization of human powers characteristic of, but not limited to, the capitalist investment in value and work and the Enlightenment allegiance to rationalism and unbounded progress," by turning to Romantic-era examples of what she calls "recessive action": an ethos of noninstrumentality as the path of least resistance (*Open Secrets: The Literature of Uncounted Experience* [Stanford: Stanford UP, 2008], xvi). Focusing on the Victorian novel, Elisha Cohn zooms in on moments of attenuated consciousness—states like "reverie, trance, and sleep"—that momentarily pause the forces of progress in "a paradoxically static intensity—still life, vibrant in its absorptive movelessness." *Still Life: Suspended Development in the Victorian Novel* (Oxford: Oxford UP, 2016), 3, 5. Connecting development to the teleology of the marriage plot in particular, Claire Jarvis finds in the Victorian novel's stylized masochistic tableaus "scenes of sustained stasis, where plot and character drop out, description thickens, and a glance, gesture, or object takes on a heightened relational significance," the capacity for novels to "stop or dislocate progress." *Exquisite Masochism: Marriage, Sex, and the Novel Form* (Baltimore: Johns Hopkins UP, 2016), viii. Anne McCarthy finds an aesthetics of suspension in nineteenth-century poetry's fascination with corpse-like figures and other arrested signs of the unknowable. *Awful Parenthesis: Suspension and the Sublime in Romantic and Victorian Poetry* (Toronto: Toronto UP, 2018). Why this emerging agreement? All these studies can be thought of as finding in literary form a counterweight to a progressive narrative underscored by more historicist work on the novel that sees in the novel's special relationship to time a necessarily progressive narrative. *Born Yesterday* joins this conversation while attempting to trace in the early novel a way of thinking about antidevelopment as durational—not momentary, as do these scholars, but as sustained. That is, the figures on which I focus do not find solace in fleeting escape from progressive logics but instead persist alongside or even above them without becoming subject to them.

11. See McKeon; Ian Duncan, *Modern Romance and the Transformations of the Novel: The Gothic, Scott, Dickens* (Cambridge: Cambridge UP, 2005); and a series of essays building toward a larger project by Scott Black, including "Fielding and the Progress of Romance," in *The Oxford Handbook of the Eighteenth-Century Novel*, ed. J. A. Downie (Oxford: Oxford UP, 2016).

12. In this vein, I am thinking of feminist historicists who have looked to counter-models of female development. For a fine example, see Susan Fraiman, *Unbecoming Women: British Women Writers and the Novel of Development* (New York: Columbia UP, 1993). For quite a different historicist account of the limits of developmental narrative, in this case centering on the conflict between progress and colonialism in the modernist novel, see Jed Esty, *Unseasonable Youth: Modernism, Colonialism, and the Fiction of Development* (Oxford: Oxford UP, 2013).

13. Caroline Levine has recently troubled the distinction I make here, arguing for the utility of the concept of "form" in describing social arrangements. See *Forms: Whole, Rhythm, Hierarchy, Network* (Princeton: Princeton UP, 2015).

14. I take this to be Franco Moretti's complaint when he provocatively calls the eighteenth-

century bildungsroman "the worst novel of the west" in *The Way of the World: The* Bildungs-roman *in European Culture*, trans. Albert Sbragia (London: Verso, 1987), 214. What Moretti calls the "judicial-fairy-tale model" of the early British novel I see as its investment in formal logics (about which more below and, indeed, throughout).

15. In a sense, then, it may be fair to think of this project as belonging to what has been called the "descriptive turn" in literary theory—the move away from the time-honored methodological pairing of critique and interpretation and toward a method that is at once more humble and more radical in its potential to remake the aesthetic object through the work of redescription. See Sharon Marcus and Stephen Best, "Surface Reading: An Introduction," in *The Way We Read Now*, special issue of *Representations* 108.1 (Fall 2009), 1–21; as well as Marcus, Best, and Heather Love, *Description across the Disciplines*, special issue of *Representations* 135.1 (Summer 2016). For a con-sideration of the descriptive turn that ultimately endorses a humbler, more aesthetically attuned interpretation, see Jarvis, esp. 155–164.

As I have presented work from this project over the past few years, it has certainly been called descriptive (and that term has not always been complimentary). While my methodology is ulti-mately more eclectic than this designation may allow (there are certainly many moments in this book that could be justly called interpretive or critical), I take from the supporters of a descriptive turn the imperative to notice what might otherwise be overlooked by a more tightly focused hermeneutic lens. I would also note that "description" names what narrative theory, to which I am indebted throughout this project, has been doing all along.

16. Readers looking for a more historically attuned account of eighteenth-century Britain's lively and contentious debates around nature and nurture, essence and education, for example, would be wise to look elsewhere. I recommend Jenny Davidson's wide-ranging and writerly *Breed-ing: A Partial History of the Eighteenth Century* (New York: Columbia UP, 2009).

17. Samuel Richardson, *Clarissa*, ed. Angus Ross (1747–48; New York: Penguin, 1985), 538; Richardson, *Clarissa*, ed. Florian Stuber et al., 8 vols., *The Clarissa Project* (1751; New York: AMS, 1990), 3:321.

18. On sensory experience as unavoidable, see John Locke: "For the Objects of our senses, do, many of them, obtrude their particular *Ideas* upon our minds, whether we will or no. . . . As the Bodies that surround us, do diversly affect our Organs, the mind is forced to receive the Impres-sions; and cannot avoid the Perception of those *Ideas* that are annexed to them." *An Essay con-cerning Human Understanding*, ed. Peter H. Nidditch (Oxford: Clarendon, 1987), 2.1.25. That ex-perience is to a significant degree unavoidable and yet nevertheless divorceable from development is a key claim of these novels.

19. The best recent reader of the eighteenth-century British novel's idealism is Thomas Pavel, who, however, subscribes to the much longer history of the novel advanced by novel theorists like Doody. See her *The True Story of the Novel* (New Brunswick: Rutgers UP, 1997). For Pavel, the eighteenth-century novel's idealism is a "new idealism," merging a time-honored tradition of el-evating morally superior characters with a new attention to the everyday. Thus, "literary histori-ans who assert the deep continuity of the novel's history from the ancient Greek novel onward are correct, as are those for whom English eighteenth-century fiction represents a new departure: they have recognized the two sides of Richardson's work." *The Lives of the Novel: A History* (Princeton: Princeton UP, 2013), 122. While I largely agree with Pavel's understanding of what I call the early realist novel, my account looks quite different, given the concentration of my focus on Britain in the later eighteenth century.

20. Samuel Johnson, *Rambler* 4, 31 March 1750, *The Works of Samuel Johnson*, vol. 3, ed. W. J. Bate and Albrecht B. Strauss (New Haven: Yale UP, 1969). See also M. H. Abrams, *The Mirror and the Lamp: Romantic Theory and the Critical Tradition* (London: Oxford UP, 1953), where Abrams

points out the selective impulse behind eighteenth-century realism, especially in his section on "the empirical ideal" (35–41). On the ambiguity of the empiricist mirror metaphor, see also Jean Hagstrum, *The Sister Arts: The Tradition of Literary Pictorialism and English Poetry from Dryden to Gray* (Chicago: U of Chicago P, 1958).

21. Jed Esty, "Realism Wars," "Worlding Realisms Now," special issue of *Novel* 49.2 (2016), 339.

22. Anna Laetitia Barbauld, "On the Origin and Progress of Novel-Writing," preface to *The British Novelists*, vol. 1 (London: 1810), 47.

23. Claudia L. Johnson, "'Let Me Make the Novels of a Country': Barbauld's *The British Novelists* (1810/1820)," "The Romantic-Era Novel," special issue of *Novel* 34.2 (2001): 163–79; 171.

24. Paul Ricoeur, *Time and Narrative*, vol. 2, trans. Kathleen McLaughlin and David Pellauer (Chicago: U of Chicago P, 1985), 43.

25. Andrew H. Miller, "Lives Unled in Realist Fiction," *Representations* 98 (2008): 118–34; 122. See also the version of this essay printed as "On Lives Unled," the conclusion to *The Burdens of Perfection: On Ethics and Reading in Nineteenth-Century British Literature* (Ithaca: Cornell UP, 2008). Miller borrows the term "optative" from Stuart Hampshire. See his *Innocence and Experience* (Cambridge, MA: Harvard UP, 1991).

26. Anahid Nersessian has argued that Romantic literature is drawn to the project of utopia as precisely a means of setting the parameters of the possible. See *Utopia, Limited: Romanticism and Adjustment* (Cambridge, MA: Harvard UP, 2015).

27. Miller, 212.

28. Dorothy Van Ghent, *The English Novel: Form and Function* (New York: Harper and Row, 1953), 14. Miller also quotes from this underappreciated passage.

29. My thinking on realism runs parallel to that of Anna Kornbluh, who has recently drawn on the architectural preoccupations of Henry James and Fredric Jameson to argue for an anti-mimetic realism that "drafts and constructs worlds." "The Realist Blueprint," *Henry James Review* 36.3 (2015), 199–211; 199.

30. I paraphrase here just some of the various meanings Johnson includes in his *Dictionary of the English Language*, s.v. "world" (London: Times Books, 1979), n.p. Laurence Sterne, creator of some of the novel's most beloved unworldly characters, is particularly fond of nesting the word's meanings, as when Tristram's midwife, "had acquired in her way—no small degree of reputation in the world:—by which word *world*, need I in this place inform your worship, that I would be understood to mean no more of it than a small circle described upon the circle of the great world, of four English miles diameter." *The Life and Opinions of Tristram Shandy*, ed. Ian Campbell Ross (Oxford: Oxford UP, 2009), 7.

31. Oliver Goldsmith, *The Vicar of Wakefield*, ed. Arthur Friedman and Robert L. Mack (Oxford: Oxford UP, 2008).

32. Aaron Kunin has recently advanced a theory of character *as* type, which is to say, character *as* form: "a device that collects every example of a kind of person." "Characters Lounge," *Modern Language Quarterly* 70.3 (2009): 291–317.

33. J. Paul Hunter, *Before Novels: The Cultural Contexts of Eighteenth-Century English Fiction* (New York: W. W. Norton, 1992), 43.

34. Samuel Johnson, *Rambler* 4, 21.

35. In an invaluable study that fruitfully crosses conventional period divisions, Teresa Michals complicates the picture Hunter gives us, arguing that the readership of early novels was "imagined not in terms of age but of social status and gender," with age-leveled reading a latter-day phenomenon tied to the emergence of adulthood as a category of experience only in the late nineteenth century. *Books for Children, Books for Adults: Age and the Novel from Defoe to James* (Cambridge: Cambridge UP, 2014), 2.

36. The classic account of the novel's indebtedness to conduct literature is Nancy Armstrong,

Desire and Domestic Fiction: A Political History of the Novel (New York: Oxford UP, 1987). For a study, aided by considerable quantitative analysis, of the ways that eighteenth-century novels were marketed to young persons, see Katherine B. Gustafson's "Coming of Age in the Eighteenth-Century Novel" (diss. U of Pennsylvania, 2012), ProQuest.

37. Michals, 62.

38. As Deidre Shauna Lynch writes, "*Identification*, the modern term for what we do with characters, . . . obscures the historical specificity, the relative novelty, of our codes of reading. With the beginnings of the late eighteenth-century's 'affective revolution' and the advent of new linkages between novel reading, moral training, and self-culture, character reading was reinvented as an occasion when readers found themselves and plumbed their own interior resources of sensibility by plumbing characters' hidden depths." *The Economy of Character: Novels, Market Culture, and the Business of Inner Meaning* (Chicago: U of Chicago P, 1998), 10. I am less cautious than is Lynch in using the word "identification," not least because my commitments to historical specificity are less pronounced, but I am likewise committed to demonstrating the ways that eighteenth-century characters tested and thwarted intense readerly response. My aim here, as will be clear later in this introduction, is to focus attention on characters who are poised between the kinds of character (to simplify: flat and deep) Lynch sees as operating on a historical continuum.

39. Hester Chapone, *Letters on the Improvement of the Mind, Addressed to a Young Lady* (London: 1777), 81.

40. For an example of the kind of study I mean, see Theresa Braunschneider, *Our Coquettes: Capacious Desire in the Eighteenth Century* (Charlottesville: U of Virginia P, 2009). Coquettes, Braunschneider argues, "exercise *choice* in ways only newly available to large numbers of women in Britain. They consume the imported luxury goods flooding domestic marketplaces in an era of expanding global trade, drinking coffee and tea out of Chinese porcelain and drawing attention to themselves through a display of 'exotic' fans, combs, laces, and silks. [The lists continue.] Offered an array of appealing options—of luxury goods, public entertainments, pets, clothes, or lovers—the coquette chooses them all" (2). Constrained in both choice and movement, tending more toward the abstemious than the voracious, the novice, by contrast, can appear to be only minimally present in her time; she is thus less amenable to the kind of analysis that would use her as a lens through which to understand her cultural moment.

41. I heartily second, then, Macpherson's skeptical reference to "character understood the way historians of the novel understand it: as *bildung*" (23).

42. By way of comparison, see Alex Woloch's *The One versus the Many: Minor Characters and the Space of the Protagonist in the Novel* (Princeton: Princeton UP, 2003), whose way of seeing character as emerging out of a formal-referential matrix both rhetorically and conceptually grafts that emergence onto tropes of maturation or development, so that the protagonist of the bildungsroman becomes the protagonist par excellence.

43. For a dense yet deft guide to this critical history, see Marc Redfield, *Phantom Formations: Aesthetic Ideology and the Bildungsroman* (Ithaca: Cornell UP, 1996). For Redfield, the success of *Bildung* as a concept creates something of a critical trap: "This genre does not properly exist, and in a sense can be proved not to exist: one can take canonical definitions of *Bildung* (itself no simple term), go to the novels most frequently called *Bildungsromane*, and with greater or lesser difficulty show that they exceed, or fall short of, or call into question the process of *Bildung* which they purportedly serve. . . . Yet despite, or because of, its referential complexity, the notion of the *Bildungsroman* is one of academic criticism's most overwhelmingly successful inventions" (vii).

44. Brigid Lowe, "The Bildungsroman," in *The Cambridge History of the English Novel*, ed. Robert L. Caserio and Clement Hawes (Cambridge: Cambridge UP, 2012), 405.

45. Patricia Meyer Spacks, *Novel Beginnings: Experiments in Eighteenth-Century English Fiction* (New Haven: Yale UP, 2008).

46. That is to say, my aim here is not to reject the utility of *Bildung* out of hand. Indeed, I use *Bildung* throughout this book to name a competing, but consistently subordinated, path of development to which I see narratives of inexperience responding. My argument is not that developmental narratives did not exist in eighteenth-century novels but rather that we have attended to their presence disproportionately. On proto-*Bildung* narratives in eighteenth-century literature, see Richard A. Barney, *Plots of Enlightenment: Education and the Novel in Eighteenth-Century England* (Stanford: Stanford UP, 1999). I extend G. A. Starr's insight about the sentimental novel to the eighteenth-century novel more generally: "The kind of ethical and epistemological workout so edifying to characters and readers alike in the Bildungsroman, and so central to the educative pretensions of most eighteenth-century novels, is largely absent from the sentimental novel." "Sentimental De-Education," in *Augustan Studies: Essays in Honour of Irvin Ehrenpreis*, ed. Douglas Lane and Timothy Keegan (Newark: U of Delaware P, 1985), 258. On this claim that sentimentalism is antagonistic to *Bildung*, see also Starr, "'Only a Boy': Notes on Sentimental Novels," *Genre* 10 (1977): 501–27; and April London, *Women and Property in the Eighteenth-Century English Novel* (Cambridge: Cambridge UP, 1999), esp. 67–85.

47. For a thorough and thoughtful study of the complex relationship between early theories of the novel and philosophical empiricism, see Roger Maioli, *Empiricism and the Early Theory of the Novel* (Cham, Switzerland: Palgrave Macmillan, 2016). For a more affirmative account of the novel's indebtedness to scientific empiricism, see John Bender's recent work, especially the essays collected in *Ends of Enlightenment* (Stanford: Stanford UP, 2012).

48. Allow me to be clear: this book does little to relitigate either philosophical empiricism itself or its place in eighteenth-century culture broadly speaking. Rather, I take up what I see as problems in literary studies that stem from an overreliance on empiricism as an answer to questions about how the early novel operates. Recent work more directly focused on eighteenth-century empiricism (especially on scientific empiricism) only promises to enrich this conversation. See, for example, Courtney Weiss Smith, *Empiricist Devotions: Science, Religion, and Poetry in Early Eighteenth-Century England* (Charlottesville: U of Virginia P, 2016). However, my book is not itself a study of empiricist thought. On empiricism itself as a literary (which is to say, rhetorical, discursive) practice, see John Richetti, *Philosophical Writing: Locke, Berkeley, Hume* (Cambridge: Harvard UP, 1983); Cathy Caruth, *Empirical Truths and Critical Fictions: Locke, Wordsworth, Kant, Freud* (Baltimore: Johns Hopkins UP, 1991); and Jules David Law, *The Rhetoric of Empiricism: Language and Perception from Locke to I. A. Richards* (Ithaca: Cornell UP, 1993).

49. Locke, 2.1.2.

50. Locke, 31.

51. Ian Watt, *The Rise of the Novel: Studies in Defoe, Richardson, and Fielding* (Berkeley: U of California P, 1959), 22.

52. We might understand this shift from sense experience to social experience as a pasting over of a gap already present in Locke's *Essay*. Nancy Yousef has pointed out, "The *Essay's* failure to distinguish between persons and things in the experiential life of the subject—an oversight which can, in its turn, be traced to the *Essay's* occlusion of the role of other persons in the formation of subjectivity." *Isolated Cases: The Anxieties of Autonomy in Enlightenment Philosophy and Romantic Literature* (Ithaca: Cornell UP, 2004), 27. See also Mark Blackwell, "The People Things Make: Locke's *Essay concerning Human Understanding* and the Properties of the Self," *Studies in Eighteenth-Century Culture* 35 (2006): 77–94.

53. The move from phenomenal to social experience is a move that recurs implicitly throughout criticism on the early novel. For a rare explicit acknowledgment of this kind of extrapolation, which generally remains tacit, see John C. O'Neill: "Focusing on the elemental origins of human behavior and thought rather than on the human activities in society that occur considerably later, I take, as do the sensationists themselves, what might best be called a phenomenological approach

to experience. Social experience is seen from [a phenomenological] perspective as an extension, albeit a highly sophisticated one, of certain fundamental early behaviors." *The Authority of Experience: Sensationist Theory in the French Enlightenment* (University Park: Pennsylvania State UP, 1996), 6n10.

54. The photo negative of (and one inspiration for) the present study is Peter Brooks's *The Novel of Worldliness: Crébillon, Marivaux, Laclos, Stendhal* (Princeton: Princeton UP, 1969).

55. For one example of such a critique, see the introduction to William Beatty Warner, *Licensing Entertainment: The Elevation of Novel Reading in Britain, 1684–1750* (Berkeley: U of California P, 1998). One of Warner's main claims is that Watt approaches the problem of accounting for the novel's rise with a series of assumptions at hand, first among them, the idea that the novel did indeed rise but also that any account of that rise must be able to comprise Defoe, Richardson, and Fielding. See also Harry E. Shaw, *Narrating Reality: Austen, Scott, Eliot* (Ithaca: Cornell UP, 1999), esp. 38–89. As Shaw notes, Watt himself acknowledges the imbalance of his book in an essay written a decade later, "Serious Reflections on *The Rise of the Novel*," *Novel* 1 (1968): 205–18. Watt reveals that his original plan for the monograph called for several more chapters on realism of assessment. However, as Shaw points out, such structural equity would not have addressed the significant problems of discontinuity between the two terms.

56. Scholars focusing on empiricist metaphor have repeatedly shown the blank slate to be a troublesome emblem for empiricism. As Davidson puts it, "Despite general acceptance of the blank slate as a suggestive metaphor for a child's mind . . . the vast majority of eighteenth-century discussions allow for natural differences between individuals" (*Breeding*, 40). Brad Pasanek provides a thorough account of the complexity of the contested blank slate and white paper metaphors (including a fascinating discussion of watermarks) in his *Metaphors of Mind: An Eighteenth-Century Dictionary* (Baltimore: Johns Hopkins UP, 2015), esp. 227–48. Pasanek cites William Walker, who even more forcefully aligns the metaphor of writing with innatist, and not empiricist, thought: "For the innatist, ideas do not enter the mind [as in the spatial cabinet metaphor], indeed cannot enter it, because the mind is not conceived as some type of space or room which an idea may enter. Rather, the mind is a substance *upon* which ideas are written, stamped, engraved, printed, or impressed. . . . [I]n the vast majority of cases, Locke claims the containment metaphor for himself while relegating the imprinting metaphor to the innatists." *Locke, Literary Criticism, and Philosophy* (Cambridge: Cambridge UP, 1994), 33–34.

57. Joseph Addison, *Spectator* 273, reprinted in *Notes upon the Twelve Books of Paradise Lost, Collected from the Spectator* (London: 1719), 11. Addison's essays on *Paradise Lost* were enormously influential in the eighteenth century, and not only on later critics of Milton like Johnson.

58. On Enlightenment ideas of probability and plausibility, see Barbara Shapiro, *Probability and Certainty in Seventeenth-Century England: A Study of the Relationship between Natural Science, Religion, History, Law, and Literature* (Princeton: Princeton UP, 1983); Douglas Lane Patey, *Probability and Literary Form* (Cambridge: 1984); Lorraine Daston, *Classical Probability in the Enlightenment* (Princeton: Princeton UP, 1988) and Robert Newsom, *A Likely Story* (New Brunswick, NJ: Rutgers UP, 1988). For a more recent account that focuses on the *im*probable (and its consequences for Enlightenment thought), see Jesse Molesworth, *Chance and the Eighteenth-Century Novel* (Cambridge: Cambridge UP 2010).

59. Richardson to Lady Bradshaigh (late 1749), in John Carroll, *Selected Letters of Samuel Richardson* (Oxford: Clarendon Press, 1965), 133.

60. See Ronald Paulson, *The Beautiful, Novel, and Strange* (Baltimore: Johns Hopkins UP, 1996). Scott Black has connected the concept of novelty explicitly to the form of the *Spectator* itself: "With the category of 'novelty,' Addison theorizes the pleasures of the *Spectator*, and so provides an aesthetics for the emerging urban and urbane public space defined by the periodical essay." "Addison's Aesthetics of Novelty," *Studies in Eighteenth-Century Culture* 30 (2001): 269–88; 271.

61. See Addison, *The Spectator* No. 50, Friday (April 27, 1711); and Voltaire, *L'Ingenu* (1767). On representations of North American indigenous peoples (including those mentioned here) as enabling the articulation of modern subjectivity, see Robbie Richardson, *The Savage and the Modern Self: North American Indians in Eighteenth-Century British Literature and Culture* (Toronto: U of Toronto P, 2018).

62. Frances Burney, letter to Samuel Crisp of 1 December 1774, in *The Early Journals and Letters of Fanny Burney*, ed. Lars E. Troide, vol. 2 (Montreal: McGill-Queen's UP, 1991), 60–63.

63. Northop Frye, "Varieties of Eighteenth-Century Sensibility," in *Northrop Frye's Writings on the Eighteenth and Nineteenth Centuries*, vol. 17 of *The Collected Works of Northrop Frye*, ed. Imre Salusinszky (Toronto: U of Toronto P, 2005), 35.

64. Mikhail Bakhtin, "Epic and Novel," in *The Dialogic Imagination: Four Essays*, ed. Michael Holquist, trans. Caryl Emerson and Michael Holquist (Austin: U of Texas Pr, 1981), 3–83; 13. Bakhtin borrows the term "absolute past" from Johann Wolfgang von Goethe and Friedrich Schiller's essay, "Uber epische und dramatische Dichtung" (written 1797, published 1827), where the original term is *vollkommen vergangen*. As their title indicates, Goethe and Schiller are actually contrasting epic to drama, and not to the novel, as Bakhtin himself acknowledges.

65. Bakhtin, 3.

66. With a nod to Bakhtin, Woloch has recently explored the issue of the novel's formlessness, especially with regard to the pressures of realist referential representation, in "Form and Formlessness in the Novel," in *The Work of Genre: Selected Essays from the English Institute*, ed. Robyn Warhol (Cambridge: English Institute, 2011), para. 227–57.

67. Bakhtin, 10. Bakhtin includes this principle, which is not actually found in Fielding, along with others such as "the novel should not be 'poetic,'" which Fielding does explicitly address in his description of his project as "a comic Epic-Poem in Prose." *Joseph Andrews*, ed. Martin C. Battestin (Middletown, CT: Wesleyan UP, 1967), 4. Bakhtin is right, however, to trace his own emphasis on character development to eighteenth-century accounts, but such an emphasis is clearer in the works of later theorists he mentions, such as Goethe and Hegel.

68. See, most influentially, Georg Lukács, *The Theory of the Novel*, trans. Anna Bostock (Cambridge, MA: MIT Press, 1971). In referring implicitly here to novel theory that does not consider character, I have in mind formalist criticism, which, far from overemphasizing *Bildung*, has been accused of ignoring character altogether in its focus on actions rather than agents. See, for both a diagnosis and a correction to this problem, Frances Ferguson, "Jane Austen, *Emma*, and the Impact of Form," *Modern Language Quarterly* 61.1 (2000): 158–80. For a useful overview of the place (or, more accurately, the absence) of character in twentieth-century literary theory, see the introduction to Woloch's *The One vs. the Many*, esp. 12–42. Woloch quotes Seymour Chatman: "It is remarkable how little has been said about the theory of character in literary history and criticism" (14). As I hope this introduction makes clear, this charge is now happily outdated, and yet I suggest that the recent contributions of character theory are still slow to be taken up by work on the novel more generally.

69. Immanuel Kant, "What Is Enlightenment?," trans. Ted Humphrey, *Perpetual Peace and Other Essays* (Indianapolis: Hackett, 1983). For an extended discussion of the common analogy between life stages and historical progress, see Ann Wierda Rowland, *Romanticism and Childhood: The Infantilization of British Literary Culture* (Cambridge: Cambridge UP, 2012). Rowland's analysis takes as its starting point Percy Shelley's articulation of the comparison in his defense of poetry: "For the savage is to ages what the child is to years."

70. Catherine Gallagher, *Nobody's Story: The Vanishing Acts of Women Writers in the Marketplace* (Berkeley: U of California P, 1994), xv.

71. Lynch, 34.

72. Locke, 2.1.15. The question of whether *innate* ideas are indelible is crucial to Locke's argument against them, though he admits that, if innate ideas are real but fragile, novices would be the ones to look to for evidence of them: "But concerning innate Principles, I desire [innatists] to say, whether they can, or cannot by Education or Custom, be blurr'd and blotted out: If they cannot, we must find them in all Mankind alike, and they must be clear in every body: And if they suffer variation from adventitious Notions, we must then find them clearest and most perspicuous, nearest the Fountain, in Children and illiterate People, who have received least impression from foreign Opinions" (1.3.20).

73. Frances Ferguson, "Rape and the Rise of the Novel," "Misogyny, Misandry, and Misanthropy" special issue of *Representations* 20 (1987): 88–112.

74. Ferguson, "Rape and the Rise of the Novel," 98.

75. Even so precise a commentator as William Blackstone points to the grayer areas of minority law. While misdemeanors are rarely enforced for those under twenty-one,

> with regard to capital crimes, the law is still more minute and circumspect; distinguishing with greater nicety the several degrees of age and discretion. By the antient Saxon law, the age of twelve years was established for the age of possible discretion, when first the understanding might open: and from thence till the offender was fourteen, it was *aetas pubertati proxima*, in which he might or might no be guilty of a crime, according to his natural capacity or incapacity. . . . But by the Law, as it now stands, and has stood at least ever since the time of Edward the third, the capacity of doing ill, or contracting guilt, is not so much measured by years and days, as by the strength of the delinquent's understanding and judgment. *Commentaries on the Laws of England*, book 4, "Of Public Wrongs," ed. Ruth Paley (Oxford: Oxford UP, 2016), 14–15.

76. See, for example, Robin Bernstein, *Racial Innocence: Performing American Childhood from Slavery to Civil Rights* (New York: New York UP, 2011).

77. As the study of the novel has returned to questions of form, Ferguson's essay has received something of a revival in attention. See, in particular, Kramnick; Macpherson; Wendy Anne Lee, "The Case for Hard-Heartedness: *Clarissa*, Indifferency, Impersonality," *Eighteenth-Century Fiction* 26.1 (2013), 33–65; and Kathleen Lubey, "Sexual Remembrance in *Clarissa*," *Eighteenth-Century Fiction* 29.2 (2016): 151–78.

78. On the promise of youth as a pervasive myth, see Patricia Meyer Spacks, *The Adolescent Idea: Myths of Youth and the Adult Imagination* (New York: Basic Books, 1981).

79. James, preface to the New York edition of *The Princess Casamassima*, in *The Art of the Novel* (Boston: Northeastern UP, 1984), 68.

80. Samuel Richardson, *Pamela, or Virtue Rewarded*, ed. Thomas Keymer and Alice Wakely (Oxford: Oxford UP, 2001), 20. All further references to this edition will be in the text.

81. Pamela is a name borrowed from Sidney's romance *Arcadia*, which Richardson printed in his shop. On Richardson and Sidney, see Gillian Beer, "*Pamela*: Rethinking *Arcadia*," in *Samuel Richardson: Tercentenary Essays*, ed. Doody and Peter Sabor (Cambridge: Cambridge UP, 1989), 23–39. It is the conjunction of Pamela's given name with her surname (the pedestrian Andrews) that, for Ian Watt, marks her as a real—that is, a novelistic—character and not a romance heroine (19). Of course, as many a critic has observed, Watt's emphasis on what he calls "the epistemological status of proper names" requires heavy qualification to yield even limited validity (18).

82. Prefatory letter to the first edition, attributed to Reverend William Webster (sometimes suspected to have been written by Richardson himself).

83. Michals observes, for *Pamela*, " 'growing up' still means moving up in the world more than it means reaching a new psychological stage. The new authority that Pamela wins is finally de-

fined by social position rather than by inner growth" (63). I would stress that what Michals calls Pamela's "new authority" after marriage is actually a ratification of the essential authority of her goodness. On the significance of Pamela's wedding—and, more precisely, her wedding night—see Kathleen Lubey, *Excitable Imaginations: Eroticism and Reading in Britain, 1660–1760* (Lewisburg: Bucknell UP, 2012). For Lubey, sex (and not virtue or class) poses the most sustained epistemological and moral puzzle in Richardson's novel: "Text, character, and reader continue to puzzle over how to 'see' sex as long as is logically possible, ceasing only after Pamela's wedding night has come to a close and she still is able to sing praises of Mr B's gentleness and good humor" (160). I would add only that it is the *anticlimax* of Pamela's long-awaited climax that I see as most illuminating here: her laboriously described anxiety about the changes conjugal bliss will bring is swiftly exchanged for a simple statement of her increased happiness: "Never, surely was so happy a Creature as your *Pamela!*" (*Pamela*, 353).

84. On the specifically "novelistic" detail, especially as compared with detail used to describe the character of an historical individual, see Jenny Davidson, "The 'Minute Particular' in Life-Writing and the Novel," *Eighteenth-Century Studies* 48.3 (2015): 263–81.

85. Jane Austen, *Mansfield Park* (Oxford: Oxford UP, 2003), 23.

CHAPTER 1: Clarissa's Conjectural History

1. Samuel Richardson, *Clarissa*, ed. Angus Ross (1747–48; New York: Penguin, 1985), 62; Richardson, *Clarissa*, ed. Florian Stuber et al., 8 vols., *The Clarissa Project* (1751; New York: AMS, 1990), 8:210. For ease of access, I quote from the Penguin edition in the text, citing both that edition and the corresponding page of the AMS reprint of the 3rd edition when possible. Further citations will be in the text.

2. James Boswell, *The Life of Samuel Johnson*, ed. R. W. Chapman and Pat Rogers (Oxford: Oxford UP, 1998), 480.

3. See Michael McKeon, *The Origins of the English Novel*, 15th anniversary ed. (1987; Baltimore: 2002); Catherine Gallagher, "The Rise of Fictionality," in *The Novel*, vol. 1: *History Geography and Culture*, ed. Franco Moretti, 2 vols. (Princeton: Princeton UP, 2006), 1:336–63; 342; Gallagher, *Nobody's Story: The Vanishing Acts of Women Writers in the Marketplace* (Berkeley: U of California P, 1994); and John Bender, "Enlightenment Fiction and the Scientific Hypothesis," "Practices of Enlightenment," special issue of *Representations* 61 (1998): 6–28, reprinted in *Ends of Enlightenment* (Stanford: Stanford UP, 2012). The quoted phrase is from Bender, 10.

4. In emphasizing this point, I break with the understanding of *Clarissa's* testing of maxims advanced by Hilary M. Schor, whose reading of Richardson's novel proceeds along parallel lines but arrives at quite a contrary conclusion. *Curious Subjects: Women and the Trials of Realism* (Oxford: Oxford UP, 2013). Schor's book is an insightful (and engagingly written) example of the experience-attained (which is to say, curiosity satisfied) paradigm that this study pushes against.

5. Anna's encomia to Clarissa balloon in the third edition. Incidentally, Richardson's use of "should-be" here predates the first *OED* entry, currently dated to 1790.

6. John Dennis, *The Grounds of Criticism in Poetry* (1704), in *John Milton: The Critical Heritage*, ed. John T. Shawcross, vol. 1, *1628–1731* (London: Routledge, 1999), 128. This endorsement of originality as individual creativity is an earlier statement of a position usually associated with Edward Young's "Conjectures on Original Composition" (1759).

7. For a nuanced argument about the novel's growth alongside emerging models of skeptical historiography, see Everett Zimmerman, *The Boundaries of Fiction: History and the Eighteenth-Century British Novel* (Ithaca: Cornell UP, 1996).

8. Gallagher, "The Rise of Fictionality," 342.

9. Aristotle, *Poetics*, trans. Richard Janko (Indianapolis: Hackett, 1987), 12. Such a distinction between historical and poetic character arises repeatedly in the accounts eighteenth-century au-

thors give of their projects. The most famous, perhaps, is Henry Fielding's: "I declare here, once for all, I describe not Men but Manners; not an Individual, but a Species." *Joseph Andrews*, ed. Martin C. Battestin (Middleton, CT: Wesleyan UP,1987), 189. The significance of Aristotle's distinction cannot be overstated. As McKeon makes clear, "The Aristotelian separation of history and poetry, the factual and the probable, the singular and the universal, is a revolutionary doctrine of great antiquity that lay like a time bomb in the cultural unconscious of the West until its 'discovery' by Renaissance modernity. . . . In the later eighteenth century, the rejuvenated Aristotelian notion of the universal truth of poetry will aid in the formulation of the modern belief in the autonomous realm of the aesthetic" (119).

10. Ian Watt, *The Rise of the Novel: Studies in Defoe, Richardson, and Fielding* (Berkeley: U of California P, 1959), 14.

11. It is important for the purposes of my argument to distinguish between conjectural and natural history, though the terms are sometimes used interchangeably (as in reference to Hume's *The Natural History of Religion* [1757]). I associate natural history with the writings of the Royal Society and the emergence of a "strange therefore true" topos of narrative historicity. See McKeon, esp. 47. On the contrary, conjectural history's emphasis on the most *simple* narrative path marginalized or eliminated the aberrant or unnatural. For a helpful discussion of conjectural history's place in Enlightenment intellectual history, see Mary Poovey, "From Conjectural History to Political Economy," in her *A History of the Modern Fact* (Chicago: U of Chicago P, 1998). While some texts referred to as conjectural were rooted in proto-anthropological accounts (which were intended to undergird a stadial theory of history), I am focusing here on those, like Rousseau's below, that disavowed empirical observation as a basis for conjecturalism.

12. Dugald Stewart, "Account of the Life and Writings of Adam Smith," introduction to Adam Smith, *Essays on Philosophical Subjects* (London: Cadell and Davies, 1795), xlvi. In part because Stewart gives the project its name, many scholars, including Poovey, associate the term "conjectural history" with the Scottish Enlightenment only; I maintain that the term usefully names a form found outside that particular movement and, indeed, outside of what we now think of as philosophical writing.

13. Historian Mark Salber Phillips locates the appeal of conjectural history in its change of scope: "The philosophical and conjectural histories that were such a marked feature of the Enlightenment were generally thought to promise a deeper understanding of the past than conventional narratives of statecraft, a claim that was principally based on the longer perspectives opened up by philosophical judgment." *Society and Sentiment: Genres of Historical Writing in Britain, 1740–1820* (Princeton: Princeton UP, 2000), 27.

14. In this respect, we might say that critics who have understood Clarissa to be participating in a project of religious typology are correct though they do not go far enough. For such a typological reading, see Paul J. Korshin, *Typologies in England, 1650–1820* (Princeton: Princeton UP, 1982). In quite another vein, Robin Valenza notes the novel's rumination on the proleptic: "*Clarissa* itself—Clarissa herself—is ultimately about the anticipation of a foregone conclusion." "How Literature Becomes Knowledge: A Case Study," *ELH* 76.1 (2009): 215–245; 232.

15. On counterfactual history, see Catherine Gallagher, *Telling It Like It Wasn't: The Counterfactual Imagination in History and Fiction* (Chicago: U of Chicago P, 2018).

16. Jean-Jacques Rousseau, "Discourse on the Origin of Inequality" in *The Discourses and Other Early Political Writings*, ed. Victor Gourevitch (Cambridge: Cambridge UP,2003), 161.

17. Rousseau, 125.

18. What these narratives could not do was solve what Hume would later identify as the problem of *induction*. As Poovey tells us, conjectural history gets its name only *after* Hume has called its very project into question, thereby necessitating its defense; "before the last quarter of the eighteenth century, British philosophers [and, I would add, many on the Continent] generally did

not admit the role conjecture played in their method, for it simply did not seem unreasonable either to postulate an origin for society or to deduce from this postulate how things that could not be observed were 'likely to have proceeded, from the principles of their nature'" (222). How, then, were these postulates determined to begin with? "A combination of introspection and assumptions about providential design and the laws of human nature" (223).

19. Rousseau, 132. Bender likewise cites Rousseau's justification of his conjectural project, taking the second discourse as an example of "the instability of the very edifice of scientific factuality that the novel may be seen as underwriting" (18). I would take Bender a step further; I understand Rousseau to mark a significant articulation of a more pervasive experiment (pun intended) with anti-empiricism—the "instability" threatens, here, to break down entirely. Moreover, I contend that Rousseau learns this gambit from *Clarissa*.

20. Rousseau, 132.

21. For a discussion of Rousseau's indebtedness to Richardson, see David Marshall, *The Frame of Art: Fictions of Aesthetic Experience, 1750–1815* (Baltimore: Johns Hopkins UP, 2005), esp. 91–126. It is likely that novels like *Clarissa* and conjectural histories shared readers. Phillips notes that some contemporary programs outlining what young women should read saw conjectural history as more relevant to girls' experience than conventional history: "The customs of primitive Britons, or the introduction of civilization into England appear far removed from cloistered female interest or experience. But these topics are not taken in isolation; rather they stand in implicit counterpoint to another kind of history writing whose preoccupations were seen as exclusively public and male. Paradoxically, then, in the library of female reading, the primitive Briton stood closer to the interests of women than a contemporary dispute over parliamentary politics" (113).

22. Joanna Picciotto reminds us that the idea of objectivity is likewise founded in the epistemological privileging of innocence; see *Labors of Innocence in Early Modern England* (Cambridge, MA: Harvard UP, 2010).

23. Recently, Jonathan Farina has made a similar claim to conjectural history's relationship to the novel, though he focuses on narrators of Victorian fiction. See "'Dickens's as If': Analogy and Victorian Virtual Reality," *Victorian Studies* 53 (2011): 427–36.

24. See Frank Palmeri, "Satire, Conjectural History, and the Bildungsroman, 1720–1795," in *Satire, History, Novel* (Cranbury, NJ: U of Delaware P, 2003), 153–77; and Palmeri, *States of Nature, States of Society: Enlightenment Conjectural History and Modern Social Discourse* (New York: Columbia UP, 2016).

25. Jean Starobinski, *Jean-Jacques Rousseau: Transparency and Obstruction* (Chicago: U of Chicago P, 1988), 19.

26. For a compelling reading of Anna and Clarissa's relationship as Sapphic, see Susan S. Lanser, *The Sexuality of History: Modernity and the Sapphic, 1565–1830* (Chicago: U of Chicago Press, 2014).

27. Aunt Harman's status as a mere device is compounded by her role at the end of the novel; it is her poor health (she is "in a declining way") that prevents Anna from visiting Clarissa on her deathbed (1087).

28. The reader Richardson refers to here is usually identified as Colley Cibber. See the headnote to this preface in Thomas Keymer, ed., *Richardson's Published Commentary on Clarissa* (London: Pickering & Chatto, 1998). Keymer reads a soft but snide pun on "experience" in the preface as a reference to Cibber's noted promiscuity. Richardson's elision of life experience and moral corruption is of central importance to my argument here.

29. Samuel Johnson, *Rambler* 4, 31 March 1750, *The Works of Samuel Johnson*, vol. 3, ed. W. J. Bate and Albrecht B. Strauss (New Haven: Yale UP, 1969), 21.

30. Richardson to Aaron Hill, letter of 5 January 1747, quoted in T. C. Duncan Eaves and Ben D. Kimpel, "The Composition of *Clarissa* and Its Revision before Publication," *PMLA* 83 (1968): 423.

31. J. Paul Hunter, *Before Novels: The Cultural Contexts of Eighteenth-Century English Fiction* (New York: W. W. Norton, 1992), 43.

32. See, for example, Martha J. Koehler, *Models of Reading: Paragons and Parasites in Richardson, Burney, and Laclos* (Cranbury, NJ: Rosemont, 2005), esp. 37–59.

33. Anna Laetitia Barbauld, "On the Origin and Progress of Novel-Writing," preface to *The British Novelists*, vol. 1 (London: 1810), 54.

34. See Ralph W. Rader's rather different account of the movement from Richardson to Austen (via Burney) in "From Richardson to Austen: 'Johnson's Rule' and the Eighteenth-Century Novel of Moral Action," in *The Novel: An Anthology of Criticism and Theory, 1900–2000*, ed. Dorothy J. Hale (Malden, MA: Blackwell, 2006), 140–53.

35. Frances Burney, *Evelina: Or, a History of a Young Lady's Entrance into the World* (Oxford: Oxford UP, 2002). For an account of the role that the ingénue plays in the development of social critique over the eighteenth century from satire to the novel, including Burney's *Evelina*, see Ronald Paulson, *Satire and the Novel in Eighteenth-Century England* (New Haven: Yale UP, 1967).

36. The novel's full title is *Clarissa, or The History of a Young Lady: Comprehending the Most Important Concerns of Private Life, and Particularly Shewing the Distresses that May Attend the Misconduct both of Parents and Children in Relation to Marriage.*

37. On Clarissa's explanations of her actions, see Jonathan Kramnick, *Actions and Objects from Hobbes to Richardson* (Stanford: Stanford UP, 2010).

38. See John Cleland, *Memoirs of a Woman of Pleasure*, ed. Peter Sabor (1748; Oxford: Oxford UP, 1999). And compare Ruth Yeazell's compelling reading of Fanny Hill's modesty in *Fictions of Modesty: Woman and Courtship in the Novel* (Chicago: U of Chicago Press, 1991), 102–21.

39. Watt, 229. For an argument that challenges Watt's reading of Clarissa's problematically opaque depths, see Wendy Anne Lee, "A Case for Hard-Heartedness: *Clarissa*, Indifference, Impersonality," *Eighteenth-Century Fiction* 26.1 (2013): 33–65.

40. See Gerald Prince, *A Dictionary of Narratology* (Lincoln: 1987); Prince, "The Disnarrated," *Style* 22 (1988): 1–8; Robyn Warhol, "Neonarrative; or, How to Render the Unnarratable in Realist Fiction and Contemporary Film," *A Companion to Narrative Theory*, ed. James Phelan and Peter J. Rabinowitz (Malden, MA: Blackwell, 2005), 220–31. Outside of narratology proper, these categories were discussed earlier by D. A. Miller in *Narrative and Its Discontents: Problems of Closure in the Early Novel* (Princeton: Princeton UP, 1981), though this is seldom acknowledged in recent work on the subject. Miller writes, "What leaves a novelist speechless is not always what makes him happiest, and there is a wide spectrum of ways in which a novel may characterize the function of the nonnarratable" (3–4). See also the forum in *Representations* 98 (2007), edited by Gallagher, on "Counterfactual Realities."

41. See Marie-Laure Ryan, *Possible Worlds, Artificial Intelligence, and Narrative Theory* (Bloomington: Indiana UP 1991); and Hilary Dannenberg, *Coincidence and Counterfactuality* (Lincoln: U of Nebraska P, 2008).

42. Of course, Clarissa's account of things is *morally* privileged by most readers, even if it is not based on a perception that is understood to be *ontologically* true. That this can be possible, even obvious, is of central interest to this chapter, and, indeed, to the book as a whole.

43. Dannenberg, 14.

44. "A novel is a work which offers the reader a focal illusion of characters acting autonomously as if in the world of real experience within a subsidiary awareness of an underlying constructive authorial purpose which gives their story an implicit and affective force which real

world experience does not have." Ralph Rader, "The Emergence of the Novel in England: Genre in History vs. History of Genre," *Narrative* 1 (1993): 72.

45. Terry Castle, *Clarissa's Ciphers* (Ithaca: Cornell UP, 1982), 101.

46. Miller, 153.

47. On inexperience as morally privileged, see Johnson, who casts real-world experience as a moral liability: "That observation which is called knowledge of the world, will be found much more frequently to make men cunning than good." *Rambler* No. 4, in *Essays from the* Rambler, Adventurer, *and* Idler, ed. W. J. Bate (New Haven: Yale UP, 1968), 11. My claim here is not that depictions of the novice are not didactic but rather that they are more than simply didactic—or, to put it another way, that the category of the didactic is amenable to formal analysis despite our (understandable) modern distaste for it.

48. Alex Woloch, *The One versus the Many* (Princeton: Princeton UP, 2003), 43.

49. Critics of *Clarissa* have tended to overlook Rosebud; however, Charlotte Sussman has similarly pointed to the way that a minor female character in *Pamela* serves to complicate our understanding of the heroine's narrative. " 'I Wonder Whether Poor Miss Sally Godfrey Be Living or Dead': The Married Woman and the Rise of the Novel," *diacritics* 20.1 (1990): 88–102. See also Lois A. Chaber on doubling in Richardson, especially as it rises to the level of self-awareness on the part of Richardson's characters. " 'Sufficient to the Day': Anxiety in Sir Charles Grandison," *Eighteenth-Century Fiction* 1:4 (1989), 291. Chaber is throughout interested in questions that are also central to the present chapter, especially regarding Richardson's use of "the language of possibility, of conditionality, of statement contrary to fact" (293). The actual difference between Clarissa and Rosebud is, of course, a difference of class. Clarissa is effectively making an anti-Pamelist argument here—that is, an argument that assumes more knowingness of a young girl from a lower social class.

50. Compare Pamela's "metamorphos[is]" in her "homespun" country clothes and Harriet Byron's "Arcadian princess" costume in the opening masquerade of *Sir Charles Grandison*. Note especially Harriet's concern that her ornate costume, with its Venetian mask, is not authentically rustic, "it falls not within my notions of the pastoral dress of Arcadia." See Samuel Richardson, *Pamela*, ed. Thomas Keymer and Alice Wakely (Oxford: Oxford UP, 2008), 55; and Richardson, *The History of Sir Charles Grandison*, 3 vol., ed. Jocelyn Harris (Oxford: Oxford UP, 1972), 1:115.

51. Dorothy Van Ghent, *The English Novel: Form and Function* (New York: Harper and Row, 1953), 62. For a trenchant examination of responses to Clarissa's rape, see Sue Warrick Doederlein, "Clarissa in the Hands of the Critics," *Eighteenth-Century Studies* 16 (1983): 401–14.

52. The act of penetration, resonating as it does with the activity of hermeneutics, was central for the poststructuralist preoccupation with Richardson's novel. See Castle; Terry Eagleton, *The Rape of Clarissa: Writing, Sexuality, and Class Struggle in Samuel Richardson* (Minneapolis: U of Minnesota P, 1982); and William Warner, *Reading "Clarissa": The Struggles of Interpretation* (New Haven: Yale UP, 1979). Sandra Macpherson has provocatively argued that the key event in the novel is not Clarissa's rape but her murder, as the rape is merely the beginning of an inexorable action to which neither Clarissa nor Lovelace can put an end. My argument echoes Macpherson's both in its redirection away from the rape itself and also in its emphasis on the slowness (even approaching stasis) of the novel rather than the sudden eventfulness of the rape. See *Harm's Way: Tragic Responsibility and the Novel Form* (Baltimore: Johns Hopkins UP, 2010), esp. 60.

53. Frances Ferguson has written about the significance of Clarissa's unconsciousness and the difficulty it raises for readers who want to read the rape through a psychological lens. "Rape and the Rise of the Novel," *Representations* 20 (1987): 88–112; 100.

54. For an argument about the pervasiveness of sexual violence in the novel, one that, like this one, subordinates the penetrative act of rape to more momentous (because less *evental*) condi-

tions, see Kathleen Lubey, "Sexual Remembrance in *Clarissa*," *Eighteenth-Century Fiction* 29.2 (2016–17): 151–78. Lubey argues that, in *Clarissa*, "Richardson portrayed sexual imposition as an unforgettable, inescapable, dispersed social condition, and that he created a particular narrative strategy for making visible its capaciousness and gravity" (154).

55. Castle, 118.

56. As Ferguson puts it, "In her white dress and increasingly childlike body, [Clarissa] represents the difference between the bildungsroman, with its project of maturation, and the psychological novel, which can never get ahead, because its way of manifesting itself in the world is to make apparent its own subjection to a stipulated state—a legal infancy—that its conditional likings and wishes can strain against and contradict but never escape" ("Rape and the Rise," 107). Lately, following Ferguson, Macpherson and Jonathan Kramnick have redirected our attention away from questions about interiority and toward questions about agency and action. This work is truly exciting, and it forces us to rethink many of the commonplaces we have brought to our readings of early novels. My contention in this chapter is that, while attention to the vicissitudes of nonindividualized agency is crucial, our work on Clarissa's epistemology remains, at the same time, incomplete.

57. Susan Stewart, *On Longing* (Durham: Duke UP, 1984), x. "Long time a-dying" is a tag that recurs in *Clarissa* criticism without attribution. As far as I can tell, it is a slight modification from a review of a Victorian dramatic adaptation of the novel, wherein the reviewer points out the unsuitability of the novel's plot for the stage: "Clarissa is an unconscionable long time dying." Rev. of "Clarissa," by Robert Buchanan, *Saturday Review* 69 (15 February 1890): 198.

58. Clarissa repeatedly figures her inexperience as a kind of self-containment. "Let me wrap myself about in the mantle of my own integrity, and take comfort in my unfaulty intention," she writes to Anna (508). "I will, now that I have escaped from you, and that I am out of the reach of your mysterious desires, wrap myself up in my own innocence (and then she passionately folded her arms about herself)," Lovelace reports (797). Clarissa's is a fantasy of chrysalid autonomy; her innocence is self-enclosing, even tautological—symbolized ultimately (and rather heavy-handedly, perhaps) by the ouroboros (the snake biting its own tail) that she inscribes on her coffin.

59. See Frances Ferguson, "Jane Austen, Emma, and the Impact of Form" *Modern Language Quarterly* 61 (2000): 157–80.

60. "And let me speak to th' yet unknowing world / How these things came about," Horatio says, before distilling Hamlet's narrative into a scant few lines. William Shakespeare, *Hamlet*, in *The Norton Shakespeare*, ed. Stephen Greenblatt (New York: W. W. Norton, 2008), 5.2.323–24.

61. The more plausible explanation is that this is a rather clumsy insertion on Richardson's part. Anna does venture that the remark was "written, I suppose, at some calamitous period *after* the day named in it" (1472; 8:322)

62. Richardson returns to this possibility of complete narrative foreclosure at the very end of the novel as well, adding in a footnote to Anna's final letter: "In [Clarissa's] Common-place book, she has the following note upon the recollection of this illness . . . [Would to Heaven I had died in it!]" (8.322).

63. Rader, "From Richardson to Austen," 145.

64. Ann Kibbie, "The Estate, the Corpse, and the Letter: Posthumous Possession in *Clarissa*," *ELH* 74 (2007): 127.

65. Kibbie, 124.

66. William Blackstone, *The Commentaries on the Laws of England*, 4 vols. (Oxford: 1765–1769), 1:128.

67. On Clarissa's Puritanism, see Cynthia Griffin Wolff, *Samuel Richardson and the Eighteenth-Century Puritan Character* (Hampden, CT: Archon Books, 1972).

68. It is worth noting here Richardson's interest in the possibility of a Protestant convent system that would provide an option for unmarried women. This is expounded upon at length in *Sir Charles Grandison.*

69. Most noteworthy in Wolff's review of Puritan diary-keeping practices is her emphasis on the character function of repeated entries, "Form and characterization merged. Recurrent events became important *because* they were recurrent; their very frequency indicated something about the narrator's life just as his reactions to them gradually revealed the inner self" (32).

70. Watt, 212.

CHAPTER 2: When Experience Matters (and When It Doesn't)

1. In an often-quoted evaluation, Coleridge considered *Tom Jones* (along with Ben Jonson's *The Alchemist* and Sophocles's *Oedipus Rex*) among "the most perfect plots ever planned." "Notes on Tom Jones," in *Table Talk and Omniana,* ed. Thomas Ashe (London: G. Bell and Sons, 1884), 295. For dissenting views, see F. R. Leavis, *The Great Tradition: George Eliot, Henry James, Joseph Conrad* (New York: New York UP, 1964); and David Goldknopf, "The Failure of Plot in Tom Jones," *Criticism* 11 (1969): 262–74. The Chicago school of neo-Aristotelian critics can be credited with keeping the plot of *Tom Jones* in critical focus; see R. S. Crane, "The Concept of Plot and the Plot of *Tom Jones*" in *Critics and Criticism,* ed. Crane (Chicago: U of Chicago P, 1952), 616–47; Sheldon Sacks, *Fiction and the Shape of Belief: A Study of Henry Fielding, with Glances at Swift, Johnson, and Richardson* (Berkeley: U of California P, 1964); and Ralph Rader, "*Tom Jones*: The Form in History," in *Ideology and Form in Eighteenth-Century Literature,* ed. David H. Richter (Lubbock: Texas Tech UP, 1999), 47–74.

2. That said, readers these days may be less surprised by the idea of a sentimental Fielding because of the influence of the work of Claudia L. Johnson, whose *Equivocal Beings: Politics, Gender, and Sentimentality in the 1790s* persuasively argued that sentimentalism's showy tears are the work of conservative masculinity (Chicago: U of Chicago P, 1995). Building on Johnson's work, Paul Kelleher has argued for a sentimental Fielding, who "represents male heterosexual passion as a source—perhaps *the* source, of moral judgment and ethical conduct." *Making Love: Sentiment and Sexuality in Eighteenth-Century British Literature* (Lewisburg: Bucknell UP, 2015), 170. Kelleher also offers a useful overview of the critical debate surrounding Fielding's sentimentalism. I depart from Kelleher's reading most clearly when it comes to attention to plot; where he sees the coincidence of sex and goodness contorted by the demands of the courtship plot into Tom's "self-mastery" (185), I see both Tom's lust and goodness as stemming from an inexperience that is maintained throughout the novel.

Likewise building on Johnson, see Sandra Macpherson, who pointedly distances *Tom Jones* from Richardson's project by revealing the comic mode to be essentially masculinist in its interest in exoneration rather than blame. "Fighting Men," in *Harm's Way: Tragic Responsibility and the Novel Form* (Baltimore: Johns Hopkins UP, 2010). I am also interested in the masculinist exoneration Fielding sets in motion, but I see more continuity between Fielding and Richardson than does Macpherson.

3. Claude Rawson, *Henry Fielding (1707–1754): Novelist, Playwright, Journalist, Magistrate* (Newark: Delaware UP, 2008), 109. The phrase "Conservation of Character" appears in Fielding's *Jonathan Wild* (1743); John S. Coolidge offers the classic account of this dramatic principle in Fielding: "Fielding and 'Conservation of Character,'" *Modern Philology* (1960): 245–59. For an important debate about the ideological implications of character consistency in Fielding's final novel, *Amelia,* see Patricia Meyer Spacks, "Female Changelessness, or, What Do Women Want," *Studies in the Novel* 19 (1987): 273–83; the response by David H. Richter, introduction, *Ideology and Form in Eighteenth-Century Literature,* ed. Richter (Lubbock: Texas Tech UP, 1999); and, fi-

nally, Spacks's response to Richter, "Ideology and Form: Novels at Work," in Richter, ed. *Ideology and Form in Eighteenth-Century Literature*.

4. See Simon Goldhill, "On Knowingness," *Critical Inquiry* 32.4 (2006): 708–23. In his playful and engaging essay, Goldhill both argues that knowingness falls outside of the (Platonic) binary of knowledge versus belief and proposes that understanding knowingness may help us move past this politically suspect binary. I am grateful to Jonah Siegal for drawing my attention to this essay.

5. Henry Fielding, *The History of Tom Jones*, ed. R. P. C. Mutter (New York: Penguin, 1985), 138. Further references to this edition will be cited parenthetically in the text.

6. Eve Kosofsky Sedgwick, *The Epistemology of the Closet* (Berkeley: U of California P, 1990), 73.

7. Like most things when it comes to sex, the idea that sex makes us stupid is thoroughly gendered, as we shall see with more specificity later in the chapter. I am reminded of the *Seinfeld* episode "The Abstinence," in which a break from sex makes Jerry and George into veritable rocket scientists while Elaine finds herself barely able to string a sentence together (episode 143).

8. More is going on here than simply the misogyny that suggests that women use their feminine wiles to lure unsuspecting men into positions of material and affective obligation (though there is certainly that, too). While Tom isn't knowing, Fielding's narrator certainly is, as critics have long noted. We need only think of the business surrounding Sophia's muff—double entendre is a verbal wink—to understand how Fielding manages both the distance between his narrator and protagonist and, moreover, the clubby, we might even say *locker-room*, camaraderie between narrator and presumably (at least, *potentially*) knowing reader. Inasmuch as Fielding's narrator takes knowingness beyond the realm of sex, he attempts to create for the reader the condition of knowingness by purporting to tell us the ending first: Tom is born to be hanged. The narrator returns to this information repeatedly in order to remind us of what we know, to cultivate in us the condition of knowingness. Only by the novel's ending is this particular procedure unraveled.

9. Tiffany Potter, *Honest Sins: Georgian Libertinism and the Plays and Novels of Henry Fielding* (Montreal: McGill-Queen's UP, 1999), 119, 6.

10. John Wilmot, Lord Rochester, "A Satyr against Reason and Mankind," in *Selected Poems*, ed. Paul Davis (Oxford: Oxford UP, 2013), lines 96–97.

11. Natalia Cecire, "An ABC of Puerility: Anderson, Britten, Crane," *New Inquiry*, 26 June 2012, https://thenewinquiry.com/blog/an-a-b-c-of-puerility-anderson-britten-crane/.

12. Samuel Johnson, *Rambler* No. 4 in *Essays from the "Rambler," "Adventurer," and "Idler,"* ed. W. J. Bate (New Haven: Yale UP, 1968), 13.

13. Johnson, *Rambler* No. 4, 12. The pun on "promiscuous" is, alas, not period. (The word as applied to the indiscriminate taking on of sexual partners dates to 1804 according to the *OED*.)

14. See Ian Watt, "Fielding as Novelist: *Tom Jones*," in *The Rise of the Novel* (Berkeley: U of California P, 1959), 260–89.

15. James Boswell, *Life of Johnson* (Oxford: Oxford UP, 1998), 389.

16. We might think of Fielding as observing quite a different kind of "uncounted experience" when compared to those that Anne-Lise François describes as "recessive action that takes itself away as it occurs." *Open Secrets: The Literature of Uncounted Experience* (Stanford: Stanford UP, 2008), xvi. Fielding notes that certain bold, seemingly decisive acts come nevertheless not to count, whereas François is interested in those experiences that tend never to come to our notice to begin with.

17. Watt is representative in reading this scene as an incident of Sophia acting out of character: "Sophia accepts Tom, and we are surprised by her very sudden and unexplained reversal" (274). For an essay that is noteworthy not only for its persuasive response to Watt's claim but also for its careful close reading of the proposal scene, see Michael Bell, "A Note on Drama and the Novel: Fielding's Contribution," *Novel: A Forum on Fiction* 3 (1970): 119–28. For quite a different

account of acting "out of character," see Sara Ahmed, "Willful Parts: Problem Characters or the Problem of Character," *New Literary History* 42.2 (2011): 231–53.

18. Martin C. Battestin, "Fielding's Definition of Wisdom: Some Functions of Ambiguity and Emblem in *Tom Jones*," *ELH* 35 (1968): 188–217; 206. A version of this essay later appeared in *The Providence of Wit: Aspects of Form in Augustan Literature and the Arts* (Charlottesville: U of Virginia P, 1974). Throughout Fielding scholarship, this tendency is clear in the ubiquitous identification of Sophia with wisdom by means of grammar of punctuation rather than through argumentation or demonstration (e.g., "Sophia or wisdom," "Sophia (wisdom)," "Sophia = wisdom"). See, among others, Peter Jan de Voogd, *Henry Fielding and William Hogarth: The Correspondence of the Arts* (Amsterdam: Rodopi, 1981); Brian McCrea, *Impotent Fathers: Patriarchy and Demographic Crisis in the Eighteenth-Century Novel* (Cranbury, NJ: Associated University Presses, 1998); and Homer Obed Brown, *Institutions of the English Novel: From Defoe to Scott* (Philadelphia: U of Pennsylvania P, 1998). I am not, of course, arguing that the name Sophia does not etymologically refer to wisdom, but I am cautioning against allegorical readings of the novel that tend to ignore the less wise, less prudent, aspects of Sophia's character.

19. To my mind, the best reading of *Tom Jones* as lingering in the tradition of romance is Scott Black's. See "The Adventures of Love in *Tom Jones*," in *Henry Fielding in Our Time*, ed. J. A. Downie (Cambridge: Cambridge Scholars Press, 2008), 27–50. While I join Black in looking for a return of formalist Fielding criticism, I am less willing (as will become clear) to call Fielding's formalism romance. This is in no small part due to the fact that I am wary of ceding the novel form to historicist approaches.

20. We might in this respect consider Sophia to be offering a complement to Tom's own powers of social observation, due in part to his illegitimacy. See Wolfram Schmidgen, "Illegitimacy and Social Observation: The Bastard in the Eighteenth-Century Novel," *ELH* 69 (2002): 133–66.

21. For a very different account of the function of prudence in the novel, see Battestin.

22. Robert D. Hume has recently argued that critics have paid too much attention to the rivalry between Richardson and Fielding, but his argument is largely that the real-world contact between the two men was limited. While this is a crucial biographical point, I nevertheless agree with those critics who find comparing the works of the two authors to illuminate (especially) the formal developments of the novel in midcentury. See Hume, "Fielding at 300: Elusive, Confusing, Misappropriated, or (Perhaps) Obvious?," *Modern Philology* 108 (2010): 224–62.

23. On the increasing dominance of fiction in this period and the emergence of fiction as a concept, see Catherine Gallagher, "The Rise of Fictionality," in *The Novel*, vol. 1: *History, Geography, and Culture*, ed. Franco Moretti, 2 vols. (Princeton: Princeton UP, 2006), 336–63.

24. We might in this regard think of the problem of naïve virtue as epitomizing the intersection of what Michael McKeon calls questions of truth and questions of virtue. See McKeon, *The Origins of the English Novel*, 15th anniversary ed. (Baltimore: Johns Hopkins UP, 2002). McKeon is right to place questions of epistemological truth at the center of the development of the early novel. I am interested here, however, in Fielding's attention to the ways that truth appears to adhere differently in different circumstances—to persons of differing socioeconomic class, for example.

25. Eliza Haywood, *Anti-Pamela: Or Feign'd Virtue Detected*, in *Anti-Pamela* by Haywood and *Shamela* by Henry Fielding, ed. Catherine Ingrassia (Peterborough, ON: Broadview, 2004), 51. Compare Parson Oliver's objection in Fielding's *Shamela*: "Young Gentlemen are here taught, that to marry their mother's chambermaids, and to indulge the Passion of Lust, at the Expence of Reason and Common Sense, is an Act of Religion, Virtue and Honour; and, indeed, the surest Road to Happiness" (239).

26. Richardson's title page reads in part, "A Narrative Which has its Foundation in Truth, and at the same time that it agreeably entertains, by a variety of curious affecting Incidents, is divested of those images which, in too many pieces calculated for amusement only, tend to inflame the

minds they should instruct." Haywood, then, borrows Richardson's caution against a reaction that is emotionally intense where it should be reasoned, but she turns Richardson's point about didactic fiction into a warning about romantic love.

27. This idea that naïveté is easily simulated does not begin with Richardson's novel, of course, but *Pamela* is read by many contemporary critics as lending credence to such claims. Fielding himself had noted the potential resemblance of vice and virtue in an issue of the *Champion* published months before *Pamela* appeared: "Tho' Virtue and Wisdom be in Reality the Opposites to Folly and Vice, they are not so in Appearance. Indeed, it requires a nicer Eye to Distinguish them, than is commonly believed. The two latter are continually industrious to disguise themselves, and wear Habits of the former." *The Champion: Containing a Series of Papers Humorous, Moral, Political, and Critical*, 4 March 1740 (London: 1741), 329. In this chapter, I contend that Fielding's dispute with Richardson moves past this rather obvious warning about deceptive appearances to include a consideration of appearances so powerful that they retroactively alter the record.

28. Peter Shaw, *The Reflector* (London: 1752), 15. See also the discussion of Shaw in Thomas Keymer and Peter Sabor, *"Pamela" in the Marketplace: Literary Controversy and the Print Culture in Eighteenth-Century Britain and Ireland* (Cambridge: Cambridge UP, 2005), 8–9. Keymer and Sabor show, following A. D. McKillop, that Shaw's source was actually an earlier Danish text, Ludwig Holberg's *Moralske Tansker* (1744).

29. The importation of the word from the context of the farce seems pointed; the play's plot features a series of prostitutes who are encouraged to cry rape for political ends. For a valuable reading of the play that provides the foundation for an argument about Fielding's equivocal response to acts of sexual violence both in his own works and in his role as magistrate, see Simon Dickie, "Fielding's Rape Jokes," *Review of English Studies* 61 (2010): 572–90. A version of this essay appears in Dickie, *Cruelty and Laughter: Forgotten Comic Literature and the Unsentimental Eighteenth Century* (Chicago: U of Chicago P, 2011). *Shamela* was published anonymously, and Fielding never acknowledged having written it, though most scholars agree that he did. The use of the term "vartue" from Fielding's dramatic work is one clue toward the establishment of *Shamela's* authorship.

30. I borrow the term "Pamela media event" from William Beatty Warner's *Licensing Entertainment: The Elevation of Novel Reading in Britain, 1684–1750* (Berkeley: U of California P, 1998).

31. Fielding, *Joseph Andrews*, ed. Martin C. Battestin (Middletown, CT: Wesleyan UP, 1967), 77; Samuel Richardson, letter to Aaron Hill, 1741, in *Selected Letters*, ed. John Carroll (Oxford: Clarendon, 1964), 41. The once common idea that *Joseph Andrews* was initially written as something more akin to *Shamela*, but then took on a life of its own, has faced criticism from scholars who maintain that Fielding intended from the beginning to write a longer romantic history in the style of Cervantes. See Ronald Paulson, *Satire and the Novel in Eighteenth-Century England* (New Haven: Yale UP, 1967). My claim here is not that Fielding's intention changed over the course of his writing *Joseph Andrews* but simply that he responds to his source material in quite a different manner in this text than he does in *Shamela*.

32. See Fielding's astonishing letter to Richardson of 15 October 1748, excerpted in William C. Slattery, ed. *The Richardson-Stinstra Correspondence and Stinstra's Prefaces to* Clarissa (Carbondale: Southern Illinois UP, 1969), 33–34. The letter is remarkable not only for corroborating Fielding's *volta face* in terms of his esteem for Richardson; it also enacts a formal concession to Richardson's "writing to the moment" as a kind of cardiography. This is Fielding narrating his own response to the aftermath of Clarissa's rape: "Here my Terror ends, and my Grief begins, which the Cause of all my tumultuous Passions soon changes into Raptures of Admiration and Astonishment, by a Behaviour the most elevated I can possibly conceive, and which is at the same time most gentle, and most natural" (34).

33. Paulson notes the similarities between the characterization of Sophia and Clarissa, and

the obvious similarity of their early domestic incarcerations. *The Life of Henry Fielding: A Critical Biography* (London: Wiley-Blackwell, 2000), esp. 201–09.

34. Thomas Keymer, introduction to Henry Fielding, *Tom Jones* (New York: Penguin, 2005), xxi.

35. Compare this moment to a strikingly similar, though morally and emotionally inverted, moment in Thomas Hardy's *Tess of the D'Urbervilles* (1891). There, Angel Clare greets the news of Tess's sexual past with an insistence that knowledge of that past conjures an entirely new Tess with whom he has no connection: "O Tess, forgiveness does not apply to the case! You were one person; now you are another. My God—how can forgiveness meet such a grotesque—prestidigitation as that!" Hardy, *Tess of the D'Urbervilles*, ed. Scott Elledge (New York: W. W. Norton, 1991), 179. Again, character continuity—even identity— is questioned in light of the introduction of new information about that character's past; see also my brief discussion of Oedipus, below.

36. Battestin calls this scene "that crucial moment of self-awareness toward which the novel has been moving" (201).

37. Samuel Taylor Coleridge, from "Notes on *Tom Jones*," found in a 1773 edition signed with Coleridge's name, reprinted in *Notes and Lectures on Shakespeare and Some of the Old Poets and Dramatists with Other Literary Remains*, vol. 4 of *The Complete Works of Samuel Taylor Coleridge*, ed. W. G. T. Shedd, 7 vols. (New York: Harper, 1884), 881. Compare book 3, ch. 1 of *The History of Tom Jones, a Foundling*, where Fielding writes that he is giving the reader "an opportunity of employing that wonderful sagacity, of which he is master, by filling up these vacant spaces of time with his own conjectures."

38. Hilary P. Dannenberg, *Coincidence and Counterfactuality: Plotting Time and Space in Narrative Fiction* (Lincoln: U of Nebraska P, 2008), 52. See also Thomas G. Pavel, *Fictional Worlds* (Cambridge, MA: Harvard UP, 1986); and Marie-Laure Ryan, *Possible Worlds, Artificial Intelligence, and Narrative Theory* (Bloomington: Indiana UP, 1992).

39. Dannenberg, 52.

40. Deidre Lynch associates the extremity of Tom's case with his status as a gentleman who must be able to circulate freely among all other types; this fluidity is indicated physically by Tom's virtually nondescript "bland handsomeness." Lynch, *The Economy of Character* (Chicago: U of Chicago P, 1998), 82. I nevertheless contend that it is the ambiguity of Tom's class status that makes his identity accordingly ambiguous; the revelation of his status as gentleman goes some way toward solidifying this identity, though, as I will argue, it is Sophia's love that ultimately confirms this.

41. Fielding, *Joseph Andrews*, 32.

42. For a compelling reading of the Tom-as-ghost scene, see Ruth Mack, *Literary Historicity: Literature and Historical Experience in Eighteenth-Century Britain* (Stanford: Stanford UP, 2009), 74.

43. Fielding, *An Enquiry into the Causes of the Late Increase in Robbers, &c.*, 2nd ed. (London, 1751), 35–36.

44. Fielding, *Enquiry*, 93. It is worth remembering that such vices that were acceptable for wealthy men were nevertheless prohibited for women, regardless of class. See, for example, Eliza Haywood's *A Present for Women Addicted to Drinking, Adapted to All the Different Stations of Life, from a Lady of Quality to a Common Servant* (London: 1750). Haywood addresses her cautionary tales explicitly to young women entering the world, or, more accurately, to their advisors: "Therefore, Ladies, when you discant upon this Subject in your instructions to a young Woman, about to enter the World, you will engage her to run over in her Mind a few of these Consequences, whenever she is invited to pass an afternoon in the Country, I mean at a Publick House, to visit any of our Suburb Fairs, to make one in a Party to *Vaux-Hall*, to partake of the Pleasures of a riotous Christening, or to taste in private a Dram" (60). "Discant" is, to my ear, so close to "decant" as to suggest a satirical undercurrent to the project even before we consider the pleasures of a

"riotous Christening"; we might, on that note, consider the prolific novelist Haywood's recommendation of novel reading as a tonic substitution for drinking.

45. Jonathan Kramnick, *Actions and Objects from Hobbes to Richardson* (Stanford: Stanford UP, 2010), 91.

46. Nancy Armstrong, *Desire and Domestic Fiction: A Political History of the Novel* (Oxford: Oxford UP, 1987), 119.

47. "to fix, v.," def. 2b, *The Oxford English Dictionary*, 2nd ed., 1989; online ed. November 2016. Note the following example for this entry, from *Pride and Prejudice*'s Charlotte Lucas: "If a woman conceals her affection with the same skill from the object of it [as from the gossiping public], she may lose the opportunity of fixing him." Here, the always-reasonable Charlotte likewise understands "fix" to be similarly transitive: the work done by a woman to a man, in this case, through the proper negotiation of an affection that is just public enough.

48. Watt, 274.

49. Richardson, *Clarissa*, ed. Angus Ross (London: Penguin, 1985), 36.

50. Richardson reported to his friend Johannes Stinstra that Fielding "had been a zealous Contender for the Piece [*Clarissa*] ending, as it is called, happily" (qtd. in Slattery, 33). In other words, Fielding wanted Lovelace to be affected and reformed by Clarissa's suffering and for the two to marry at the end of the novel. As Richardson's sneering aside implies ("as it is called"), he thought a "reformed rake" ending to be antithetical to his aims in writing the novel. He was certainly not alone in such hopes, nor was he the only reader of the novel's early volumes to entreat Richardson to alter his plan. Richardson's friend Lady Bradshaigh sketched out an alternative ending where the rape is thwarted and Clarissa lives a single life. Her sister, Lady Echlin, wrote an even more elaborate version, where the rape is absent, Lovelace dies reformed, and Clarissa dies of grief soon after. See Lady Dorothy Bradshaigh, *The Annotations in Lady Bradshaigh's Copy of "Clarissa,"* ed. Janine Barchas with Gordon D. Fulton (Victoria: U of Victoria English Literary Studies, 1998); and Lady Elizabeth Echlin, *An Alternative Ending to Richardson's "Clarissa,"* ed. Dimiter Daphinoff (Bern: Francke Verlag, 1982).

CHAPTER 3: Simple and Sublime

1. C. J. Pitt, "The Age: A Poem Moral, Political, and Metaphysical, with Illustrative Annotations" (London: 1810), 209n1.

2. Markman Ellis, *The History of Gothic Fiction* (Edinburgh: Edinburgh UP, 2003), 29.

3. Ann Radcliffe, *The Italian, or, the Confessional of the Black Penitents: A Romance*, ed. Robert Miles (Oxford: Oxford UP, 2000), 91.

4. Radcliffe, *The Mysteries of Udolpho*, ed. Bonamy Dobrée (Oxford: Oxford UP, 2008), 319. Hereafter abbreviated *MU* and cited parenthetically within the text. See Jayne Lewis on the interpenetration of character and atmosphere in Radcliffe, where a heroine's "airs cannot be said to realize [her] 'as if' she were a person. But they do realize the air of as-ifness itself." *Air's Appearance: Literary Atmosphere in British Fiction, 1660–1794* (Chicago: Chicago UP, 2012), 227–28.

5. Horace Walpole, *The Castle of Otranto*, with Henry Mackenzie, *The Man of Feeling*, ed. Laura Mandell (New York: Longman, 2006), 7–8. Further references to this edition will be cited parenthetically in the text.

6. The best example of such a reading of Shakespeare's influence on Walpole is Cynthia Wall, "*The Castle of Otranto*: A Shakespeareo-Political Satire?," in *Historical Boundaries, Narrative Forms: Essays on British Literature in Honor of Everett Zimmerman* (Cranbury, NJ: Rosemont, 2007), 184–98. There, however, as in her book (*The Prose of Things: Transformations of Description in the Eighteenth Century* [Chicago: Chicago UP, 2006]), Wall is more interested in the objects found in Otranto than in the domestics who point to them. I will trouble this distinction below.

7. See Vladimir Propp, *The Morphology of the Folktale*, trans. Laurence Scott and Louis A. Wagner (Austin: U of Texas P, 1990), esp. the section "The Hero Acquires the Use of a Magical Agent," which includes as agents "objects possessing a magical property, such as cudgels, swords, guslas, balls, and many others" (44). See also Frances Ferguson's discussion of Propp and object-character in "Jane Austen, *Emma*, and the Impact of Form," *Modern Language Quarterly* 61.1 (2000): 157–80.

8. These characters are not, however, commonly read alongside each other. The final group, young women, has received considerably more critical attention, especially in work that considers Radcliffe to be the founder of what is known as the "female Gothic," as opposed to the "male Gothic" of Radcliffe's contemporary Matthew "Monk" Lewis. Ellen Moers was the first to coin the term "female Gothic" to describe the Radcliffean strain of novels featuring female protagonists; see "Female Gothic," in *Literary Women* (New York: Oxford UP, 1976), 90–98. See also Julianne Fleenor, ed., *The Female Gothic* (Montreal: Eden, 1983); Kate Ellis, *The Contested Castle: Gothic Novels and the Subversion of Domestic Ideology* (Urbana: U of Illinois P, 1989); Anne Williams, *Art of Darkness: A Poetics of Gothic* (Chicago: Chicago UP, 1995); Diane Hoeveler, *Gothic Feminism: The Professionalization of Gender from Charlotte Smith to the Brontës* (University Park: Pennsylvania State UP, 1988). As George E. Haggerty puts it, "Feminist readings of the Gothic have taught us to look deeply into the souls of Radcliffe's characters—more deeply than earlier Gothic critics had asked us to." *Unnatural Affections: Women and Fiction in the Later Eighteenth Century* (Bloomington: Indiana UP, 1998), 158. While I am sympathetic to the concerns that lead to such a deepening, I would also caution against readings that look for depth where it is pointedly absent, especially in the aligning of depth with the achievement of maturity over time.

9. Radcliffe, "On the Supernatural in Poetry," *New Monthly Magazine* 16 (1826): 145–52.

10. *MU*, 697n249.

11. Jane Austen, *Northanger Abbey*, with *Lady Susan*, *The Watsons*, and *Sanditon*, ed. James Kinsley and John Davie (Oxford: Oxford UP, 2008), 26.

12. It helps, perhaps, to note that the object was designed less for personal betterment than for punishment: "A member of the house of Udolpho, having committed some offence against the prerogative of the church, had been condemned to the penance of contemplating, during certain hours of the day, a waxen image, made to resemble a human body in the state, to which it is reduced after death" (*MU*, 662).

13. M. Ellis, 3.

14. Samuel Taylor Coleridge, rev. of *The Mysteries of Udolpho*, by Ann Radcliffe, *Critical Review* (August 1794): 361–72. This observation was fairly common; compare the 1796 reader quoted by Leah Price in *The Anthology and the Rise of the Novel*: "[Radcliffe's] plan of writing . . . raises expectations, which it never gratifies" ([Cambridge: Cambridge UP, 2003], qtd. 98).

15. See E. J. Clery, *The Rise of Supernatural Fiction, 1762–1800* (Cambridge: Cambridge UP, 1995); and D. L. Macdonald, "Bathos and Repetition: The Uncanny in Radcliffe," *Journal of Narrative Technique* 19.2 (1989): 197–204.

16. Ian Duncan, *Modern Romance and Transformations of the Novel: The Gothic, Scott, Dickens* (Cambridge: Cambridge UP, 1992), 37.

17. As in Walpole, servants in Radcliffe are agents of plot but also validations of the heroine's supernatural belief. Adeline's servant Annette, unlike Peter, and also unlike the servant to Emily St. Aubert in *Udolpho* (who bears the same name), appears infrequently in the novel, as if she were being introduced only to signal her absence. At the close of volume 1, Adeline, awaking from a series of especially vivid nightmares, is "almost determined to call Annette," only to have the thought disappear as quickly as the dreamscape (110). The novel's early climax comes when a frightened Adeline sleeps in Annette's room, only to find a secret passageway that contains the manuscript. If *Udolpho*'s Emily and *her* omnipresent Annette form two halves of a single naïve

figure, a Pamela cleft in twain (servant/heroine as servant-and-heroine), then Annette's virtual absence in *The Romance of the Forest* requires Adeline to bear even more of the burden of naïveté's narrative oscillations. Emily can, and does, seek validation of her perceptions from Annette (though we might justly question the precise value of such validation), but Adeline is nearly always on her own. This places considerably more pressure on the heroine's independent and unvalidated registration of Gothic phenomena.

18. See Duncan, 37; Duncan associates the tradition of the female *bildungsroman* with the novels of Samuel Richardson.

19. Radcliffe, *The Romance of the Forest*, ed. Chloe Chard (Oxford: Oxford UP, 2009), 31. Hereafter abbreviated *RF* and cited parenthetically in the text.

20. This scene of exposition, in other words, demonstrates what Eve Sedgwick has referred to as the significance of surface over depth in the Gothic novel; the mystery pervades without eliciting penetration. See Sedgwick, *The Coherence of Gothic Conventions* (New York: Arno, 1980).

21. On defamiliarization and wonder, see Sarah Tindal Kareem, *Eighteenth-Century Fiction and the Reinvention of Wonder* (Oxford: Oxford UP, 2014).

22. See *The Oxford English Dictionary*, s.v. "elastic," def. 3a, 2nd ed., 1989; online version March 2012: "Of material substances, whether solid, liquid, or gaseous: That spontaneously resumes (after a longer or shorter interval) its normal bulk or shape after having been contracted, dilated, or distorted by external force." While this definitely dates to the late seventeenth century, the metaphorical application to persons begins in the 1780s. "Plastic" suggests instead a permanent change in shape and has a considerably older provenance.

23. For critical works devoted to unpacking that influence, see Malcolm Ware, *Sublimity in the Novels of Ann Radcliffe* (Uppsala: Lindequist, 1963); David Hills Smith, *Edmund Burke and Ann Radcliffe: A Psychology of Nature and the Sublime* (Cambridge, MA: Harvard UP, 1969); and, from the wave of feminist reevaluation of Radcliffe, Anne K. Mellor, *Romanticism and Gender* (London: Routledge, 1993); and Elizabeth Bohls, *Women Travel Writers and the Language of Aesthetics, 1716–1818* (Cambridge: Cambridge UP, 1995). To my mind the best essay on Radcliffe's aesthetics, which offers a timely reconsideration of the feminist readings of the 1990s, is Jayne Lewis's " 'No Colour of Language': Radcliffe's Aesthetic Unbound," *Eighteenth-Century Studies* 39 (2006): 377–90.

24. Gerald Prince, *A Dictionary of Narratology* (Lincoln: U of Nebraska P, 1987), 19. See also Janice Hewlett Koelb, *The Poetics of Description: Imagined Places in European Literature* (New York: Palgrave Macmillan, 2006). For the classic Marxist privileging of narrative over description, see Georg Lukács, "Narrate or Describe?," in *Writer and Critic and Other Essays* (New York: Grosst & Dunlap, 1971), 110–48. A contrary view is offered by Ruth Ronan, "Description, Narrative and Representation," *Narrative* 5 (1997): 274–86. See also Cannon Schmidt, "Interpret or Describe?," "Description Across the Disciplines," special issue of *Representations* 135.1 (Summer 2016): 102–18. For more on description in Radcliffe specifically, see Lynne Epstein Heller, "Mrs. Radcliffe's Landscapes: The Influence of Three Landscape Painters on Her Nature Descriptions," *Hartford Studies in Literature* 1 (1969): 107–20; Charles C. Murrah, "Mrs. Radcliffe's Landscapes: The Eye and the Fancy," *University of Windsor Review* 18 (1984): 7–23.

25. See, esp., Lukács, though the association is, following him, quite commonly held.

26. Frances Ferguson, *Solitude and the Sublime: Romanticism and the Aesthetics of Individuation* (New York: Routledge, 1992), 37.

27. Edmund Burke, *A Philosophical Enquiry into the Origins of Our Ideas of the Sublime and the Beautiful*, ed. James T. Boulton (London: Routledge, 2008), 61–62.

28. In this sense, they are also ideal readers, since suspense requires suspension, the forestalling of satisfaction (in knowledge and experience). See Margaret Russett, "Narrative as Enchantment in *The Mysteries of Udolpho*," *ELH* 65 (1998): 159–86. I will return to this point below.

29. Ferguson, *Solitude*, 2. She continues, "The problem that arises for Burke's *Enquiry* is, then, that the mental images of past or future objects of experience clutter the tablet of experience to such an extent that one cannot differentiate the responses to objects from the response to one's representations of them" (2).

30. *OED*, s.v. "deceive, v.," def. 2c.

31. This sentiment is delivered in the narrative as speech, though Adeline appears to be speaking only to herself. The effect, then, is of a more formal declaration rather than mere musing.

32. Michel Foucault, "What Is an Author?," in *The Foucault Reader*, ed. Paul Rabinow (New York: Pantheon, 1980), 114.

33. Susie I. Tucker, *Protean Shape: A Study of Eighteenth-Century Vocabulary and Usage* (London: Bloomsbury, 2013), 119.

34. Hester Lynch Piozzi, *British Synonymy* (London: 1794), 1:86. See Ingrid Tieken-Boon van Ostade, *In Search of Jane Austen: The Language of the Letters* (Oxford: Oxford UP, 2014), 123. For a more precise (and more thorough) discussion of ingenuousness, see Helen Thompson, *Ingenuous Subjection: Compliance and Power in the Eighteenth-Century Domestic Novel* (Philadelphia: U of Pennsylvania P, 2005).

35. For example, the Marquis's observation, "It is the first proof of a superior mind to liberate itself from prejudices of country, or of education" (*RF*, 222). In this quite long speech, the Marquis is justifying murder. Sade, a contemporary of Radcliffe, predictably praises Lewis's *The Monk* as the best of Gothic fiction, even as he dismisses the genre's deployment of supernatural elements. See "An Essay on Novels," in *The Crimes of Love*, trans. David Coward (Oxford: Oxford UP, 2005), 3–19.

36. I refer here to R. F. Brissenden's classic study, *Virtue in Distress: Studies in the Novel of Sentiment from Richardson to Sade* (New York: Harper and Rowe, 1974).

37. Terry Castle, "The Spectralization of the Other in *The Mysteries of Udolpho*," in *The Female Thermometer: Eighteenth-Century Culture and the Invention of the Uncanny* (Oxford: Oxford UP, 1995), 124.

38. Castle, 123.

39. On Victorian interest in supernatural mediation, see Nicola Brown and Carolyn Burdett, eds., *The Victorian Supernatural* (Cambridge: Cambridge UP, 2004); and Sarah A. Willburn, *Possessed Victorians: Extra Spheres in Nineteenth-Century Mystical Writings* (Aldershot: Ashgate, 2006).

40. Unsigned review of *Harrington and Ormond, Tales*, by Maria Edgeworth, *British Review and London Critical Journal* 11 (1818): 48.

41. It might be helpful here to think about Radcliffe's own exclusion from the world (at least in the anecdotes about her life) as related to the depiction of retirement in the novels. See Claudia Johnson on Radcliffe's relationship to her historical moment: *Equivocal Beings: Politics, Gender, and Sentimentality; Wollstonecraft, Radcliffe, Burney, Austen* (Chicago: U of Chicago P, 1995), esp. 76.

42. Tobias Smollett, who possessed a rather poor command of Castillian, based his translation in large part on a literal translation by Alexander Pope's friend Charles Jarvis, published in 1742, which did retain the "Ingenious Knight" of the original. Even before it was published, Smollett's translation was widely regarded as amateurish. For reception and problems with the translation, see Carmine Rocco Linsalata, *Smollett's Hoax: Don Quixote in English* (Stanford: Stanford UP, 1956). Hester Lynch Piozzi also translated parts of Don Quixote into English at sixteen to practice her Spanish. See Marianna D'Enzio, *Hester Lynch Thrale Piozzi: A Taste for Eccentricity* (Cambridge: Cambridge Scholars, 2010), 3.

43. See Miriam Borham Puyal, "For the Amusement of the Merry Little Subjects: How British Children Met Don Quixote in the Long Eighteenth Century," *Anales Cervantinos* 47 (2015): 133–58.

44. Samuel Johnson, *Rambler* 2, 24 March 1750, in *The Works of Samuel Johnson*, vol. 3, ed. W. J. Bate and Albrecht B. Strauss (New Haven: Yale UP, 1969).

45. Henry Fielding, *The Covent Garden Journal*, Number 24 (March 24, 1752) in *The Criticism of Henry Fielding*, ed. Ioan Williams (London: Routledge, 1970), 191–92. Fielding makes a canny observation about the difference gender makes to quixotism: "Don Quixote is ridiculous in performing Feats of Absurdity himself; Arabella can only become so, in provoking and admiring the Absurdities of others."

46. See Catherine Gallagher, "The Rise of Fictionality," in *The Novel*, vol. 1, ed. Franco Moretti (Princeton: Princeton UP, 2006), 336–61.

47. Gallagher, 345–46.

48. Gallagher, 350.

49. Sarah Fielding, *The Adventures of David Simple*, ed. Peter Sabor (Lexington: UP of Kentucky, 1998), 35. This edition reprints the first edition of the novel, published in May 1744. Previous modern editions—including the widely used Oxford, edited by Malcolm Kelsell—instead reproduce the second edition (published just two months later), which featured a preface and extensive editing by Sarah's brother Henry.

50. Sarah Fielding, "Prologue to the Fifth Part," *The Cry: A New Dramatic Fable*, 3 vols. (London: 1754), 3:122.

51. Sarah Fielding, *The Cry*, 3:122.

52. Compare also Scott Paul Gordon, *The Practice of Quixotism: Postmodern Theory and Eighteenth-Century Women's Writing* (New York: Palgrave Macmillan, 2006).

53. Deidre Shauna Lynch also notices this in *The Economy of Character: Novels, Market Culture, and the Business of Inner Meaning* (Chicago: U of Chicago P, 1998), 130.

54. Deidre Shauna Lynch, "Gothic Fiction," in *The Cambridge Companion to Fiction in the Romantic Period*, ed. Richard Maxwell and Katie Trumpener (Cambridge: Cambridge UP, 2008), 47–64; 47. Compare Janice H. Radway's study of readers of modern romance novels, wherein she demonstrates that knowledge of the conventions of the genre serves only to reinforce the connection readers find there. *Reading the Romance: Women, Patriarchy, and Popular Culture* (Chapel Hill: U of North Carolina P, 1984). For a more general account of how readerly assumptions factor into reading practices, see Peter J. Rabinowitz, *Before Reading: Narrative Conventions and the Politics of Interpretation* (Columbus: Ohio State UP, 1998).

55. One line of literary criticism has looked askance at such readerly absorption. As Rachel Ablow describes it, according to Foucauldian literary criticism, especially of the Victorian novel, "readerly absorption has tended to be regarded as an insidious means by which we are interpellated into a social order." Introduction to *The Feeling of Reading: Affective Experience and Victorian Literature*, ed. Ablow (Ann Arbor: U of Michigan P, 2010), 1. The central text of this tradition is D. A. Miller's *The Novel and the Police* (Berkeley: U of California P, 1988).

56. Austen, 23. Here it is worth noting that Austen cannily suspends Catherine Morland alongside Emily; we never get to know what she thinks about her favorite novel's ending.

57. See William C. Slattery, ed., *The Richardson-Stinstra Correspondence and Stinstra's Prefaces to "Clarissa,"* (Carbondale: Southern Illinois UP, 1969), 6:158; cited in Deidre Shauna Lynch, "The Shandean Lifetime Reading Plan," in *The Work of Genre: Selected Essays from the English Institute* (Cambridge: English Institute, 2011).

CHAPTER 4: Frances Burney and the Appeals of Inexperience

1. "Kimmy Goes Outside!," *The Unbreakable Kimmy Schmidt*, directed by Tristram Shapeero (New York: Netflix, 2015). Each episode title is a breathless exclamation naming a new experience. While the darkness of Kimmy's background is clear from the outset, the show is somewhat elliptical about specifics. Only in season 3, episode 3 is the word "rape" used.

2. Hillary Busis, "Tina Fey and Robert Carlock talk *The Unbreakable Kimmy Schmidt*," January 7, 2015, https://www.ew.com/article/2015/01/07/unbreakable-kimmy-schmidt-tina-fey/.

3. Fred H. Goldner, "Pronoia," *Social Problems* 30.1 (October 1982): 82–91.

4. Henry Fielding, *The History of the Adventures of Joseph Andrews and of His Friend Mr. Abraham Adams* and *An Apology for the Life of Mrs. Shamela Andrews*, ed. Douglas Brooks-Davies (Oxford: Oxford UP, 2008), 19.

5. Sarah Fielding, *The Adventures of David Simple* and *Volume the Last*, ed. Peter Sabor (Lexington: U of Kentucky P, 1998), 8.

6. From scrap marked 2a/b in "Scraps: Plots Hints Dialogues— for *Camilla*," in MSS Arblay, housed in the New York Public Library's Berg Collection.

7. Frances Burney, *Camilla, or a Picture of Youth*, ed. Edward Bloom and Lillian D. Bloom (Oxford: Oxford UP, 2009), 7. All further references to the novel will be parenthetically cited.

8. Burney clearly wrestles with this language. A remarkably similar articulation can be found on the reverse of a manuscript page on which she drafts a preface for *Cecilia*: Back of second MS page: "the intricacies of the human heart are various as innumerable, + its feelings, upon all interesting occasions, are so minute + complex, as to baffle all the power of language" (British Library Egerton MS 3696).

9. Jacquetta Agneta Mariana Jenks [William Beckford], "Exordium Extraordinary" to *Azemia, a Descriptive and Sentimental Novel* (London: Sampson Low, 1797) ix–xii.

10. John 3.3. On the "new man" trope of rebirth in Methodist writing and its destabilization of identity, see Misty Anderson, *Imagining Methodism in Eighteenth-Century Britain: Enthusiasm, Belief, and the Borders of the Self* (Baltimore: Johns Hopkins UP, 2012).

11. Margaret Anne Doody, *Frances Burney: A Life in the Works* (New Brunswick: Rutgers UP, 1988), 220. Doody is one of the few critics to take seriously the ways that Burney's preface undermines attempts to read the novel as didactic.

12. Frances Burney, *The Wanderer; or Female Difficulties*, ed. Margaret Anne Doody, Robert L. Mack, and Peter Sabor (Oxford: Oxford UP, 2001), 8.

13. See the account in Burney's memoir of her father: "She was wholly unnoticed in the nursery for any talents or quickness of study: indeed, at eight years old she did not know her letters; and her brother, the tar, who in his boyhood had a natural genius for hoaxing, used to pretend to teach her to read; and gave her a book topsy-turvy, which he said she never found out!" Burney, *Memoirs of Doctor Burney, Arranged from His Own Manuscripts, from Family Papers, and from Personal Recollections*, 3 vols. (London: Edward Moxon, 1832), 2:168. This prolonged naturalness (contrasted with her brother's more malicious "natural genius for hoaxing") is complicated by the fact that young Fanny, shy and serious around company, was known as "The Old Lady" (168).

14. Doody, 21. While some have speculated that Burney may have been dyslexic, Doody dismisses these claims as unpersuasive.

15. Burney, *The Early Journals and Letters of Fanny Burney*, vol. 3, *The Streatham Years: Part I, 1778–1779*, ed. Lars E. Troide and Stewart J. Cooke (Montreal: McGill-Queen's UP, 1994), post 26 June 1779, p. 329.

16. This story is also recounted in the preface to *The Wanderer*, nestled in an oddly unelaborated footnote (5). She gives a bit more context in her journal, again explaining that this was communicated by Johnson, who told her "he [Burke] has talked very finely, indeed, about you! so finely, & in such Language, that you can do nothing better for *yourself*, than *die to Night*! for you *can* rise no higher, nor be more illustrious!—" Burney, writing to her sister, responds with considerable understatement: "This was solemn praise indeed!" Burney, *The Early Journals and Letters of Fanny Burney*, vol. 5, *1782–1783*, ed. Lars E. Troide and Stewart J. Cooke (Montreal: McGill-Queen's UP, 2012), December 1782, p. 196.

17. John Wilson Croker, review of *Memoir of Dr. Burney*, *Quarterly Review* 49 (1833): 97–125;

109. For more in the same vein, see Croker's review of *Diary and Letters of Mme D'Arblay, Quarterly Review* 70 (1842): 243–87. Croker is the notorious critic who was blamed by Keats' friends for hastening his death.

18. Croker, review of *Diary and Letters of Mme D'Arblay*, 255. Croker likely alludes here to a farce written by David Garrick: *Miss in Her Teens; or the Medley of Lovers* (1747).

19. While researching this chapter, I came across a remarkable self-published monograph that claims that the works of Jane Austen and Frances Burney are all *actually* the work of Austen's cousin (and later sister-in-law) Eliza Hancock (Madame la Comtesse de Feuillide). This (patently ludicrous) argument is, to a significant degree, founded on the supposition that Burney would have been, at the time of her novels' publication, too old to write youthful protagonists convincingly. That is, it launches something of the inverse of Croker's claim: while Croker believes Burney's maturity to account for the gifts of her novels (and thus render them unremarkable), this skeptical critic sees her as too old to have produced those same effects. See Nicholas Ennos, *Jane Austen: A New Revelation* (Leicester: Troubadour, 2013). Ennos—who is also a Holocaust denier and 9/11 truther—likewise argues that Austen, as an unmarried woman, could not have written so convincingly of marriage. The question of whether the representation of experience must be grounded in experience—a question not asked by conspiracy theorists alone—is of central interest to this book.

20. Here's Doody: " 'Fanny' is a patronizing diminutive. It makes the author sound the harmless, childish, priggish girl-woman that many critics want her to be—as if the heroine of *Mansfield Park* had set up as a novelist. Let her have an adult full name" (6).

21. Doody, 41.

22. Catherine Gallagher, *Nobody's Story: The Vanishing Acts of Women Writers in the Marketplace* (Berkeley: U of California P, 1994), 207.

23. Susan Fraiman, *Unbecoming Women: British Women Writers and the Novel of Development* (New York: Columbia UP, 1993), x.

24. British Library Egerton MS 3696, p. 58. In both cases, "culpable" is an addition, inserted over an illegible crossed-out word.

25. Likewise investigating the novel's publication history, Hilary Havens comes to essentially the opposite conclusion. For Havens, the draft version is more daring in its formal experimentation with the aftermath of the marriage plot. See "Revising the 'prose Epic': Frances Burney's *Camilla*," *The Age of Johnson* 22 (2012): 299–320. While Havens's archival research is impressive, my thinking about the published novel's defiance of *Bildung* leads me to side with Doody.

26. Julia Epstein, "Marginality in Frances Burney's Novels," in *The Cambridge Companion to the English Novel*, ed. John Richetti (Cambridge: Cambridge UP, 1996), 199.

27. Compare Lovelace's determination to "test" Clarissa's virtue. As he puts it to Belford: "But let me ask thee, is not calamity the test of virtue? and wouldst though not have me value this charming creature upon *proof* of her merits?—Do I not intend to reward her by marriage, if she stand that *proof?*" (emphasis in original). On the intersection of questions of truth and questions of virtue, see Michael McKeon, *The Origins of the English Novel, 1600–1740*, 15th anniversary edition (Baltimore: Johns Hopkins UP, 2002).

28. As critics have noted, this introduction of the necessity of proof into a relationship already founded on mutual affection raises the specter of *Othello*, with Marchmont playing a version of Iago. This reference is literalized later in the novel, when Camilla attends a production of the play. Fittingly, given the novel's aversion to closure, she misses the ending.

29. Though Camilla is of respectable birth, the class implications of this model nevertheless apply here, as Edgar is wealthy and Camilla, though no one ever believes her, has been disinherited from her uncle's fortune in favor of her sister on the event of the latter's disfigurement.

30. Joanna Picciotto argues that the Enlightenment value of objectivity is founded on a privi-

leging of innocence. *Labors of Innocence in Early Modern England* (Cambridge, MA: Harvard UP, 2010). Piccioto's account is quite different from that of Amanda Anderson, who, in *The Powers of Distance: Cosmopolitanism and the Cultivation of Detachment* (Princeton: Princeton UP, 2001), argues that the aspiration toward critical objectivity depends on the ability, however partial, to detach from one's own particularity in lived experience.

31. Note that Madame Arlbury has a clearly innatist understanding of courtship: "O, assure yourself, that of the first young man who has come in her sight. Every damsel, as she enters the world, has some picture ready painted upon her imagination, of an object worthy to enslave her: and before any experience forms her judgment, or any comparison her taste, she is the dupe of the first youth who presents himself to her, in the firm persuasion of her ductile fancy, that he is just the model it had previously created" (366).

32. Samuel Johnson, *Idler* 45, in *Essays from the "Rambler," "Adventurer," and "Idler,"* ed. W. J. Bate (New Haven: Yale UP, 1968), 304–05.

33. "Twice betrayed in his dearest expectations, he had formed two criterions from his peculiar experience, by which he had settled his opinion of the whole female sex; and where opinion may humour systematic prepossession, who shall build upon his virtue or wisdom to guard the transparency of his impartiality?" (903).

34. *Edinburgh Review* 24 (1815).

35. *British Critic* 8 (November 1796): 535.

36. Croker, review of *Diary and Letters of Mme D'Arblay*, 271.

37. Deidre Lynch is the best reader of Burney's treatment of debt (and the marketplace) as the production of character psychology; still, I am stressing here that the ephemerality of those debts is as important as their acquisition. See Lynch, *The Economy of Character: Novels, Market Culture, and the Business of Character* (Chicago: U of Chicago P, 1998).

38. Doody, 13.

39. *Critical Review* 18 (November 1796): 40.

40. See Sandra Macpherson, *Harm's Way* (Baltimore: Johns Hopkins UP, 2010).

41. Samuel Comyn, *A Treatise of the Law relative to Contracts and Agreements Not under a Seal: With Cases and Decisions Thereon in the Action of Assumpsit* (London, 1807), 1:155.

42. Holly Brewer, *By Birth or Consent: Children, Law, and the Anglo-American Revolution in Authority* (Chapel Hill: North Carolina UP, 2005), 267.

43. Jane Austen, *Mansfield Park*, ed. James Kinsley (Oxford: Oxford UP, 2008), 39.

44. Frances Ferguson, "Rape and the Rise of the Novel," "Misogyny, Misandry, and Misanthropy," special issue of *Representations* 20 (1987): 95.

45. See note to page 760: "The rate of interest upon the lending of money was legally five per cent as fixed by the statute 12 Annae, st. 2. c. 16."

46. Macpherson, 66.

EPILOGUE: Emma's Dystopia

1. For endings themselves as providing "consolation," see the classic study by Frank Kermode, *The Sense of an Ending: Studies in the Theory of Fiction* (Oxford: Oxford UP, 2000).

2. Edmund Wilson, "A Long Talk about Jane Austen" (1945), in *Jane Austen's "Emma": A Sourcebook*, ed. Paula Byrne (London: Routledge, 2004), 55.

3. See Eve Kosofsky Sedgwick, "Jane Austen and the Masturbating Girl," *Critical Inquiry* 17 (Summer 1991): 818–37.

4. Wayne C. Booth, *The Rhetoric of Fiction* (Chicago: U of Chicago P, 1983), 260.

5. Claudia L. Johnson, *Equivocal Beings: Politics, Gender, and Sentimentality in the 1790s* (Chicago: U of Chicago P, 1995), 194. See also Johnson, "The Divine Miss Jane: Jane Austen, Janeites,

and the Discipline of Novel Studies," in *Janeites: Austen's Disciples and Devotees*, ed. Deidre Lynch (Princeton: Princeton UP, 2000): 25–44.

6. For one move in this direction, see Caroline Levine and Mario Ortiz-Robles, eds., *Narrative Middles: Navigating the Nineteenth-Century British Novel* (Columbus: Ohio State UP, 2010).

7. On the alternate endings to *Clarissa*, see Peter Sabor, "Rewriting *Clarissa*: Alternative Endings by Lady Echlin, Lady Bradshaigh, and Samuel Richardson," *Eighteenth-Century Fiction* 29.2 (2016–17): 131–50. On where eighteenth-century readers placed emphasis when reading *Don Quixote*, see Miriam Borham Puyal, "For the Amusement of the Merry Little Subjects: How British Children Met Don Quixote in the Long Eighteenth Century," *Anales Cervantinos* 47 (2015): 133–58. On the eighteenth-century defiance of closure with respect to character, see David A. Brewer, *The Afterlives of Character, 1726–1825* (Philadelphia: U of Pennsylvania P, 2005).

8. See Lisa Zunshine, *Bastards and Foundlings: Illegitimacy in Eighteenth-Century England* (Columbus: Ohio State UP, 2005).

9. Not to mention Austen's most anguished teen, Marianne Dashwood, on whom see Shawn Lisa Maurer, "At Seventeen: Adolescence in *Sense and Sensibility*," *Eighteenth-Century Fiction* 25.4 (2013): 721–50.

10. William Galperin, "Adapting Jane Austen: The Surprising Fidelity of *Clueless*," *Wordsworth Circle* 42.3 (Summer 2011): 187–93; 190.

11. *Clueless*, directed by Amy Heckerling (Paramount, 1995).

12. As Thomas Pavel has observed, the principle of coupledom governs the novel form: "The novel has traditionally focused on love and the formation of couples." "The Novel in Search of Itself: A Historical Morphology," in *The Novel: Forms and Themes*, ed. Franco Moretti (Princeton: Princeton UP, 2006), 23.

13. Jane Austen, *Emma* (Oxford: Oxford UP, 2008), 11. Hereafter cited parenthetically within the text.

14. D. A. Miller, *Jane Austen and the Secret of Style* (Princeton: Princeton UP, 2003), 34. For Miller, Emma's style effectively coincides with her youth: "Let me suggest that what in the end overtakes Emma's style, despite all the godlike timelessness to which its utterances lay claim, is nothing less than a sense of its temporality—a temporality measured not against the large, event-filled scale of world-historical time, but in the minor unit of social pressure within which the Novel typically begins and ends: the time of a *generation*, from youth to eventual settlement" (50).

15. Teresa Michals notes that YA fiction "triggers strong reactions that range from praise for regaining an inner Romantic child to condemnation for infantilizing culture, such as William Safire's protest that when adults read Harry Potter, it 'is not just dumbing down; it is growing down.'" *Books for Children, Books for Adults: Age and the Novel from Defoe to James* (Cambridge: Cambridge UP, 2014), 18.

16. Dystopian YA Novel, Twitter post, 24 August 2015, 8:43 a.m., https://twitter.com/Dystopian YA/status/635839899669766144; Anthony Oliviera, Twitter post, 17 December 2016, 7:52 p.m., https://twitter.com/meakoopa/status/810331787717214208.

17. Suzanne Collins, *The Hunger Games* (New York: Scholastic, 2008), 26.

18. Collins, *Hunger Games*, 9.

19. Collins, *Hunger Games*, 10.

20. While my reading places pressure on the series' insightful conflation of courtship and suspense, the bulk of the book is at the same time composed of a Crusoe story—and not only for the way that Katniss must survive in an unfamiliar wilderness, taking advantage of her prior experience as a hunter while also learning new skills on the fly. The turns of the story map uncannily to Defoe's, from a serious fever that threatens to unsettle her fragile progress, to her contemplation of the gravity of murder, to her repeated calculation of the interventions of Providence (in

this case, the Gamemakers who contrive and provoke the episodes that will give the bloodbath of the Games a shape, a plot).

21. Collins, *Mockingjay* (New York: Scholastic, 2010), 389.

22. See Susan Dominus, "Suzanne Collins's War Stories for Kids," *New York Times*, April 8, 2011. For The Hunger Games Trilogy as an allegory of adolescence, see Laura Miller, "Fresh Hell," *New Yorker*, June 14 and 21, 2010.

Index